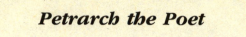

Petrarch the Poet

PETRARCH THE POET

An introduction to the
Rerum vulgarium fragmenta

Peter Hainsworth

ROUTLEDGE
London and New York

First published in 1988 by
Routledge
11 New Fetter Lane, London EC4P 4EE

Published in the USA by
Routledge
a division of Routledge, Chapman and Hall, Inc.
29 West 35th Street, New York NY 10001

© Peter Hainsworth 1988

Set in 10/12 Sabon by Columns of Reading
Printed in Great Britain by
TJ Press Ltd., Padstow, Cornwall

British Library Cataloguing in Publication Data
Hainsworth, Peter,   1942–
    Petrarch the poet : an introduction to
    the Rerum vulgarium fragmenta.
    1. Poetry in Italian. Petrarch, Francesco –
    Critical Studies
    I. Title
    851'.1

Library of Congress Cataloguing in Publication Data
Hainsworth, Peter.
    Petrarch the poet : an introduction to the Rerum vulgarium
    fragmenta / Peter Hainsworth.
       p.   cm.
    Bibliography: p.
    Includes index.
    1. Petrarca, Francesco, 1304–1374.   Rime.   I. Title.
    PQ4478.H35 1988
    851'.1—dc19
                                                    88–9681
                                                    CIP

ISBN 0-415-00270-2

Contents

Preface   vii

Abbreviations   ix

1   Introduction   1

1 Two languages   1
2 The Italian context   9
3 The *Rerum vulgarium fragmenta*   17
4 Petrarch's career as an Italian poet   20

2   Composition   30
1 The premisses   30
2 Making the collection   34
3 Making poems   41

3   Structure   49
1 What kind of structure?   49
2 Problems   51
3 The emergent patterns   54
4 In the labyrinth   65

4   The tradition   78
1 The self and the past   78
2 The Latin self   80
3 Assimilating the past   84
4 Viewing the tradition   92
5 Anti-medievalism   100

5 **Themes** 103

1 The introduction   103
2 History   108
3 The senses   118
4 Laura and the laurel   135
5 Transcendence   153

6 **Art** 172

1 Poetic disunity   172
2 Metre and rhythm   175
3 Sound   181
4 Words and images   189
5 Syntax   199
6 Poetic forms   210

Bibliographical notes   221

Bibliography   224

Principal references to
individual poems in the *RVF*   232

Name Index   235

Preface

This book is an introduction to Petrarch's major work in Italian, the collection of poems which he called the *Rerum vulgarium fragmenta*, though it is also known as the *Canzoniere* or the *Rime sparse*. My aim is in part to provide information. It is also to give a critical and historical interpretation of Petrarch's poetry. Some recent studies have presented Petrarch primarily as a medieval writer and a moralist who composed a form of perhaps exemplary autobiography in poetry. My approach is rather to see him as a poet whose moral and religious concerns are intimately bound up with an examination of the nature of poetry in the post-Dantesque era and whose work constitutes its ambiguous renewal, largely within a framework which derives from early Italian humanism. A more deep-rooted attitude towards Petrarch with which I also implicitly take issue is Anglo-Saxon mistrustfulness of him, which begins with Sidney's indifference to his 'long-deceasèd woes' and extends through nineteenth-century puzzlement or horror at what were variously seen as vacuousness, scholasticism, bad puns, impossible imagery and immoral refinement, to Ezra Pound's forthright condemnation of his 'fustian and ornament'. The Petrarch I have tried to describe is an extremely serious poet — self-conscious, scholarly, subtle, diverse, absorbed in problems which regard poetry generally, absorbed too in the problem of the bewildering beauty of his own poetry. Now that the great figures of twentieth-century modernism, who tended to look to Dante as a model of total literature, have themselves become part of the past, Petrarch's equivocal solutions to the problems which he faced may strike chords, though his humanism necessarily preserves a distance between himself and any post-modernism.

Without the work of Petrarchan scholars and interpreters of the last hundred years this book would not exist. As will be evident to those who know, its particular perspective is dependent on synthesising what others have done, though the synthesis is necessarily selective and the perspective necessarily partial. As has become increasingly evident, Petrarch is an immensely complex and multifaceted figure. Any single study can only hope to do justice to him through being open-ended, through leading the reader into his work, not out of it. Although I have arrived at conclusions, which I make as explicit as possible, I have aimed at this form of introduction too.

Petrarch is concerned with words even more than most poets. Whilst I have tried to avoid technical jargon, a great deal of what I have to say is about language – about its meanings, suggested or explicit, about the forms it takes and their poetic significance. I have quoted extensively, providing translations which are as literal as is decently possible and intended solely to facilitate understanding of the bare meaning of the words in English.

I have reduced bibliographical references in the text to a minimum. The bibliographical notes at the end of the book indicate further reading on the topics covered in each chapter. The Bibliography itself is restricted to works cited, and, together with the bibliographical notes, is intended to be useful, not comprehensive, even in its coverage of recent writing about Petrarch. I have used the author–date system of reference throughout.

Various friends and colleagues helped me, directly or indirectly, to complete what often seemed an impossible task. I wish particularly to thank Michael Caesar, who provided the original impulse to write a book about Petrarch, David Thomas, who gave me unfailing assistance with the resources of the Taylorian Library in Oxford, and, most of all, John Woodhouse, whose detailed reading of the typescript was invaluable. Faults and inadequacies are, of course, mine.

Peter Hainsworth,
Lady Margaret Hall, Oxford

Abbreviations

Petrarch

Af.	Africa
Buc. carm.	Bucolicum carmen
De rem.	De remediis utriusque fortune
Ep. met.	Epistole metrice
Fam.	Familiares
Fr.	Frammenti
Ot. rel.	De otio religioso
RD	Rime disperse
RVF	Rerum vulgarium fragmenta
Sec.	Secretum
Sen.	Seniles
Tr. Cup.	Triumphus Cupidinis
Var.	Epistolae variae
Vit. sol.	De vita solitaria

Dante

DVE	De vulgari eloquentia
Inf.	Inferno
Par.	Paradiso
Purg.	Purgatorio
VN	Vita nuova

Otherwise full forms are given.

1

Introduction

1.1 Two languages

Italian literature of the Middle Ages and the Renaissance is composed in the shadow of Latin. The shadow may seem sometimes shorter, sometimes longer, but it is inevitably there, evoking an alternately benign and threatening presence whose roots stretch back into antiquity and whose branches extend across Europe. Latin asserts repeatedly that it has the exclusive right to knowledge and excellence, and continually demands that its authors and authority should be attended to. When it seems most displaced, it infiltrates the less prestigious, less stable language with its words, its turns of phrase, its rhetoric and its standards. If there is such a thing as popular literature, the index of popularity is the distance from Latin. Literature which makes implicit or explicit claims to refinement, let alone to greatness, does so in virtue of its power to assimilate what Latin has to offer and to become like it. Only in the sixteenth century does literary culture in Italy make a general commitment to Italian, and even then the result is symbiosis with Latin rather than its eviction. For earlier writers the two languages are mostly in tension. Even Dante, who declared Italian the nobler language in the *De vulgari eloquentia* and gave an overwhelming demonstration of its power in the *Divina commedia*, was the victor in a battle, not the war.

There were many reasons, some stemming from the *Commedia* itself, others from the linguistic and cultural pressures at work in fourteenth-century Italy, why Dante's example could not be wholeheartedly embraced by the generation that followed him. But one of the prime factors was the emergence of a humanist

1

movement which was intent on the recovery and renewal of
Latinity, with, at its centre, the figure who dominated the literary
culture of his time. Petrarch wrote with equal seriousness in both
Latin and Italian and redrew the lines of demarcation between the
two languages. In one way the result was a return to orthodoxy,
in another it was a radical revision with implications for both
literatures. The effects were immediate, deep, widely felt, and, in
the longer term, asymmetrically bi-focal in a way that reflected the
actual constitution of Petrarch's work. For a century and more
after his death humanism evolved within the perspective defined in
his Latin writings, whilst Italian retreated to the literary margins.
Then in the sixteenth century his Italian poems, which had always
been influential within vernacular literature, were pronounced the
supreme examples of modern poetry. They were the paradigms of
language, style, and, to a lesser degree, of love, and were to exert a
profound influence upon poetry inside and outside Italy. By then
the Latin works were already fading from view: henceforth it
would be the Italian poems which spoke for Petrarch and defined
him. Only since the later nineteenth century has the eclipse been
slowly rectified. Gradually it has become evident that the whole of
Petrarch is not contained within what he wrote in either language
considered in isolation, though it has become equally clear that
any composite picture has to take as much account of contrasts
and contradictions as of similarities or underlying consistencies.

In themselves neither his bilingualism nor his humanism is
surprising. His father, Ser Petracco, was a notary who lived and
worked in Florence, though his family was from Incisa, a small
town not far from Arezzo. In 1302, a few months after Dante, he
too was exiled. He first returned to Incisa and Arezzo, where
Petrarch was born in 1304. But in 1312 he moved with his family
to Provence, where, like other White Guelphs exiled from
Florence, he found work and refuge in the ambit of the Papal
Court at Avignon. From now until his definitive departure for
Northern Italy in 1353, Provence would be Petrarch's base,
though a base which he would frequently leave, more often than
not, for lengthy visits to Italy. There were also Italian friends,
some of whom at least had an interest in vernacular literature,
notably the poet Sennuccio del Bene. But Papal Provence was
primarily international and its culture was enthusiastically Latinate,
particularly amongst its Italian members. Petrarch's father direc-

ted him as a boy towards Virgil and Cicero, and, in the light of his ability in the language and his enthusiasm for classical antiquity, brought him to the notice of the Colonna family, whose centre was Rome but whose members were currently important figures in the Church in Southern France. The Colonna were to be Petrarch's patrons and friends until his support for the revolutionary attempts of Cola di Rienzo to re-create the Roman republic led to a cooling of relations during his last years in Provence. With their own humanist interests, their contacts in both France and Italy, and their sheer political and financial power, they provided a springboard for Petrarch's studies and writings. They also provided material support: Petrarch took minor orders and was granted a canonry at Lombez, where Giacomo Colonna was bishop. Like other livings which he acquired later, the canonry made minimal demands. Petrarch always insisted that his means were modest, though they were sufficient for him to acquire, sometime in the early 1330s, the famous villa at Vaucluse which became his country retreat. With Colonna help and careful manipulation of his own myth, the culminating point of which was his coronation as poet laureate in Rome in 1341, he made himself famous and respected. From his thirties onwards, kings, princes, emperors and popes would correspond with him, or at least receive his letters, would welcome him as the greatest adornment of learning in contemporary Europe, would use him as an ambassador or seek his advice. When he moved to Italy in 1353, he had no difficulty in finding support, first from the Visconti in Milan, then from the Venetian republic, and finally from Francescoda Carrara of Padua, who provided him with the land in Arquà in the Euganean hills where he built the house in which he was to die in 1374.

Petrarch's life was a remarkable achievement in itself, and one accomplished in virtue of his work in Latin, not Italian. It marked the emergence of a new kind of writer. Petrarch was not a member of any university or any other institution, and was not directly in the service of any of his patrons, not even the Colonna, or of any state organisation. Though he was continually negotiating his position and continually threatened by the powers amongst which he moved, he created an independence for himself and for his work which no other intellectual had enjoyed since antiquity. With him high literature established a distance between itself and the vocationalism and institutionalism to which it had been subjected throughout the Middle Ages. Its arbiter was the author, a figure who created himself in and through his writing and who was dignified in his own eyes and those of society for his literary excellence and for no other reason.

At the base of Petrarch's work was textual mastery. As a young man he brought together the surviving decades of Livy, which had been separated from each other throughout the medieval period, and emended the text of accretions and corruptions in a way that presupposed a respect both for classical Latin and for the wishes of the author. He went on to emend, copy and make available other texts, including some which had been lost to the intellectual life of Europe for centuries. One of his early discoveries was Cicero's *Pro Archia*; another, still more important, was the collection of Cicero's letters to Atticus, which he found in the cathedral library of Verona in 1345. These and other texts became part of the largest private library that had existed in Europe since ancient times. Though Petrarch's readings in medieval literature were much more extensive than he cared to admit, the texts he chooses to edit and, even more, those which he values, signal a reaction against literary and intellectual concerns that were dominant in the preceding century. He has no truck with scholastic or Aristotelian thought. In place of speculative metaphysical systems, of scientific, especially medical, investigation, of legal codification, he puts grammar, rhetoric, poetry, history, moral philosophy. Virgil and the other classical poets, Cicero, Seneca, Livy are his authors, not Aristotle, Aquinas, Averroes, let alone the jurists and the decretalists. When he turns to Christian philosophy, it is above all to Augustine, with whose position *vis-à-vis* pagan thought he felt bound at times to identify. In all this there is evident a desire to recover what had been lost in the Middle Ages (though the term, like the term 'humanism', was still to be invented) and to present a historically accurate version of it to the present, or, given the decadence of the present – which episodes such as that of Cola, and lasting sores such as the exile of the Papacy from Rome, made seem all too apparent – to a future that was yet to take shape.

There was little dissociation of sensibility in Petrarch. Knowing was doing. Though the next generation of humanists would easily surpass him, his Latin was more classical than that of any of his contemporaries or medieval predecessors, and made its classical connections evident through a web of allusions, citations, and reformulations or phrases taken from great and not so great authors. At the same time Petrarch insisted on his individuality. None of his works are totally subservient to ancient models, in some cases perhaps inadvertently. His unfinished epic poem, the *Africa*, unreleased in his lifetime apart from one short passage and the greatest literary flop when it eventually emerged after his death, was less epic than it was discursive and personal. The large collections of letters, principally the *Familiares* and the *Seniles*, which were apparently inspired by his Ciceronian discoveries, were less anecdotal and occasional than measured moral discourses, miniature treatises, self-analyses and self-portraits. But these are only part of a literary production which is amazing in its diversity and abundance. It includes allegorical eclogues, verse epistles, biographies, treatises, polemical defences of humanistic studies and of Petrarch's own position within them, a self-analysis in the form of a dialogue with St Augustine (*Secretum*), and moral dialogues (*De remediis utriusque fortune*), as well as relatively minor pieces such as the oration he delivered on his coronation (*Collatio laureationis*) or the letter addressed to posterity (*Posteritati*).

In that letter, as throughout his writings, Petrarch is primarily concerned with himself, or rather with formulating some version of himself which caters for his continual shifts of perspective on himself and on his work, and for the doubts and contradictions which he never fully resolves. He continually debates the nature of his studies and his writing, exploring their relationship to a truth which his disavowal of metaphysics prevents him from even beginning to express, but which impinges as an absence, or as a matter of faith. In the course of his career he entertains every possibility: he normally dismisses simple restoration of classical glories as something which he foolishly entertained in his youth, but he moves between a humanism which is also Christian, a Christianity which has a humanist colouring, and a Christianity which has nothing to do with the folly of writing. Though he liked to present himself as evolving from a more or less Christian but distinctly humanist poet into a distinctly Christian moral philosopher, the phases blur together. Almost everything we have of Petrarch belongs to his maturity. Although the passage of time

and the changes it brings is one of his constant themes, there is a
sense in which all his surviving writings are an encyclopaedia
which includes as many kinds of writing and as many attitudes to
the nature and function of writing as they possibly can, all united
not by any reference to some external truth but by a self which is
present in all of them, though complete in none, and whose
boundaries are determined by the totality of the authorised
oeuvre.

Much of Petrarch is incomplete or composed of short units in
different states of elaboration. Most betokens a state of unease or
even of crisis. But the assurance is also striking. However much
rewritten, however much they might have been further revised, the
fragments and incomplete works are formally and stylistically
accomplished. What is more important, the fundamental decisions
are unhesitatingly held to. From the beginning there is a rejection
of the conceptual and literary practices of the previous generation
of Italian writers (especially those of Dante) and a conviction that
all matters of intellectual and moral importance should find
expression in a renovated form of Latin. What is left to Italian is
poetry, and poetry of a particular kind.

Petrarch's work in Italian falls into three parts. Most important
are the 366 lyric poems which make up the collection often called
the *Canzoniere*, sometimes the *Rime sparse* (from the first line of
the first poem), but which Petrarch himself entitled *Rerum
vulgarium fragmenta*, literally 'Fragments of vernacular matters': I
shall follow Petrarch, at least to some degree, by using the
acronym *RVF*. Then there are some poems excluded from the
major collection: at least twenty-nine of these *Rime disperse* (*RD*),
as they are conventionally called, are genuine, though there may
well be others amongst the vast body of poems attributed to
Petrarch between the fourteenth and the sixteenth century. Lastly
there are the *Triumphi* (*Triumphs*), a sequence of six visionary
poems which was never quite completed. It is a substantial body
of work: the *RVF* alone is larger than the total surviving
production of any earlier lyric poet, except perhaps Guittone
d'Arezzo, and at least as large as the production of some of his
prolific contemporaries. But it is dwarfed by the Latin writings. In
the Basle edition of 1554, which is still the only comprehensive, if
not quite complete, edition of his works, the Italian poems are
crammed into some 78 pages: the Latin writings fill nearly 1,400.

The contrast is not solely of scale. In Latin Petrarch looks to the ancient world, in Italian to the lyric tradition of Tuscany and Provence, and to the love-poetry that had always been at its centre. Though the poems are much more than the expression of passion and at least some turn explicitly away from love, the great majority centre on Petrarch's love for the woman he called Laura, whom he claims to have first seen in 1327 and to have loved from then until long after her death in 1348. Love is largely absent from the Latin works. There are love-poems for Laura amongst the verse epistles (*Epistole metrice*): she is allegorised as the laurel in some of the eclogues (*Bucolicum carmen*); but she becomes a major issue only in the dialogue with Augustine in the *Secretum*, which debates some of the dangers of love in a comparable way to some of the poems. In the self-portrait given in the letter to posterity there is only a cursory dismissal of a passion which, to judge by the Italian poems, obsessed their author from the ages of twenty-three until at least his sixties.

Laura may or may not have existed as an individual. But poetically the obsession was certainly real and long-lasting. Some of the poems in the *RVF* were written in the 1330s or perhaps even earlier, though Petrarch probably began work on making a collection in the 1340s at the earliest. But it was in his later years that he did most of the work on the composition of the whole, and, in all probability, wrote a considerable number of the individual poems. He gave the arrangement of the collection its final form something less than a year before his death.

His Latin work offers a different picture. By the 1350s he was presenting himself as having abandoned poetry altogether, and, so far as poetry in Latin was concerned, this was true. As for the work on his Italian poetry, he declares that he is merely collecting together youthful trifles: he is now ashamed of them, but they are in demand from friends whom he cannot refuse: he also wishes to protect them from abuse and distortion. But the disparities are comprehensible. Italian poetry, as he conceived and wrote it, was not to be reconciled with humanism in any intellectually coherent fashion, even if humanists and their patrons enjoyed writing and reading it. There could be no justification for indulgence in sexual love, however refined, nor for love-poetry. It was available to the vulgar at large, and, what was perhaps worse, available to women. It had to be judged frivolous, immoral, and, as literature, inferior in every way to what might be written in Latin. Such a poetry might perhaps have been justified if it were allegorical – if, that is, Laura were indeed the laurel, the symbol of glory and poetry, which she became in the *Bucolicum carmen*. But that was a step whose ambiguous possibilities Petrarch explored in the *RVF* without totally committing himself. Instead he risked the absurdity and ridicule of being a man in his fifties and sixties who wrote love-poetry. Contemporaries seem to have been indifferent to this contradiction of the equation between love and youth which goes back to antiquity and which had been particularly strong in Provençal poetry. Petrarch himself was not. For him there had to be some degree of shame in such a display, as the poems themselves indicate. In spite of public appreciation and the protracted work of composition, it was unthinkable that the results could be called poetry: had that been done, they would have entered the same category as the *Aeneid* or the *Africa*, with implications for the possible status of the vernacular generally which Petrarch the humanist was anxious to avoid.

Clearly he was also anxious to orient writing in the two languages in two separate, even opposed directions. That does not mean that what he writes in the one is radically different from what he writes in the other. The very professions of shame, the slighting dismissals as trifles of works on which he spent years, are applied to his Latin writings as well as to the Italian. And the more we look, the more the points of contact proliferate, ranging from turns of phrase, favoured images, direct cross-references to fundamental concerns. If Petrarch writes in Italian of despair, confusion, frustration, that is only a reformulation in the terms of the lyric of much that appears in his Latin works. If he puts at the centre of his Latin works a self who is continually reshaped and re-examined, it is a similar fluctuating and uncertain self which is created and explored in Italian. If he voices and investigates in Latin various contradictory positions *vis-à-vis* the purposes and nature of writing, so in Italian he articulates and examines a series of poetic possibilities, embracing all and settling for none. As in Latin, writing is less a way of making statements about the world or reality than an area in which multiple pathways alternately diverge and cross each other, their contradictions being reconciled (though not annulled) in the writing itself rather than in any point of arrival or final judgment. The difference is one of quality; for

Italian, in Petrarch's hands, has the advantage: in a way that he could not quite achieve in Latin, he is able, in the inferior language, to create a style which is consistent whilst constantly varied, which can absorb literature of the past whilst retaining its own identity, which is always beautiful in a convincing, if sometimes bewildering way. There is no disparity of aspiration or literary attention between the Latin and the Italian Petrarch: but the latter presupposes the former in a way that is not true if we invert the terms. As Petrarch's Latin title suggests, the *Rerum vulgarium fragmenta* are the vernacular poems of a humanist.

1.2 The Italian context

Though there are important difference of perspective between them, Dante and Petrarch both make historical interpretations of Italian poetry which, taken together, suggest the idea of a poetic tradition running fairly smoothly from the Sicilians, or perhaps even from Provence, through to Petrarch. But in many ways the tradition was, and is, a retrospective construction. In reality continuity was neither automatic nor linear. At any point – and at some more than others – connections with the past had to be affirmed or denied, interferences had to be assimilated or rejected, and the past itself reassessed. There were always risks of rupture or dispersal. In the first half of the fourteenth century they were particularly intense. For Petrarch and his contemporaries, writing poetry in Italian was a quite different enterprise from what it had been in thirteenth-century Tuscany. At the same time the later poetry came into being largely in the shadow of the earlier. Petrarch was able to reshape the past in the light of the contradictory exigencies at work in himself and in fourteenth-century culture generally. His contemporaries often had similar aspirations, but were repeatedly thrown into confusion or confined to epigonal roles.

The tradition was no more than a hundred years old when Petrarch wrote the earliest poems which he included in the *RVF*. It had been initiated, quite abruptly it seems, by a loose-knit group of administrators, lawyers and notaries connected with the court of the Emperor Frederick II in Sicily and Southern Italy. Perhaps the Emperor himself encouraged, or ordered, the production in an Italian language of a poetry similar in kind and quality to that

produced by the minnesinger and troubadours whom he patronised. At all events the Sicilians (as they have been called since at
least the time of Petrarch, though not all of them were from Sicily)
produced a quite sophisticated love-poetry which owed a great
deal to Provençal *fin' amors*. They made the Sicilian language in
which they wrote acceptable by giving it a Provençal and, to a
lesser extent, a Latin flavour, as well as by importing idioms,
images and conventions from the troubadours. So Italian poetry
began on the elevated level which it was to maintain up to and
beyond Petrarch. It also acquired its fundamental poetic forms –
the major form, the canzone, deriving from the Provençal *canso*;
the minor one, the sonnet, being an invention of the Sicilians, and
probably of the dominant figure amongst them, the notary
Giacomo da Lentini.

Sicilian poetry came to an abrupt end when the German power
on which it depended was shattered by the French at the battles of
Benevento (1265) and Tagliacozzo (1267). But by then it had long
penetrated Central Italy. Bologna and the cities of Tuscany were
to be the centres in which it developed and to which it was
confined until almost exactly the end of the thirteenth century.
Broadly speaking, the first phase was one of expansion. It was
centred around Guittone d'Arezzo (*c.* 1230–94), who produced
the first sizeable body of work in Italian lyric poetry and who was
considerably more ambitious than the Sicilians had been, drawing
on some of the techniques of the Provençal *trobar clus* and also on
the refinements of the *Ars dictaminis*. Guittone also wrote political
and moral poetry, eventually denouncing love as carnal and
adulterous when he became one of the new lay order of *Frati
gaudenti* in the early 1260s. Nor was the expansion simply
internal. Canzoni and sonnets in the Sicilian and Guittonian mode
proliferated amongst notaries, merchants, bankers in the various
Tuscan towns. There may even have been a woman poet, the so-
called 'Compiuta Donzella'.

This too was sophisticated poetry, aware of its own conventions
and aware of European ideas of literary hierarchy. Overall the
Tuscans aimed to be elevated, whether celebrating or denouncing
love. But they also made moves in the direction of a more
colloquial register in political and occasional verse, whilst in
Florence, probably in the 1270s, the antithesis of high poetry
suddenly appeared in some of the poems of Rustico Filippi.

Vulgar, idiomatic, morally perverse, what is now called *poesia giocosa* was less a questioning of high poetry than its parasitical inversion, written in complete accordance with the accepted rules for low-style poetry.

But the limitations were evident, at least by contemporary standards. The early Tuscans were the voices of a provincial culture which had emerged quite suddenly into literacy as a result of rapid commercial expansion. Their points of reference were principally Sicilian and Provençal poetry and contemporary Latin rhetoric. Though the debates about the nature of love echo scholastic procedures of argument and suggest some acquaintance with contemporary medical and psychological thought, intellectual vitality is largely limited to the manipulation of commonplaces. The practitioners, whether we call them poets or not, were in contemporary parlance *rimatori, dettatori, trovatori,* not *poeti* or *auctores* whose names were to be respected and whose texts were to be commented on or glossed. In a sense their poetry was public property. Though it was certainly literate and, to judge from the evidence, it differed from Provençal poetry in not being directly associated with music, it quickly passed outside its authors' control into anthologies where it was at the mercy of scribal whim and regional variation.

This last problem would continue into Petrarch's time. But in the later years of the century there were major revisions of Tuscan poetic habits. What is now generally called the *dolce stil novo* (though Dante's phrase may well have a different emphasis in its original context in *Purg.* 24. 57) began in Bologna with Guido Guinizzelli (?1230–?1276), whose slender surviving *oeuvre* includes poems in the Guittonian style, but also some others which are conspicuously both more harmonious and more complex intellectually. What Bonagiunta da Lucca, one of his contemporary critics from the old school, considered an excess of Bolognese learning (*Poeti* 2. 481) is especially strong in the famous canzone on the nature of love, *Al cor gentil rempaira sempre Amore*. But it was in Florence in the work of Guido Cavalcanti (*c.* 1259–1300) that the new style really developed both its characteristic 'sweetness' and its conceptual scope, the latter being formidably displayed in Cavalcanti's philosophical canzone *Donna me prega*, the former being more apparent in his other poems. The new poetry was aimed at a circle of initiates, presupposing an intellectual and literary sophistication far exceeding that demanded by the run of previous poets. In other words with Cavalcanti the modes of high literature began to be reproduced in the vernacular.

It was Dante (1265–1321) who made the claims of the vernacular explicit. In the *Vita nuova* (*c.* 1294) he gathered together a selection of his youthful poetry and, with the help of a prose commentary, made its coherence evident. Love, reason and vernacular poetry were, he argued, complementary. At this stage he thought poetry in Italian should restrict itself thematically to love, but, since there was as much sense and order in the best vernacular poetry as traditional theory held there to be in the Latin masters, it followed that there was no difference in kind between the *rimatori* and the *poeti* (*VN* 25).

The rest of Dante's work is, amongst other things, a demonstration of the truth of this radical proposition. He had already gone beyond Cavalcanti in the *Vita nuova*. Over the next decade or so he wrote a series of poems which were conceptually more substantial and technically stricter than anything so far written in Italian. Concurrently he supported practice with theory, moving from the relatively restricted claims of his first book to the eventual proclamation of the *De vulgari eloquentia* (1. 1. 4) that 'nobilior est vulgaris' (the vernacular is the nobler language), and that meant that it could deal with the noblest of themes – moral and spiritual well-being, political and military struggle, as well as love.

For all his theoretical pronouncements, all the poetry which Dante had written was just about containable within the confines of the tradition and within traditional ways of seeing the relationship between Latin and the vernacular. The *Divina commedia* was not. It was finished not long before Dante died in Ravenna in 1321. Within ten years it was well known and widely read in Northern and Central Italy. Though one or two dissenters were to be heard, it was quickly recognised that here was a work in Italian which rivalled any work of ancient poetry. It satisfied all criteria for poetic excellence. It showed a complete mastery of rhetoric: it was immensely learned in philosophy, science and theology: and it was rich in moral lessons for its readers' improvement. If it quickly became popular with the people at large, it was also clear that its appealing surface concealed difficult, even arcane truths. Learned commentaries began to appear almost at once. By 1333 there were at least four in existence which have survived (Jacopo di Dante, Graziolo Bambaglioli, il Lana and l'Ottimo), indicating a *de facto* recognition that the text required the same depth of exegesis as, say, the *Aeneid*. The theoretical recognition was voiced most forcefully by Boccaccio. Dante, he proclaimed in his celebratory biography, is a great and glorious *poeta*: his work has the sweetness and beauty which appeals to everyone, including women and young people, but it also has a wealth of deep meaning which first puzzles and then 'refreshes and nourishes serious minds' ('ricrea e pasce gli solenni intelletti': *Opere* 384).

Boccaccio may have been right, but the *Commedia* posed enormous problems for any subsequent poet. Apart from its assault upon linguistic certainties which had been presumed valid for centuries, there was the question of how Italian poetry was to deal with a literary father who seemed simultaneously to have created the poetic language and to have exhausted all its resources. Indeed, if the implications of his poem are taken seriously, he had said everything worth saying. One response was to attempt encyclopaedical poems on the Dantesque model, but with different matter; another, already evident in Dante's friend, the canon lawyer Cino da Pistoia (*c.* 1270–1336/7), was to incorporate phrases, words, images from the *Commedia* into lyric poems of a familiar kind, in Cino's case a generally more subdued *dolce stil novo*.

Both responses are signs that Dante's great synthesis could only collapse. Perhaps it was in any case a more fragile, idiosyncratic creation than it pretended: the attempt to demonstrate the truth of the assumption that everything which existed did somehow cohere could perhaps only convince within the terms of the poem. Outside there were too many disruptive forces. Dante's universalist politics were already outmoded when he was writing. The exile of the Papacy to Avignon, the weakness of successive emperors, the increasing importance of national monarchs, the rise of the new *signorie* in Northern Italy – all these political realities made one of the major struts of his work outmoded except as literature. The republican city-states of Central Italy which had obsessed him were reduced in numbers in the course of the fourteenth century, and the strongest of them, Florence, developed in precisely the direction he wished it not to take. The commercialism which Dante detested was absorbed into a culture which found its image in the human world of the *Decameron*. Philosophically, too, the unity was broken. Dante made a unique fusion of Aristotelian and Neo-Platonic thinking: in the fourteenth century the two divided again, with humanists of the Petrarchan stamp rejecting out of hand all the speculative thought that was fundamental to the *Commedia*. If its commentators are anything to go by, even the poem itself could only be read as a series of episodes or of difficulties whose place in the whole was not to be considered.

Cultural and political fragmentation was linked with geographic dispersal. In the early years of the century lyric poetry spread out of Tuscany to the North, partly, it seems, as a result of the banishment of the White Guelphs from Florence in 1302. According to Boccaccio's biography (*Opere* 338), Dante himself made converts to the cause of poetry in general and vernacular poetry in particular during his last years in Ravenna. Already between 1325 and 1335 Niccolò de' Rossi, a notary in Treviso, assembled an anthology of poems that ran back through Dante and Cavalcanti all the way to goliardic Latin. Niccolò also wrote a great deal of largely old-fashioned lyric verse of his own. His manuscript of his poems, completed probably before 1330, is the earliest example we have of an Italian poet making an 'edition' of his own work (see Brugnolo ed.).

As in the previous century, many poets were notaries, like Niccolò, or merchants. But they were not dominant voices as their Tuscan equivalents had been. There is an immense profusion of fourteenth-century poetry, in which many conflicting tendencies are visible. A major one is the rise of court-poetry, which to all intents and purposes did not exist in thirteenth-century Tuscany. The rule of absolute *signori* meant a return to the situation of the troubadours or even of their *jongleurs*, at least for some of the most important Northern poets. Dante himself had become a dependant of princes, though protected by his prestige against the worst indignities of such a position, in spite of his gloomy comments in *Paradiso* (17. 58–60). Some of his successors, such as Antonio da Ferrara (1315–71/4) and Francesco di Vannozzo (*c.* 1340–90?), were less fortunate. Of poor birth, with relatively little education and no material resources, they found themselves continually moving from court to court, looking for support and patronage, and often producing poems at their patrons' requests. As Francesco di Vannozzo put it in one of his poems, 'vo cantando fole / su per le tole altrui / con questo e con colui / per un bicchier di vino' ('I go singing fables / at others' tables / with this fellow and that / for a glass of wine': ed. Medin, p. 248).

In this kind of poetry, and in much written by sober notaries and merchants, the sense of poetry as a means of investigating and articulating serious and complex issues has all but evaporated. So too has the linguistic and stylistic homogeneity of Tuscan poetry, with its strict distinction between styles and its careful cultivation of the high style as the supreme form of poetic expression. Antonio da Tempo, a Paduan who wrote a pedantic treatise on vernacular lyric forms, datable to 1332, said that the Tuscan language was more appropriate to literature ('ad literam sive literaturam') than other idioms, because it was 'magis communis et intelligibilis', that is, because it had more features that were general and hence was more widely understood, though he also allowed that other idioms could be used too (ed. Andrews, p. 99). Other Northern poets would probably have agreed with Antonio, although they did not have the means to act on even this uncertain programme. There was no grammar detailing the rules and forms of Tuscan. In practice Northerners were limited to reworking Tuscan poems and to embedding words and phrases from Dante and the other poets in a language based on their own usage, with *ad libitum* admixtures from Latin. Much is written in a more or less conversational vein, with overtly autobiographical or occasional content (such as the lines from Vannozzo given above). Much too is written expressly to be set to music, especially *madrigali*, which were probably not cultivated by the earlier Tuscan poets, if they existed at all.

Though these developments suggest a resurgence of orality, poetry was also becoming more distinctly literate, as the example of Niccolò de' Rossi shows. Manuscript collections, both of earlier and contemporary poetry proliferate in the course of the century. There were also clear aspirations towards higher styles of writing. Dante, the new learning of humanism and, from at least the middle of the century and perhaps before, Petrarch's own Italian poetry, all had their effects. But the results often flaunt classical learning, or else become heterogeneous mixtures which, by Petrarchan standards, are medieval rather than humanist. Brizio

Visconti (d. 1357), the bastard son of Luchino, wrote a canzone on the beauty of his *donna, Mal d'Amor parla chi d'amor non sente* ('He who has no feeling of love speaks ill of love': *Rimatori* 184). Each stanza ends with a comparison to a famous figure: viz. Ovid's Actaeon, St Paul, Apuleius' Psyche, Absalom, the Polyxena of Daretes Phrygius, Virgil's Lavinia, Solomon, Isolde, Aristotle, Polycletus (the sculptor), and St Augustine. Brizio has mixed together the classical, the vernacular, the biblical, in a sequence that has no rationale which I can discover. But he does give his poem more of a structure than this. He described the lady in accordance with the rules for female description laid down in textbooks of poetics: he begins with her hair and works downwards feature by feature until the limits of decency are reached. There is nothing comparable in thirteenth-century poetry, nor will there be in Petrarch, but such curious combinations of haphazard learning and rigid structuring are quite frequent amongst other fourteenth-century poets.

To a large extent it is the context of Northern poetry which is relevant to Petrarch. He composed the *RVF* largely in Northern Italy and it was for Northern *signori* that he made various intermediate versions of the collection. His contacts with contemporary Tuscan poets, other than Boccaccio, belong principally to the earlier phases of his career. The most important of these was probably with Sennuccio del Bene (see section 4 below), though he certainly knew the work of Cino da Pistoia, and may even have known him personally. In any case, whilst Florentines and Tuscans were protected against linguistic heterogeneity to some degree, their poetry shows many of the same tendencies as that of the Northerners. Cino, Sennuccio and others continued to write in the manner of the *stil novo*, though in less exalted vein than their predecessors. There were also Dantesque imitations, classicising poetry of various kinds, and, increasingly as the century went on, homely occasional verse, speaking good sense in colloquial language. The most important Tuscan writer is of course Boccaccio (1313–75), who was a personal friend of Petrarch from 1351 until the end of his life. Before he largely abandoned the vernacular, Boccaccio continually opened up new avenues in prose and verse, principally in the area of narrative, exploiting his large, unsystematic readings in medieval and classical literature to produce a series of works which combined the two in unprecedented amalgamations. Within the terms of the mercantile culture in which he worked, he, like Petrarch, found a series of solutions, some perhaps more successful than others, to the problem of reconciling different cultural pressures and energies in complex wholes. His surviving lyric poetry is largely occasional, sometimes classicising, sometimes popularising, even casual from a technical point of view.

The story that Boccaccio burnt his poems after seeing Petrarch's may or may not be true, but the letter by Petrarch (*Sen 5*. 2) consoling him for his sense of literary inferiority affirms what will become the dominant perspective on Italian literature of the thirteenth and fourteenth centuries. In whatever order of precedence they are to be arranged, the three authors are Dante, Petrarch and Boccaccio. For the rest there is silence. The historical reality was of course much less clear cut. In the last section of this chapter I shall look briefly at what can be deduced of Petrarch's involvement in the common situation of the poets of his time and at his relations with other poets.

1.3 The *Rerum vulgarium fragmenta*

The *RVF* was a major poetic enterprise beyond the powers of any of Petrarch's contemporaries, none of whom had a comparable experience of literature, or an equivalent critical and historical awareness. It is conditioned throughout by Petrarch's humanism. Though the poems do not flaunt classicism, it is in the light of his work in Latin that he carries through a reassessment of the possibilities of poetry in Italian. Alone of fourteenth-century poets, Petrarch rethinks and remakes the tradition, finding solutions to some of the major problems which poetry faced in his own time, whilst recognising that some of the fundamental ones were, unhappily, intractable, except, perhaps, in the contradictions of which poetry itself is made. At the same time he absorbs into his work the main tendencies evident in his contemporaries, even, when it suited him (or his poetry), drawing directly on their work. For, in spite of his sheer egocentricity and the effacement which he inflicted on them, Petrarch spoke for, not against, other Italian poets of his time.

The foundation of the work was the making of a text. Whilst at least one partly autograph collection (by Niccolò de' Rossi) predates the *RVF*, it is Petrarch's text which is historically significant. Here we have a major author expressly recognising the destruction that his poems were exposed to at the hands of performers to whom he released them (*Fam.* 21. 15 and *Sen.* 5. 3). In the manuscript which he made in the last years of his life Petrarch created a defence against the absorption of his poetry into an oral culture, and also made a humanist resolution of the textual problems of contemporary and preceding poetry generally. He takes control as author of his production, making the same provisions as he makes with any of his Latin works to resist the forces of dispersal and corruption, and presuming implicitly that the poems have the same status as his works in Latin. It is on this act of control and preservation that everything about his poetry depends, from the finest and most subtle of musical effects, to the complexities of the relations between poems. In the fullest sense these are literary poems.

Within the collection the poems are autonomous. Petrarch excludes poems by others and refuses to specify any of the occasions which gave rise to poems, whether these are *tenzoni* with other poets, incidents in his life, or the ups and downs, true or invented, of a peculiarly protracted love-affair. At the same time the autobiographical and occasional character of poetry after Dante is not denied. The *RVF* tells a story, but it does so indirectly in the full recognition that poetic narrative, especially that of lyric poetry, is subject to other pressures, some of which run counter to narrative demands. As well as the partial autobiography which a collection of lyric poems might easily furnish, Petrarch creates a complex interplay between poems, in which narrative possibilities, formal and thematic patterning, and variety (or disorder) compete with each other. On the whole the poems are abstracted from history. When they do display a sense of poetry having an active role to play, it is primarily with reference to some moment in the future which they themselves can only anticipate. (See Chapter 5.4 below.)

Like his contemporaries Petrarch looks to the past. Unlike them, he makes a serious and lucid recuperation of the central features of the tradition. Although he admits political poems and poems of other kinds, he gives overwhelming priority to love-poetry, almost as if he were following Dante's dictates in the *Vita nuova*, and certainly in accordance with the general practice of thirteenth-century poets. And with the choice of the canonical theme he makes a choice of language and poetic forms which also looks back to the earlier Tuscan lyric. The hybridism and outrageous classicism of his contemporaries, their liking for extended or irregular forms, their conversational tone are all discarded. So too are they: the references, the echoes, the different varieties of metrical organisation are all cast primarily as reassessments of the past, not the present.

All the same there are fundamental modifications. In Italian, as in Latin, Petrarch rejects the scholastic and speculative tendency which had been the strength of later thirteenth-century poetry, and re-forms the style or styles of his predecessors in the light of his own criteria of selfhood, recasting the figure of the *donna* and creating a psychological complexity in poetry for which there were no precedents. He also finds a solution to the problem of Dante. Beatrice is remade as Laura and questions of transcendental love and transcendental poetry are re-formed in a poetry which is far more sceptical, although unhappily so. The *Commedia* itself is ousted. It becomes the prodigy which it had to be, something quite distinct from lyric poetry, not its point of arrival. In its place there is a reaffirmation of order: the progress of the lyric in Italian ran (as we still tend to think it does) from the Sicilians through the lyric Dante to Petrarch, who in his turn became its culmination. The *RVF* is a representation of the poet's self, but the self represented is also poetic. The changes and fluctuations which the collection represents make up a selective encyclopaedia of Italian poetry, which absorbs and reinterprets the practices of earlier poets, simultaneously casting them as having no greater role than that of being its precursors.

All is accomplished by accepting even more than his contemporaries the cultural dispersal in which they and Petrarch wrote. Earlier poetry in Provençal and Italian reappears in the *RVF* in fragmentary, even pulverised form. So too do fragments from the full range of Petrarch's vast reading. The difference lies in the reconstitution: in the *RVF* there is no literary pastiche, no embedding of literary jewels in drab or uncertain language. Everything is re-formed as an aspect of the self, which is constantly changing but constantly the same, and which finds poetic identity in all the forms it takes, however uncertain it may be about their meaning or status.

The combination of order and disorder, of resolution and indecision, is one of the most disquieting and deep-rooted attractions of the *RVF*. Thematically the poems raise questions about the meaning and scope of poetry which had been voiced by earlier poets (though not, it seems, by other poets of the fourteenth century) and by Petrarch himself in Latin. Simultaneously, they reshape those questions and answer them in some measure, only to discard the answers as provisional, or as only the material of a poetry which can never find a single formulation to embrace its multiple ambiguities (see Chapter 5). The very stylistic and formal brilliance of the poetry, so evidently not present in the work of his contemporaries, is itself dependent on conflicts and unresolved contrasts, on elements of language which are never rid of their irrational and ambiguous overtones, as much as it is dependent on the creation of lucidly balanced structures. In the course of the Renaissance the *RVF* will become a paradigm of aesthetic achievement in poetry. As we look at the collection now, it betrays constant unease as well as pleasure in the artefacts of which it is made. In some sense it recognises and includes its own negativity, never excluding the aura of death and vanity which surrounds all of Petrarch's work. A combination of the uncombinable, in what may or may not be an integrated whole, is achieved in each poem of the *RVF* and in the totality of the collection, with resonances which extend far beyond the specific personal and cultural crises from which the work historically evolved.

1.4 Petrarch's career as an Italian poet

Whilst it is possible to outline the general context from which the *RVF* emerged, the specifics largely elude us. It is hard to speak with any confidence about Petrarch's evolution as a vernacular poet or his personal and literary relations with contemporaries who wrote in Italian. The main collection of poems is at best an ambiguous guide, and other evidence – principally the *Rime disperse (RD)* – is fragmentary and insubstantial. All the same, it is possible to map out a little of the itinerary which Petrarch must have traced, and to explore one or two points of contact with a poetic culture from which he was clearly not so divorced as the *RVF* as a whole seems to suggest.

We do not know when Petrarch began to write Italian poems. His earliest surviving poem is a Latin elegy on the death of his mother written when he was eighteen (*Ep. met.* 1. 7), though a letter to his brother Gherardo probably written in 1348 (*Fam.* 10. 3) talks disparagingly of love-poems which they wrote during their student days. None of these have survived, if indeed they ever existed. The earliest poems we can identify belong to a group of twenty-five which Petrarch copied out into his rough manuscript in the years 1336–8, forming what Wilkins called a 'reference collection' on the grounds that the poems seem to have been transcribed in no significant order for personal use (1951: 81–92). Eighteen of the poems would eventually enter the *RVF* as 23, 34–6, 41–6, 49, 58, 60, 64, 69, 77, 78, 179. According to a later note, *RVF* 23 (*Nel dolce tempo de la prima etade*) was one of the earliest poems which Petrarch wrote (Romanò 1955: 169; see Chapter 2.2 below). The discarded poems comprise five by Petrarch himself (*RD* 1–5), and two poems by a certain Geri dei Gianfigliazzi and the equally obscure figure of Ser Pietro Dietisalvi, to which two of his own poems were originally replies. In all probability two other excluded poems (*RD* 17 and 18), addressed to Sennuccio del Bene, which were not amongst those transcribed in 1336–8, are also very early.

Taken as a group, these poems are less distinct from much other poetry of their time than are the *RVF* as a whole. Although the poems admitted into the collection are fully integrated, they make a more open display of classical mythology than most of the *RVF*. In the rejected poems myth seems to be used relatively or uncertainly. *Quando talor, da giusta ira commosso* (*RD* 1) uneasily fits the myth of Hercules into a generally Cavalcantian poem: from its first line *Se Febo al primo amor non è bugiardo* (*RD* 5) introduces the myth of Apollo, which is fundamental to much of the *RVF*, in an emphatic conversational register which the later Petrarch avoids: *Sí come il padre del folle Fetonte* (*RD* 17) strings together one Ovidian myth after another, with an explicit mention of the name Daphne, which is to be excluded from the *RVF* (see Chapter 5.4). This poem is also exceptional in apparently making a pun between Laura's name and 'l'ora' (time), and, like one or two other excluded poems (and many poems by other fourteenth-century poets) in being an extended sonnet.

At this stage, or at least in the poems he rejected, Petrarch has

not completely established the voice which he will have in the
RVF. He is also and quite so autonomous. He is willing to write
poems on request: *RD* 3 and 4, which are love-poems of a sort,
have notes saying that they were written to order, the second note
making it plain that the unknown commissioner also told him
what matter ('materiam') to put into the poem. At least two other
poems were written, if not to order, with the express purpose of
furthering his patrons' interests. The sonnet *Vinse Hanibàl*
(*RVF* 103), urging Stefano Colonna to press on and destroy the
Orsini after his victory over them in 1333, is almost certainly the
short piece ('breve quiddam') which, according to a letter on the
same theme (*Fam.* 4.3), was composed in the vernacular so that
his feelings would be known to the soldiers in Stefano's army. The
canzone *Quel c'ha nostra natura in sé più degno* (*RD* 29), written
after the bloody recovery of Parma by Azzo da Correggio and his
brothers in 1341, makes it plain in its *congedo* that it is intended
to celebrate their achievement and to make it known particularly
in Tuscany. But perhaps these are exceptional. Taken together,
poems to patrons included in the *RVF* suggest a picture, perhaps
somewhat idealised, of relations between a great humanist and the
powerful. Those to the Colonna, Agapito (58), Stefano (10, 103)
and Giovanni (266, 269, 322), like those to Orso dell'Anguillara
(38) and Pandolfo Malatesta (104), suggest a shared interest in
Roman virtue and in ancient poetry. Here there are no requests
for gifts, no indignities, but instead a friendship not so distant in
tone from that of Ennius and Scipio in the *Africa*.

The poems from the 1330s also include poetic exchanges
(*tenzoni*). It appears that Petrarch was willing to continue taking
part in these until well into the 1340s. Two are with friends in
humanist circles or on its edges, whose poems (often printed at the
end of the *RVF* in Renaissance editions) show that they too can
turn a reasonable sonnet. One friend was the schoolmaster
Stramazzo da Perugia, mentioned in *Fam.* 14. 12 as one of the few
men in Italy to know Greek, the other Giovanni Dondi, the
Paduan mathematician and astronomer; *RVF* 24 was originally a
reply to the first, 244 to the second. But Petrarch's principal poetic
correspondents are Sennuccio del Bene and Antonio da Ferrara,
two figures who represent quite different trends in fourteenth-
century poetry and whose relations with Petrarch are of rather
different kinds.

Sennuccio (*c.* 1275–1349) wrote in the somewhat toned-down version of the *stil novo* which had become common amongst Tuscans in the early part of the fourteenth century, although it is significant, in the light of Petrarch's development, that amongst the small number of his surviving poems are two on the theme of the elderly lover (*Canz.* 9 and 10). He is probably Petrarch's main direct link with poetry of the previous century. The two became friends when Petrarch was quite young. The older poet was exiled from Florence as a result of his involvement with other Whites in Henry VII's siege of the city in 1312. From 1316 to 1326 he was in Avignon, where he too entered humanist circles and was also a protégé of the Colonna. He also made at least one further visit after being allowed to return to Florence. Petrarch addressed seven poems to him which have survived, five of them (the last on his death) being included in the *RVF* (108, 112, 113, 114, 287: for a discussion of 113 see Chapter 6.5), the two classicising poems already mentioned being excluded (*RD* 17 and 18). The poems on both sides have a tone of relaxed intimacy that does not appear elsewhere in the *RVF*, though one of the poems by Sennuccio is written in the name of Giovanni Colonna as a reply to Petrarch's poem to the latter, *Signor mio caro* (*RVF* 266). Petrarch thought enough of his work to mention him, with another friend and minor poet, Franceschino degli Albizzi (who died of the plague in 1348), at the end of his selective survey of Italian poets in the *Triumphus Cupidinis* (4. 37–8), though admittedly in words that suggest personal rather than poetic excellence: 'Senneccio e Franceschin, che fur sí umani, / come ogni uom vide' ('Sennuccio and Franceschino, who were so human, / as every man saw). As always on poetic matters, Petrarch was ruthless but right.

Petrarch's exchanges with Antonio da Ferrara belong to a time when his position as an eminent writer was assured. To a large extent they reflect the differences in prestige and education between the two, but they also show Petrarch stepping outside his familiar persona. Antonio (1315–71/74) was the son of a butcher, an autodidact, and, throughout his life, a second- or third-grade courtier, dependent on the various Northern *signori* for whom he wrote. The acquaintance with Petrarch began in 1343 when a report spread that he had died of an illness in Sicily. Antonio wrote a fullsome canzone of lament and celebration, *I' ho già letto*

el pianto d'i Troiani ('I have read in the past the lament of the
Trjoans': *Rime* 67a), the first line of which gives a hint of the
display of text-book erudition which is to follow, though the
canzone ends with a characteristically forthright and modest
admonition to the poem to say that it is by 'Antonio Beccar, un da
Ferrara, / che poco sa ma volenter impara' ('Antonio Beccari, one
from Ferrara, / who knows little, but learns willingly'). Antonio
eventually received a sonnet in return (to become *RVF* 120), in
which Petrarch assured him that he was still alive though he had
been ill, and disclaimed his worthiness to receive such a tribute.
Sooner or later there followed other *tenzoni* (texts in Antonio,
Rime, 78–82). In the first two Petrarch is surprisingly willing to
debate – playfully, no doubt – worn commonplaces about love
and hope, and the difference between honourable love and carnal
passion, though the authenticity of the second poem (*Rime* 79b)
has been doubted, in part because it ends with the statement that
he has been in love himself more than twenty-two times. Another
tenzone is initiated by Petrarch: in a poem beginning 'Antonio cos'
ha fatto la tua terra?' (*RD* 15: Antonio, *Rime* 80a) Petrarch says
that he has fallen passionately in love with a Ferrarese girl and
asks Antonio who she is. In his reply (*Rime* 80b) Antonio regrets
that Petrarch has become so enamoured that he has forgotten their
friendship, but hopes that the outcome will be that he will stay in
Ferrara, so that he can enjoy his company once again. Obviously
enough we are a long way here from the serious, complex figure of
the *RVF*, though it may just be that the Ferrarese girl is the new
love who appears in *RVF* 270 and 271, from which Petrarch is
glad to say he is quickly liberated, once again by death.

The *tenzoni* are not all there is to Petrarch's poetic relationship
with Antonio. There are three sonnets, one by Antonio (*Rime* 11),
one by Petrarch (*RVF* 102), and one attributed to Boccaccio
(*Rime* 41) (though its authenticity has been doubted), which
rework the same material in almost exactly the same order. The
texts of all three are given at the end of this section. The first
quattrain of each begins with the example of Caesar concealing
his joy at receiving the head of Pompey; the second takes the
opposite case of Hannibal concealing his grief when the head of
his brother Hasdrubal was sent to him; in the sestet the poet
applies the examples to himself, saying that he is obliged to
present to the world the image of someone happier than he really

is. It is quite possible that the original sonnet was by Antonio. An early biography of Petrarch by Lelio de' Lelii (quoted by Bellucci in her notes to Antonio, *Rime* 11) says that Antonio's sonnet came into his hands, and, feeling that the idea was a good one ('l'invenzione era buona') but that the sound of the verse was inadequate, he wrote another, much better sonnet which followed Antonio 'verse by verse with different and much more ornate words' ('verso per verso con diverse e molto piú ornate parole').

The interdependence of the three poems is not simply a matter of the use they make of classical history or the organisation of their material. They also seem to demonstrate a shared sense of what is poetically desirable. All three are based on antitheses of thought and expression which they attempt to integrate with flowing syntax and imagery to give an impression of ease and yet decorum. Antonio has grave difficulties: hampered by Northern forms ('fazzol', 'pianȝendo', 'soa' etc) which contrast uneasily with the Tuscan of the greater part of the poem, he is also semantically loose (eg l.3), melodically awkward (eg in the rhyme between the two proper names in ll.6 and 7), uncertain in his Latinisms (eg 'intrinseche' in l.14) and clumsy in some of his phrases ('la gran testa reverente' in l.5). His main technique for enriching the texture of his verse is lexical repetition ('testa', 'allegrezza', 'canto', 'celar', etc), which gives the poem an air of old-fashioned rigidity, particularly since some of the repeated items appear at the same point in the line. The sonnet attributed to Boccaccio errs in the contrary direction, that is, towards becoming excessively conversational, even casual. In spite of elevated moments (especially l.2), it is willing to be dully prosaic (above all ll.6–7), and, like some poems of Boccaccio which certainly are genuine, it can accept a quite imperfect rhyme (l.8). Petrarch alone maintains throughout his poem (certainly not one of his most important) an evenness of register and tone, which is at the same time subtly varied, creating a whole which is complex, musical and apparently effortless. As elsewhere, he appears not so much to depart from the aesthetic implicit in the work of his fellow-poets as to realise their aspirations more successfully.

There is a point in the *RVF* where we can trace the outlines of another victory over the poetically unfortunate Antonio, a victory which also betrays some of the basic dynamics of the collection. I said above that relations between the two poets began with

Antonio's canzone of lament on Petrarch's reported death in 1343, in response to which Petrarch wrote the sonnet which was to become *RVF* 120. In the *RVF* there is no hint of the destinatee or of the occasion of the poem, but the issue is not forgotten. This sonnet of self-deprecation is placed immediately after the canzone in which Petrarch presents his coronation of 1341 in allegorical form. A *donna*, representing Glory, appears to Petrarch, and enters into a dialogue with him, in the course of which another *donna* representing Virtue also appears. The dialogue is measured, decorous, raising questions of moral and cultural decline and presenting Petrarch as a lonely and devoted aspirant who is eventually symbolically rewarded with the laurel crown. The contrasts with Antonio's poem are striking: for Antonio had simply packed in allegorical figures and authoritative names ranging from Priscian to the Muses, all of whom he represents as coming to pay tribute to the dead Petrarch. There may or may not be any connection so far as the actual composition of Petrarch's canzone is concerned. But it effectively corrects what Antonio had written, and demonstrates how a celebratory poem might be managed. When it is put together with the following sonnet, Antonio's effacement is complete: the issues of celebration and modest refusal of celebration are poetically counterposed within the collection. The link with another poet is reduced to an imprecise occasion preceding the second poem: the poems are now internally related and autonomous. Poetry outside the *RVF* has been absorbed and excluded.

It may be that some of Boccaccio's poetry underwent a similar fate. The friendship between the two writers was largely a humanist one, in which Petrarch played the senior role, and Boccaccio that of admiring disciple. In Italian, although there are broad analogies to be drawn between their treatment of the problem of variety and disorder, their paths mostly diverge. However, in some ways Petrarch was willing to be the learner. His principal model for the *Triumphi* is the *Amorosa visione* and he probably drew on other poems for one or two sonnets in the *RVF*. More importantly, Boccaccio's enthusiasm seems to have made him write directly about the issue of Dante in the late 1350s, which he had previously hoped to pass over in silence, and, more important still, to have confirmed the making of the *RVF* as a serious enterprise. (See 2.2.) So far as the *RVF* are concerned, Boccaccio's shadowy presence is not to be underestimated.

Appendix
Three poems on Caesar and Hannibal

Antonio da Ferrara

Cesare, poi che recevé 'l presente
de la tradita testa in sommo fallo,
dentro fece allegrezza, canto e ballo,
e de for pianse e mostrosse dolente.

E quando la gran testa reverente
del poderoso tartaro Asdruballo
fo presentata al so frate Anniballo,
rise, pianʒendo tutta la soa ʒente.

Per simil piú fiate egli addivene
ch'a l'om conven celar zò ch'ha nel core
per allegrezza o caso de dolore.

E però, se già mai canto d'amore,
fazzol perché celar e' me convene
le 'ntrinseche mie triste e grave pene.
(Bellucci ed., Rime 11)

(Caesar, when he received the present / of the head [of Pompey] most heinously betrayed, / within made mirth, song and dance, / and without wept and showed himself in pain. / And when the great revered head / of the powerful barbarian Hasdrudal / was presented to his brother Hannibal, / he laughed, as all his nation wept. / Similarly often it befits / a man to conceal what he has in his heart / through joy or some painful happening. / And so, if I ever sing with love, / I do so, because it befits me to conceal / my sad and heavy inner torments.)

Petrarch

Cesare, poi che 'l traditor d'Egitto
li fece il don de l'onorata testa,
celando l'allegrezza manifesta,
pianse per gli occhi fuor sí come è scritto;

et Hanibàl, quando a l'imperio afflitto
vide farsi Fortuna sí molesta,
rise fra gente lagrimosa et mesta
per isfogare il suo acerbo despitto.

Et cosí aven che l'animo ciascuna
sua passion sotto 'l contrario manto
ricopre co la vista or chiara or bruna:

però, s'alcuna volta io rido o canto,
facciol, perch'i'non ò se non quest'una
via da celare il mio angoscioso pianto.

(*RVF* 102)

(Caesar, when the traitor of Egypt [Ptolemy] / made him a gift
of the honoured head [of Pompey], / concealing his manifest
joy, / let the tears flow openly from his eyes as it is written. /
And Hannibal, when he saw Fortune make herself so inimical to
his afflicted empire, / laughed amongst people who were tearful
and gloomy, / in order to vent his bitter rancour. / And so it
happens that the inner self / covers each passion that it feels
under the contrary cloak / with an appearance which is now of
cheer, now of gloom. / Hence, if I sometimes laugh or sing, / I
do so because I have none but this one / way to hide my
anguished tears.)

Boccaccio

Cesare, poi ch'ebbe, per tradimento
dell'egiziano duttor, l'orrate chiome,
rallegrossi nel core, en vista come
sí fa qual che di nuovo è discontento.

E allor ch'Annibàl ebbe 'l presento
del capo del fratel, ch'aveva nome
Asdrubal, ricoprí suo grave some
ridendo alla suo gente, ch'era in pianto.

Per somigliante ciascun uom tal volta
per atto allegro o per turbato viso
mostra 'l contrario di ciò che 'l cor sente.

Però, s'i' canto, non dimostro riso:
fo per mostrare a chi mi mira e ascolta
ch'ai dolor gravi i' sia forte e possente.

(*Rime* 41)

(Caesar, when he received, through treachery / of the Egyptian
leader [Ptolemy], the honoured head of hair [of Pompey], /
rejoiced in his heart, in appearance [behaving] as / does one
who is unhappy at an unexpected event. / And when Hannibal
received the present / of the head of his brother, who was
named / Hasdrubal, he covered up the heavy burden [of grief], /
laughing at his people, who were in tears. / Similarly each man
sometimes, / through joyous behaviour or through his disturbed
features / shows the contrary of what he feels in his heart. /
Hence, if I sing, I do not demonstrate [real] mirth: / I act so to
show to those who see and hear me / that I am strong and
powerful in the face of heavy woes.)

2

Composition

2.1 The premisses

The *RVF* is a work with a past. Though there are serious gaps and
even more serious ambiguities, the evidence we have of its
composition is detailed and authoritative. In a way that is not true
of any preceding work and a great many that follow, we are in a
position to write an account of how it evolved and to interpret the
reasons why it should have evolved in that particular way. In
other words, we can begin to write its history.

The major evidence stems directly from Petrarch. Most
importantly, there exists, in modern terminology, a final and fully
authorised edition of the poems: the manuscript now in the
Vatican (Vat. Lat. 3195, conventionally referred to in this context
as V1), which was transcribed at intervals between 1367 and 1374
partly by Giovanni Malpaghini, working under Petrarch's supervision, and partly by Petrarch himself. There is also an autograph
manuscript containing earlier drafts of some poems and notes on
them (Vat. Lat. 3196, conventionally V2). In addition, apart from
snippets of information about individual poems derived from later
manuscripts, there are other manuscripts representing different
stages in the elaboration of the collection, the most important of
which was probably copied out by Boccaccio in consultation with
Petrarch in the early 1360s.

That so much survives is only partly a matter of luck. Though
their importance was publicly acknowledged only in the sixteenth
century with the rise of vernacular humanism, the autograph
manuscripts were already objects of value before then. That they

30

were written by Petrarch, and they contained works by him, was enough to draw them into the humanist tradition. Perhaps initially by mere association with the more prestigious works, they were part of a literary and literate culture which gave primacy to the preservation and transmission of texts, particularly the texts of those who were perceived as masters.

But the initiator of the association was Petrarch himself, who made no distinction in composition between Latin and Italian. In both languages writing meant rewriting, an obsessive revision, reorganisation and supplementation of what was already written. Thus poetry in Italian becomes as literate as that written in Latin. The last residues of orality, and of the textual instability connected with it, are swept away. Changes in the poem are changes made by the author, validated in and by his name, and under his exclusive control. Other changes are illegitimate perversions. When in 1368 Petrarch gave the collection of Italian poems their Latin title, *F[rancisci] P[etrarce] laureati poete rerum vulgarium fragmenta* (literally: *The fragments of vernacular matters of the laureate poet Francesco Petrarca*), he was acknowledging, defensively and disingenuously, the discontinuity and lack of wholeness of his collection of lyric poems (cf. *RVF* 1. 1) and the cultural inferiority of a work written in the 'vulgar' language. But he was also pointing to an identity: these were the writings of a poet crowned for his work in Latin and they merited a Latin title in the same idiom as his other works. Whatever the ideological and theoretical problems, they were part of the same textual universe.

We are thus in a position to see the collection not as a static, closed system, but as a group of texts changing gradually over time. The work becomes a work-in-progress, absorbing into itself the very processes of its own creation rather than eliminating them, and never quite reaching the terminus of perfection. Though the individual poems were all probably finished to Petrarch's satisfaction, their final arrangement could still have undergone further adjustments or additions. At Petrarch's death ending and completion were very close together, but, as with most of his major works, they were still asymptotic. I shall argue in the next chapter that incompletion is fundamental to the structure of the work even in what for us is its definitive form.

The work enters history and we write the history of the work.

But in doing so we can only speak with any confidence of dates, of additions, subtractions, insertions, of style and language. We can make little use of the story of Petrarch and Laura. For that story, which is vitally important for the interpretation of the collection, has come more and more to appear a perfidious guide to its composition. The poems refer to a period running from Good Friday (*RVF* 3), 6 April 1327 (211), when Petrarch first saw Laura, to 1358 or soon after (364). This is the last year registered in a series of fifteen 'anniversary' poems which mark the years that have passed since the first meeting, or, in Part 2, since Laura's death on 6 April 1348 (336). The inaccuracies and coincidences in this story and some of its literary functions in the collection will be discussed in Chapter 5.2. Here it is sufficient to note that the dates marked in the anniversary poems are unreliable pointers to their own dates of composition and to those of surrounding poems. Again and again, when there is further evidence, it runs counter to Petrarch's apparent chronology. Perhaps a few poems already existed before 1327 (such as the first, incomplete version of 23); others that are apparently early were written after 1348; and the collection as a whole was certainly not finished by 1358 or thereabouts. Most of the poems that can be identified as existing in one form or another in the later 1330s do appear in the first hundred poems, but not consecutively, not in chronological sequence and not in an order that corresponds to the times marked in the anniversary poems. In general it seems that the earlier the position of a poem, the earlier is likely to be the date of its first drafting, though there are many important areas of doubt. It is quite possible, for example, that the first twenty and more poems were composed whenever it was that Petrarch decided to make an organised collection of his poems, which may well have been as late as 1349. It may be that many others among the poems written apparently before Laura's death in 1348 were written later, particularly coherent sequences, such as the last twenty poems in Part 1 which only appear very late in the composition of the collection. Petrarch's own comments in the letter which he wrote in 1373 to accompany the version which he sent to Pandolfo Malatesta (*Var.* 9, later revised as *Sen.* 13. 10) create an appealing picture of an old man assembling youthful poems when he has time. It may be that he is partly telling the truth, but the dubious status of vernacular love-poetry, especially for an ageing writer who claims to have renounced poetry altogether, is reason enough why such a picture should be manufactured.

Whilst the poems project one story as history, they resolutely conceal another which we might expect to find. The story of Petrarch's love for Laura merges with the story of a poet's love-affair with poetry (see Chapter 5.4). But the poetry evoking these intermingled stories undergoes no changes which allow us to distinguish between early, middle and late styles. There are variations and differences, some with important narrative implications, but there is no evolutionary dynamic. Romantic and post-Romantic poets develop in the course of their writing career, or so we say. So too does Dante, who both within and across his major works (*Vita nuova, Convivio, Divina commedia*) continually reassesses what he has already written from every point of view in order to push further forward. As far as Petrarch's Italian poetry is concerned, such changes in his aesthetic as occurred took place before the *RVF* (see Chapter 1.4). Within the collection there is no appreciable difference between poems known to have been written in the 1330s (e.g. *Solo e pensoso* (35)) and those known to have been written much later (e.g. *L'aura serena* (196)). At most the later poems seem to have a more complex texture, a greater rhythmical and harmonic density, but more measurable features, such as imagery, lexis, metaphor, are not significantly changed. By the same token the progress of a poem from first draft to final version does not involve radical change: what was already implicit is realised by dint of punctilious refinement, and any reshaping or experiment occurs almost entirely within lines that have been already drawn. In not presenting a dynamic of composition Petrarch is a characteristic writer of the Middle Ages and of the Renaissance, whilst, as in so much else, Dante is the exception. But the consequence for any history of the *RVF* is a serious undermining, and perhaps collapse, of a convenient poetic teleology.

The account of the composition of the *RVF* which follows is more incomplete and sceptical than most which have been published. It is heavily indebted to the scholarship of E.H. Wilkins (1951), whilst following more recent work by Francisco Rico (1976) in departing from some of Wilkins's conclusions. It largely discounts the story of Laura and the dating of the poems projected in the anniversary poems. Tempting though the prospect is, a full history of the *RVF* is not to be written. Any history which is made must be reconstruction linking together the fragments which we have, in much the same way as Petrarch himself wrote history outside the *RVF*. The analogy is not gratuitous. Once we have accepted the invitation which Petrarch's texts extend, we are drawn into an imitation of his processes of composition. That the imitation should be incomplete is written into the texts as we have them: Petrarch knew well enough that even a literary past does not return in its entirety.

2.2 Making the collection

The beginnings are obscure. The group of poems transcribed by Petrarch in the years 1336–8, which was discussed in Chapter 1.4, contained eighteen poems which would eventually be included in the *RVF*. But it does not appear that the group can be thought of as the nucleus around which the rest of the collection was to be built, since it had no particular order and it included poems by other poets. Wilkins termed it a 'reference collection', on the grounds that it was made for further use at some later date.

The period between 1338 and 1360 or thereabouts is extremely shadowy. At some point Petrarch decided to make a collection of his Italian poems which had a significant order to it, but it is not clear when he made the decision or how large the collection was in its early stages. He began to transcribe a selection of poems on 21 August 1342, which Wilkins (1951: 146) thought was the first nucleus of the *RVF* (the 'first form'), but the poems included were probably only about fourteen in number and all would be scattered amongst the first seventy poems of the final version. However, notes that Petrarch made at various times in the years 1349–51 intimate that by then he was at work on a larger collection, and one that was, in some sense, 'in order'. One note, to a draft of what would become *Che debb'io far?* (268), reads:

Transcriptum, non in ordine, sed in alia papiro. 1349.
novembris 28. mane. (Romanò 1955:190)

(Transcribed not in order, but on another sheet of paper. 1349. November 28. morning).

Another, this time to the much-revised *Nel dolce tempo* (23), is fuller, though less easy to interpret:

> post multos annos, 1350 Aprilis 3 mane quoniam triduo exacto institi ad supremam manum vulgarium, ne diutius inter curas distrahar, visum est et hanc in ordine transcribere; sed prius hic ex aliis papiris elicitam scribere. (Romanò, p. 168)

> (After many years, 1350, April 3, morning. Since at the end of three days I pressed on to give the last touch to the vernacular pieces, in order not to be further distracted in the midst of my cares, I decided to transcribe this poem too in order, but first to transcribe it here [i.e. on a sheet now in V2] after extracting it from some other papers.)

There are also other notes which show that Petrarch worked on 265, 270 and 324 about this time, as well as on some poems that were never completed (*Fr.* 1, 3, 7).

Wilkins thought that the composition of the *RVF* was quite well advanced by this time, and describes (1951: 150–3) a 'second form', containing about 150 poems, and divided into two parts, each with their introductory poems, that is, *Voi ch'ascoltate* (*RVF* 1) and *I' vo pensando* (264). But Wilkins's views now seem speculative. Francisco Rico (1976) has proposed that the basic idea and the first phases of elaboration are to be linked with two similar projects in Latin. In January 1350 Petrarch wrote the first letters of the *Familiares* and began collecting and revising others which already existed. In the spring of the same year he also decided to collect his Latin verse letters as the *Epistole metrice*. Like the *RVF*, both projects involved assembling, revising, supplementing and arranging short (or shortish) pieces of writing, and both have introductory pieces, which, like *RVF* 1, allude to the disunity and diversity of the pieces to follow, and suggest the detachment which their author now feels from them and his doubts about their value. Since the first letter in the *Familiares* also mentions that vernacular poems form part of the mass of material which Petrarch is trying to sort through and set in some kind of order, it may well be that it was in fact in 1350 that Petrarch set about making his collection of Italian poems, introducing it with *Voi ch'ascoltate* as in the final version. So far as it went, the collection could well have prefigured the shape of later versions, although it could well not have been divided at 264, since at this stage in all probability few of the poems in Part 2 actually existed. It may also be that, just as Petrarch composed a number of fictional letters about this time to represent his early correspondence in Book 1 of the *Familiares*, so he also wrote the first twenty or so poems in the *RVF*.

Presumably Petrarch continued to work on the collection at intervals during the 1350s, though his notes show a certain lack of enthusiasm. The note to 23 quoted on page 35 suggests that he wished to be done with Italian poetry and to turn to more important matters. Further notes have the same air:

1356, novembris 4, sero. dum cogito de fine harum nugarum. (To 23: Romanò, p. 169)

(in the evening, whilst thinking of [making] an end of these trifles)

Transcripti isti duo in ordine post mille annos, 1357. mercurii. hora 3. novembris 29 dum volo his omnino finem dare. ne unquam amplius me teneant. et jam Jerolimus ut puto primum quaternum scribere est adortus pergameno pro domino Azone postea pro me idem facturus. (To 77: Romanò, p. 118)

(These two transcribed in order after a thousand years, in 1357, on Wednesday November 29 at the third hour, whilst wishing to bring these [poems] to an end altogether, so that they should not ever occupy me any further, and already Jerolimus [a scribe?] has begun to write out the first quaternion on parchment for master Azzo [da Correggio]. Afterwards he is to do the same for me.)

It is generally assumed that Azzo da Correggio, the tyrant of Parma, who had protected Petrarch during his visit to war-torn central Italy in the 1340s and for whom he wrote the canzone *Quel c' ha nostra natura in sé più degno* (*RD* 29) (which was always excluded from the *RVF*), got his copy of the poems, and that this 'Correggio' form, the third in Wilkins's classification, only needed to be extended, with some adaptation of its two *termini*, to become the next version, the first actually to survive.

Working from the latter, the 'Chigi' or fourth form on his scheme, Wilkins (1951: 93ff) argued that the Correggio form contained *RVF* 1–142 in its first part and 264–92 in its second, the one notable difference being at *RVF* 121: as would continue to be the case until late in the composition of V1, the madrigale was one beginning *Donna mi vene* (*RD* 13), not the eventual *Or vedi ben*.

The next stage is crucial. Whatever the previous forms, the Chigi version (so called from Agostino Chigi, of whose manuscript collection it became part) exists, and quite clearly the final version would develop from it. It is also the version that appears to have effectively resolved Petrarch's doubts, though he would continue in more public statements to decry the poems to be included as juvenilia.

Boccaccio seems to have played the roles of both catalyst and scribe. He had known Petrarch personally since 1351, and, apparently, the redirection of his own work away from the vernacular into Latin during the 1350s was influenced by Petrarch's example. But, as I remarked at the end of the previous chapter (1. 4), the influence was not all in one direction. Boccaccio had pressed upon Petrarch the need to recognise the value of Italian poetry and in particular of Dante. If Petrarch's notes to his poems and his letter about Dante to Boccaccio of 1359 (*Fam.* 21. 15: see Chapter 4.4) signal deep uncertainties about the issue, by the early 1360s he seems to have changed his mind completely. In 1362 Boccaccio visited Petrarch in Venice. In all probability he took away with him from the visit a manuscript of the collection of Italian poems as it then stood. This he then transcribed sometime between 1363 and 1366. It has been convincingly argued by De Robertis (1974) that this manuscript (Chigiano L. V. 176) was originally joined with another, now quite separate manuscript (Chigiano L. VI. 213), the whole containing Boccaccio's biography of Dante, the *Vita nuova*, the *Divina commedia*, fifteen of Dante's canzoni, Boccaccio's poem to Petrarch, *Italie iam certus honos*, and the incomplete *RVF*. The implications are plain: by this stage Petrarch was ready to accept the validity of vernacular poetry and to allow his work to be linked with that of Dante, competing with, or, perhaps, complementing the work of the 'leader of eloquence in our vernacular' ('ille nostri eloquii dux vulgaris'), as he would call Dante in the second, much more approving letter which he wrote about him in 1366 (*Sen.* 5. 2).

There was much else to encourage such a change of mind. The early work on the *RVF* had been carried out whilst Petrarch's centre was still Provence, where Italian poetry counted for little except amongst Italian exiles. But in 1353 he had made his definitive move to Italy. After a period in Milan, his centre had become the North-East, where, since, the time of Dante, rulers had encouraged and patronised Italian poets (see Chapter 1.2). One after another, Azzo da Correggio, Pandolfo Malatesta and a further unknown patron demanded and received versions of the collection. Whatever the private reasons or the insistences of friends such as Boccaccio, there were also public pressures and public support for composition in the vernacular.

The Chigi form contains *RVF* 1–189 in its first part (with *Donna mi vene* at 121, and minus fifteen other poems that would eventually be included) and 264–304 in its second. The division between the two parts is marked by a page and a half which are left blank. Given the restricted scope of the second part, the division was probably provisional and the empty page and a half were to be filled by other poems at some later date. Certainly the opening poem of the second part (264) does not have an illuminated initial indicating that it is a new beginning as it will have in the final version. All the same, the collection had viable conclusions to its two parts: *Passa la nave mia* (189) is a poem of despair, and *Mentre che 'l cor* (304) recognises the futility of continuing to write verse. Provisionally the collection was shaped at its two terminal points. It also had a title: *Francisci Petrarche de Florentia nuper laureati fragmentorum liber* (*The book of fragments of Francesco Petrarca lately crowned poet laureate*). The 'lately', as Rico has argued (1976: 117), is not evidence that the title was invented soon after Petrarch's coronation in 1341 (as has been thought), but rather that Petrarch, or perhaps Boccaccio, wanted to stress that the author was the one poet to have been crowned in modern times. Again the humanist quality of the project is to the fore.

The rest is mainly the story of the making of the final manuscript (V1) as reconstructed by Wilkins. In the latter part of 1366 Petrarch set his amanuensis, Giovanni Malpaghini, to elaborate on the Chigi version. Working under Petrarch's supervision, Malpaghini transcribed into V1 poems 1–190 (still with *Donna mi vene* but now making all the insertions except for

179) and, in the second part, 264–318. He also added the definitive title. Then, on 21 April 1367, he suddenly decided to stop working for Petrarch. Wilkins suggested that six months of copying Italian poetry was too much for a young man eager to work on prestigious Latin texts. Whether this was so or not, Malpaghini did no more work on V1 and soon left Petrarch altogether, first for a few weeks, and then after a year of further employment, for good. (See *Sen. 5. 5* and 6.)

What Malpaghini had written makes up Wilkins's fifth ('Johannine') form of the collection, though, given the abruptness with which transcription was broken off, it cannot be considered to have even the provisional finish of the Chigi version. There is certainly no sign that Petrarch thought of it as in any way complete: within a few months he had begun to add more poems in his own hand. The last, remarkably active phase of elaboration had begun. Work on the manuscript would continue, with frequent brief interruptions, from now until not long before Petrarch's death in 1374. There would also be two more provisional versions. The one made for Pandolfo Malatesta (Wilkins's sixth form) was sent to him on 4 January 1373 with an accompanying letter (*Var.* 9, later *Sen.* 13. 10). The other, the seventh or 'Quiriniano' form (so called from the library in Brescia where a copy is preserved), was prepared for an unknown patron during the same year.

The final stages of composition are bewilderingly complex, since more than with any other phase the abundance of the evidence means that we can see here Petrarch's detailed and piecemeal methods in operation. But the general pattern is clear. Within V1 Petrarch made minimal alterations to the parts transcribed by Malpaghini, only inserting the early poem to Geri dei Gianfigliazzi at 179 and replacing, probably not before 1373, *Donna mi vene* with *Or vedi ben* (121). His main work consisted of the addition of poems, usually in small groups, to the two ends of the two parts of the collection, the division of which seems to have been made definitive in 1368 when the opening of 264 was decorated with an ornate initial. In Part 1 the additions proceeded in largely linear fashion. By the time of the Malatesta and Quiriniano versions Petrarch had reached 243, and added the last twenty poems (244–63) later in 1373 or even in 1374. The later poems in Part 2 caused him more hesitation. When he sent the Malatesta version off, he said in the accompanying letter that he had left spaces at the ends of both parts so that further poems could be inserted 'if anything turns up' ('si quidquam occurret': *Var. 9*). On the evidence of a manuscript derived from the Malatesta version, it seems that the poem to the Virgin and some others amongst the last thirty were included. Petrarch was already clear that it would be the poem to the Virgin which would conclude the whole work, since the manuscript contains a note saying that it should be put at the end ('in fine libri ponatur'), but he was uncertain about the poems preceding it from 337 onwards. He sent to Pandolfo Malatesta a supplement containing some of the omitted poems perhaps for insertion in any order that Pandolfo thought suitable, though these poems reappear in the same order in the Quiriniano version. Then, when he finally inserted these poems in V1, he rearranged them considerably, whilst keeping the poem to the Virgin at the end. But he seems to have been dissatisfied with this arrangement too, and at some point later in 1373 or during the last year of his life, he put Arabic numerals by poems 336–66 to indicate the new and, as it turned out, final order. This last alteration would not be effected in V1, nor in the mass of editions deriving from it. It is, however, the arrangement (and numeration) followed in all modern editions, and which I follow in all my references to the later poems.

The later stages of composition make it almost certain that the *RVF* was not composed to a pre-established plan. The Malatesta and Quiriniano versions, as we have them, have minor discrepancies at various points with V1, which suggest that Petrarch was willing even in 1373 to allow for almost impromptu readjustments. From the addition of the last poems to Part 1 and the rearrangements at the end of Part 2, it seems that it was at this time that he decided to emphasise narrative and dramatic elements in his arrangement. Poems 244–63 are those in which anticipations of Laura's death are most accented, whilst in the last poems of the sequence (261–3) there is a climatic celebration of her virtues that stands in strong contrast to the opening of Part 2. The original order of 337–66 plays on formal contrasts of tone and theme, especially in the placing of the pathetic and nostalgic *Vago augelletto* (now 353) before the canzone to the Virgin. It is only in the revised order (which may seem now the most natural one but which Petrarch seems not to have first entertained) that the drama of ending comes to the fore, first with two opposed and in a sense conclusive canzoni (359 and 360) and then in the sequence of poems marking a turning towards God (363–6). (See also Chapter 3.3.)

There is no reason for thinking that other adjustments were not possible or would not have been made. As Wilkins remarked (1951: 186), other poems could have been inserted in the blank pages left after 263. In a sense the *RVF* is a work-in-progress even when finished. Even at the end Petrarch's aesthetic does not turn on that kind of necessity which allows no change to be imagined. It is the authorial text which ultimately makes the order of the poems unchangeable, and, up to a point, arbitrarily so (see also Chapter 3.1).

2.3 Making poems

Petrarch cultivated the impression that the *RVF* is made up of youthful poems which he collected late in life. The first sonnet speaks of poems written 'in sul mio primo giovenile errore / quand' era in parte altr' uom da quel ch'io sono' ('at the time of my first youthful error / when I was in part a different man from the one I am': 1.3–4). The letter accompanying the Malatesta version of the collection of 1373 is fuller and almost throwaway in tone: 'I still have with me many pieces of vernacular poetry of this kind, on extremely old sheets which are so eaten away by age that they can barely be read. When one day or another dawns without commitments, I usually extract one sheet or another from the pile as a form of relaxation' ('Sunt apud me huius generis vulgarium adhuc multa, et vetustissimis schedulis, et sic senio exesis ut vix legi queant. E quibus, si quando unus aut alter dies otiosus affulserit, nunc unum, nunc aliud elicere soleo, pro quodam diverticulo laborum': *Var.* 9).

This appealing picture, shorn of its casual air, fits well enough with the process of mosaic-like composition outlined in the previous section. But in fact the pieces in the mosaic were not inert. Some were written specially for the collection, others were extensively revised, sometimes over years. The metamorphosis canzone, *Nel dolce tempo* (23), is the extreme case, so far as we know. One of Petrarch's notes signals it out as 'one of my first compositions' ('est de primis inventionibus nostris': Romanò,

p. 169). It first appears in incomplete forms in the 'reference collection' of 1336–8 and then passes through various intermediate stages before its eventual transcription by Malpaghini into V1 in 1367. But that a poem was relatively early did not necessarily mean that it required much modification. The one later alteration to *Solo et pensoso* (35), which was also written by 1336–8, was the substitution of a single word in its fourth line ('ove' for 'dove', both meaning 'where'). And conversely, that a poem was relatively late did not mean that it would not undergo many more modifications, the canzone *Standomi un giorno* (323), written in the 1350s, being the outstanding example.

I remarked in the first section of this chapter that the revisions never became radical remodelling of the first draft. Lines were reordered, particular words were re-placed, rhythms were adjusted, but, however extensive the revisions, the poem as a whole remained the same: the aim was to polish and to perfect, not to reorient or to bring to light something obscurely felt. The best-known of Petrarch's rewritings shows just how thorough and painstaking these revisions could be. Originally the first canzone on the death of Laura (268) began:

> Amore, in pianto ogni mio riso è volto,
> ogni allegrezza in doglia,
> ed è oscurato il sole agli occhi miei;
> ogni dolce pensier dal cor m'è tolto,
> e sola ivi una voglia
> rimasa m'è di finir gli anni rei
> e di seguir colei,
> la qual omai di qua veder non spero.
>   (Romanò, p. 202 = *Fr.* 4)

(Love, all my laughter is turned to tears, / all my joy to grief, / and the sun is darkened before my eyes. / Any sweet thought is taken from my heart, / and I have one wish alone / remaining there, to finish the bad years of life / and to follow her / whom I no longer hope to see this side of the grave.)

Petrarch was dissatisfied with this uninteresting and inconsequential phrasing. He transcribed the poem in V2 on 28 November 1349, and soon after, he wrote above it: 'non videtur satis triste principium' ('the beginning does not seem sad enough'). At some later date he remembered, or reread, an epigram by Q. Catulus given by Aulus Gellius:

> Ibimus quaesitum: verum ne ipsi teneamur
> formido. Quid ago? Da, Venus, consilium.

(We shall go to ask: but I am afraid lest we ourselves should be ensnared. / What shall I do? Venus, give advice.)

From the second line came a new opening that eventually emerged as:

> Che debb'io far? Che mi consigli, Amore?

(What must I do? What do you advise me, Love?)

although for some time Petrarch hesitated over 'debb'io far', trying out also 'farò' ('shall I do') and 'faccio omai' ('do I do now'), before arriving at the version we now read.

The lines that followed were also rewritten:

Tempo è ben di morire,	2
et ò tardato piú ch'i' non vorrei.	3
Madonna è morta, et à seco il mio core;	4
et volendol seguire,	5
interromper conven quest'anni rei,	6
perché mai veder lei,	7
di qua non spero, et l'aspettar m'è noia.	8

(It is well time to die / and I have delayed longer than I would wish. / My lady is dead, and she has my heart with her; / and wishing to follow it, / I should interrupt the course of these bad years of life, / because I do not hope to see her / this side of the grave, and writing is an aggravation for me.)

Though the general sense and some phrases are retained, the improvement is obvious: the phrasing is more musical, the syntax more varied, the sense denser and more allusive. But the new version was itself reached after many hesitations and revisions. In line 4 Petrarch tried: 'Madonna è gita e portane il mio core' ('My lady has gone and bears away my heart'), but he noted on 28 December 1351 that he should resolve the ambiguity ('. . . attende ambiguitatem sententie dicendo'), alluding presumably to the possibility that 'gita' could mean 'gone away' rather than 'gone to the other world': 'portane' ('carries away') was also rejected, probably because it introduces action in the present where stillness is required. Line 5 had a particularly involved development: the first attempt, 'parmi il me' di seguire' ('it appears to me the better thing to follow'), was rhythmically awkward and anomalous as a locution in the *RVF*. Petrarch followed it with 's'io vo' lei seguire' ('if I wish to follow her'), and then 's'io gli vo' seguire' ('if I want to follow it [my heart]'), before arriving (via 'volendo io') at his final solution, the more resonant, rhythmically regular 'volendol seguire' ('wishing to follow it'), which preserves the continuity with the heart of the previous line without the emphasis on it, or on Laura, or on himself that all the previous attempts had shown. Line 6 was also considerably weaker: 'romper conven quest'anni acerbi e rei' ('I should break off these bitter bad years'), in which 'romper' lacks the weight of 'interromper', though the new word means losing one of the pairs of balanced words ('acerbi et rei') that Petrarch characteristically was drawn to. In l.7 he hesitated between three ways of saying 'since' – 'perché', 'che già' and 'poiché'. He had first chosen 'perché' and eventually came back to it, presumably because it accords with the immediate sound context ('ved*er*', 'sp*er*o'), whereas 'che già' overloads lines 7–8 with monosyllables and 'poiché' makes an awkward pararhyme with 'n*oi*a' (line 8). These are only the most significant modifications in the opening lines of the poem, and the punctilious revisions continue with similar intensity through to its end.

If there is torment in Petrarch, it is in this work of refinement. But it is a torment that comes to an end. Eventually Petrarch is satisfied, as he often indicates by noting by the final version of a line 'hoc placet' ('approved'). And inevitably he is right: the rhythms are smoothed, ambiguities disappear, transitions are eased, the syntax varied and the whole texture made dense, clear, even. *Labor limae* conceals art and creates naturalness and spontaneity.

The poem by Q. Catulus was obviously crucial for the

rewriting of 268. In all probability other poems were similarly affected by Petrarch's reading. In some cases the original starting-point was another text, such as poems by Horace and Arnaut Daniel (see Chapter 4.3), or else poems by Petrarch himself. He makes the idea of being inspired by the act of writing a motif in the canzoni on Laura's eyes (especially 71. 108–10). It seems, from another note to 268, written in November 1349, that he was not exaggerating:

Videtur nunc animus ad hec expedienda pronus propter sonitia de morte sennucij et de Aurora, que his diebus dixi. et erexerunt animum. (Romanò, p. 190)

(My frame of mind now seems eager to get these [lines? poems?] finished, on account of the sonnets on the deaths of Sennuccio (287) and Aurora (267), which I composed in the last few days, and they have stimulated my mental energies.)

Traces of the process remain in the texts. In 1368 Petrarch reworked *L'aura serena* (196), a poem apparently written during Laura's lifetime. He discarded the original sestet, but instead of rejecting the lines completely he revised them and incorporated them into a related poem, *L'aura gentil* (194), which, together with *L'aura celeste* (197), was either first composed or rewritten at this time (Wilkins 1951: 171). Poems 155 (*Non fur ma' Giove*) and 156 (*I' vidi in terra*) seem to have had a similar genesis, the latter having originally had the tercets of the former (Romanò, pp. 79–84). These are presumably not isolated cases. The remarkable number of lexical links between contiguous poems (see Chapter 3.4) make it likely that many other poems came into being through interference of one poem with another of this kind, as if, in conformity with Mallarmé's famous dictum, Petrarch really did make poems with words, not ideas.

One instance of rewriting, on what were perhaps originally stylistic or formal grounds, has implications for the collection as a whole. In June 1369 Petrarch turned up the sonnet *Voglia mi sprona* (*RVF* 211), which he had previously rejected. The note he made is not entirely clear though its general sense is evident:

Mirum, hoc cancellatum et damnatum post multos annos, casu

relegens, absolui et transcripsi in ordine statim, non obstante 1369, Junii 22, hora 23, veneris; pauca postea, die 27, in vesperis, mutavi fine (?); et de hoc f[inis] erit al[ius]. (Romanò, p. 101)

(Amazing, rereading by chance after many years this [sonnet] which had been crossed out and condemned, I absolved it and transcribed it in order immediately, in spite of [having rejected it], on Friday, June 22, 1369, at the 23rd hour(?). A few days later, on the 27th, at the time of vespers, I changed the end. And the end of this will be different.)

Originally the tercet concluding the poem read as follows:

> Nel laberinto intrai, né veggio ond'esca
> su l'ora prima il dí sesto d'aprile.
> Lasso che insieme presi l'esca e l'amo.

(I entered the labyrinth, and cannot see how to leave, / at the first hour on the sixth day of April. / Alas, I took the hook and the bait together.)

Petrarch was right: the last line in this version is very weak. The revised version is much better:

> Mille trecento ventisette, a punto
> su l'ora prima, il dí sesto d'aprile,
> nel laberinto entrai, né veggio ond'esca.

(In 1327, precisely / at the first hour on the sixth day of April / I entered the labyrinth, and cannot see how to leave.)

But this sonnet, so nearly damned, is vital for the narrative of the *RVF*. Without it the reader would not gather from the poems alone that Petrarch fell in love with Laura on 6 April, and without the revision would not have known that the year was 1327. It appears that it was only in 1369 that Petrarch decided to give the *RVF* a precise historical starting-point.

Tornami a mente (336) is the parallel sonnet in Part 2. Its final tercet specifies the moment of Laura's death in exactly the same way:

. . .

> Sai che 'n mille trecento quarantotto,
> il dí sesto d'aprile, in l'ora prima,
> del corpo uscío quell'anima beata.

(. . . You know that in 1348 / on the sixth day of April, at the first hour, / that blessed soul left her body.)

Wilkins (p. 175) puts this poem amongst a number transcribed into V1 in late 1369 or early 1370, that is a few months after the recuperation of the corresponding poem in Part 1. It is more than likely that it was written or rewritten at this stage on the basis of the first poem and inserted in Part 2 with a similar narrative function.

The repercussions of the work Petrarch had carried out on *Voglia mi sprona* did not stop there. He had expunged the original last line of that poem ('Lasso che insieme presi l'esca e l'amo') but it seems that he still thought of it as harbouring a potential conclusion to a sonnet. The very next poem, *Beato in sogno* (212), provides the occasion:

> Cosí venti anni, grave et lungo affanno,
> pur lagrime et sospiri et dolor merco:
> in tale stella *presi l'esca et l'amo*.

(So for twenty years, in long oppressive labour, / I have dealt only in tears and sighs and pain: / such were the stars when I *took the bait and the hook*.)

As these lines show, the poem is one of the apparently self-dating anniversary poems, the twenty years that have gone by situating it in 1347. In the light of the other two poems I have discussed it is hard not to believe that it was either composed from scratch or substantially rewritten in 1369, at a moment when Petrarch had become interested in reinforcing the chronology of the collection and perhaps only as a result of dissatisfaction with the ending of a particular poem.

Though copious, the evidence we have does not allow more than a little of the interaction between the composition of the whole and the composition of separate poems to be even tentatively reconstructed. But it seems certain that such an interaction occurred on a considerable scale. As will become evident in the next chapter, the eventual structure of the collection presupposes more interplay of that kind than it does general planning either before or during its making. Indeed the *RVF* absorbs at least some developments which occurred in the course of composition (whether rejected lines or the division into two parts) and gives them a permanent place. The changefulness and disorder of experience which were a constant preoccupation for Petrarch also generate poetic chances which he is happy to seize.

3

Structure

3.1 What kind of structure?

It is tempting to ignore the precise arrangement that Petrarch gave to his poems. Apart from moments which are highlighted, such as the beginning and end, the collection offers the freedom to move backwards and forwards, comparing and contrasting at will, which most collections of short poems offer their readers. Though some poems are obviously set off against each other or linked in some way through their positioning, most seem to ask to be fitted only loosely into the minimal narrative that they project or presuppose, whether we class the narrative as love-story, auto-biography or exemplary moral tale. Poems are early or late, belong to a time when Laura was away or ill, when she was dead or Petrarch was old. It always seems possible to work out a more exact story and chronology from internal and external informa-tion, but from many points of view exactitude on these counts does not matter. The circumstances are always rudimentarily imaginable, and that is sufficient, at least up to a point.

Many readers, perhaps most, have undoubtedly read the *RVF* in this way, and with justification. A whole tradition, stretching back to antiquity and forward from Petrarch, assumes that the individual lyric poem is the thing and that the arrangement of a poetic sequence is secondary, even incidental. Petrarch himself never made a fetish of completeness. He allowed for some circulation of versions of the collection that were incomplete and slightly differently arranged. He sent poems in ones and twos to friends (Wilkins 1951: 289). His own hesitations particularly

49

during the later stages of making the collection might suggest
fundamental uncertainties in the face of an intractable problem
rather than a working towards its solution. And yet to settle for a
reading of the poems which pays little or no attention to the final
outcome is to settle for something partial, refusing the invitations
which the collection extends to take account of its structure and
relegating to some limbo of curious obsessions the long elaboration that it underwent.

What kind of structure might we expect? Petrarch's notes speak
of the transcription of poems 'in ordine' ('in order') during the
composition of the collection. One possibility is that the 'order' is
a comprehensive design regulating the deployment of the whole
and the position and meaning of each poem. In this perspective
the *RVF* will not be loosely connected poems, the 'rime sparse' of
the first line of poem 1 or the 'fragments' of the title, but a unified
whole – what Italian criticism terms a *poema* – a large-scale work
comparable to the *Divina commedia* or the *Aeneid*.

I shall argue in this chapter that the collection has no order of
this kind, no intricate architecture that can eventually be
intellectually mastered. Instead it has a complex arrangement
(*ordo*), in which order and disorder continually interact, or, to
state the same thing in different words, a series of orders interact
which are not reconcilable in a superior synthesis. The poems are
present on the page in a fixed arrangement. In other respects their
ordering shifts according to the perspective within which it is seen
and the distance at which it is seen. Overall, certain regularities
emerge, although, since there are always exceptions, they never
fully define themselves or are totally consistent. Looked at more
closely, the *RVF* appears more as an ever-changing network of
variations, with continually renewed patterns, within and across
even the most established of the rules which Petrarch creates for
himself and for subsequent Italian poetry. The play of instability is
central to the collection: it gives rise to some of its important
pleasures, as well as to the literary and moral problems which it
confronts. From many points of view, the structure is best seen, in
Petrarch's own metaphors, as a labyrinth, a wood, an unpeopled
landscape crossed by no paths or by numberless ones. Modern
criticism might speak of a process, a poetic practice disturbing the
very ideas of order and orthodoxy which it simultaneously
affirms.

3.2 Problems

Three general principles on which the collection might be organised immediately suggest themselves. They are chronological sequence, whether historically accurate or not, arrangement by theme, and arrangement by metrical form. All are identifiable in the *RVF*, but each is an inadequate explanation of structure in isolation. Nor can they be easily reconciled with each other, since there is no logical connection between them. Indeed, there may be some degree of contradiction.

Chronological sequence is the most humble and most tyrannical way of arranging discrete poems, since in itself it presupposes no order at all except succession. Petrarch obviously asks the reader to take account of the years going by, situating along that arc of time from 1327 to 1358, or thereabouts, the specific incidents and events from which the poems appear to spring. But structurally there is no subservience to temporal succession. Whilst continually acknowledging the power of time, within the limited compass of poetic organisation Petrarch also neutralises it. Many poems are imprecisely located in historical time and few enjoy any dynamic temporal relation with each other. Chronology itself is sparingly indicated in the irregularly distributed anniversary poems, two of which (145 and 266) are in any case out of sequence (see Chapter 5.2). Repeatedly formal patterning obtrudes as being at least as important as succession, if not more so. Most strikingly Laura's death, which seems to divide the story, does not correspond with Petrarch's division of the collection. The break after 263 leaves Laura apparently alive for the first three poems of Part 2, her death being first registered in *Oimè il bel viso* (267).

There are also thematic and formal disparities. The great majority of poems are homogeneous in the sense that, whatever their further implications, they are concerned with Laura and with loving her. But scattered amongst the Laura poems there are some eighteen political, moral or occasional poems which are not love-poems in any obvious sense, and another seven or eight borderline cases. There are precedents enough for including non-amorous material in earlier collections of poetry, but these provide no guide to the logic of their distribution, other than reinforcing an impression of randomness.

And then there is metre. The forms of poem which Petrarch uses are themselves clearly defined, but their arrangement is irregular and unprecedented. Earlier anthologies of lyrics by different authors had been arranged on the basis of metrical form: all the canzoni were set before all the sonnets, other forms being grouped with one or the other of these two (Wilkins 1951: 266). In the *Vita nuova* Dante had abandoned this crude system, in favour of a complex almost symmetrical patterning of different forms, the rationale for which can be largely elicited from the prose narrative and commentary intercutting and surrounding the poems. Petrarch also brings poems of different kinds together, but he presents no comparable explanation and creates no overall symmetries. The 317 sonnets make up the metrical norm. Amongst them, appearing either singly or in various combinations, are forty-nine poems in other forms. The positioning of some (such as closing the collection with the canzone to the Virgin) seems quite explicable in both narrative and formal terms. For most the rationale is not at all apparent, though it is noticeable that the majority of deviations from the norm are concentrated in the first half of Part 1.

Not surprisingly there has always been a temptation to bring order to this apparent confusion or to complete an order that seems to be potentially there but to have eluded Petrarch himself. It is a temptation to which editors have been particularly prone. Some, even in the 19th century, applied the dodoesque criterion of metrical form (Wilkins 1951: 273–4), but most stuck to something like Petrarch's organisation, except at the point of transition between Part 1 and Part 2. The traditional titles for the two parts, *Rime in vita di M.L.* (*Poems written in the lifetime of Lady Laura*) and *Rime in morte di M.L.* (*Poems written after the death of Lady Laura*) had crept into the original manuscript after Petrarch's death (Carducci and Ferrari eds 1899: xxiii), and were readily taken up. With them came a tendency to regularise the transition by beginning the *rime in morte* with *Oimè il bel viso*, the poem announcing Laura's death. In the sixteenth century Alessandro Vellutello's widely read edition combined a division based on Laura's death with a thematic division, to give the whole collection three clear and roughly coherent parts. That particular solution was almost as extreme as one based on metrical form, but the practice of dividing the collection before *Oimè il bel viso* hung on. Even Giosuè Carducci and Severino Ferrari, in their indispensable edition of 1899, felt that in this instance 'the almost religious custom' (as they called it in their preface) overrode philological exactitude. Ferdinando Neri (1951) adopted the converse solution, sweeping the issue away by abolishing any distinction between the two parts. Nowadays, largely through the example and influence of Gianfranco Contini (1964, but originally 1949), the original division has generally been restored, usually with a purely functional nomenclature, such as Part 1 and Part 2. I shall argue later that it is a division that has several important purposes.

But it may be that any apparent disorder will fall into shape, if only we can find the correct key. There have recently been various interpretations of the *RVF* as a form of spiritual autobiography, perhaps more exemplary than personal, in which number symbolism has played a prominent part. It is just possible that the 366 poems correspond to the days of the year, either a normal year (such as 1327), in which case the first poem will be a prelude, or a leap year (such as 1348). If the poems are then read against the Christian calendar, beginning on Good Friday, 6 April (when Petrarch first saw Laura), some surprising results can be obtained. Most strikingly, *I' vo pensando*, the canzone opening Part 2, corresponds to Christmas Day. The implications are plain: Part 1, beginning with the Crucifixion, is the period without God, and Part 2, beginning with the Nativity, is the period when God is reborn in the soul of the sinner.

It is impossible to prove or disprove the existence of such a 'calendrical structure', but as a solution, it seems to give rise to more difficulties than it resolves. The composition of the collection does not give any hints of following any detailed plan of this kind. The poems themselves do not allude to Christian festivals other than the Crucifixion. On the face of it *I' vo pensando* is concerned with separation from God, not Christ's rebirth. There are other problems too, most conspicuously the fact that in reality the basic date, 6 April 1327 (mentioned in poem 211) was not Good Friday (indicated in poem 3) (see Chapter 5.2). Although it is not completely satisfactory to do so, it seems best to consider the coincidence between the number of poems and the number of days in a leap year as a secondary, decorative attribute of the collection, with no further significance.

3.3   The emergent patterns

If the arrangement of the poems resists explanation in terms of rational order, it does not follow that it is haphazard or confused. The disorder may be calculated randomness, a carefully nourished variety. Wilkins (1951: 154) thought that, up to and including the Correggio version of 1357, Petrarch applied the three principles already mentioned – variety of theme, variety of form and chronological sequence – but that thereafter, beyond the careful adjustments at the end of the collection, he added poems more or less as they came to hand and as his habits of intermittent work and frequent movements from place to place allowed. The final result for Wilkins was a rather ramshackle edifice in parts of which some elements of systematic building were still visible.

Wilkins's view flies in the face of the intuitive conviction that there is much more to the later development and final structure of the collection than coacervation. From at least the first surviving version (the Chigi of the early 1360s) its mosaic growth is quite consistent. Completion could have come about in several ways, and, in the event, it involved some rethinking. But the alternatives were already implicit in the text as it stood then. If there was an element of arbitrariness in the solutions eventually adopted, that was because arbitrariness was a constituent feature of the work, not a signal of organisational failure.

But in putting the accent on variety Wilkins evoked a fertile notion or complex of notions, the ambiguous attractions of which Petrarch knew very well. As usual he is not a theoretical innovator, though he returns with more subtlety and more insistence to the terms 'varietas' and 'varius' than had ancient rhetoricians, who had merely said that variety was needed to maintain the pleasure and interest of the reader or listener (e.g. Cicero, *De oratore* 1. 118, 2. 177, and Quintilian, *Institutio oratoria* 4. 2. 118, 11.3. 44). As one version of John of Garland's *Poetria nova* pointed out (Lawler ed. 1974: 830) in one of the rare comments by medieval rhetoricians on the subject, it is implicit in Horace's injunction to mix the useful and the sweet. In a similar vein Petrarch suggests in the *De vita solitaria* that diversity enhances meaning (making it 'significantius'), so that the reader 'can easily judge the difference in importance between very different things that are juxtaposed' ('facile iudicet quid inter res diversissimas iuxta se positas intersit': *Prose*: 300). But he is generally less moralistic. For him variety is primarily a source of pleasure in literature, as he remarks particularly in prefaces and conclusions to his works, and also, as he remarks on other occasions, a source of pleasure in life. Literature itself varies the tedium of existence (*Fam.* 24. 2); he hopes the variety of his writings will make up for their qualitative defects (*Fam.* 1. 1; 24. 13; *De rem.* 2, Praefatio); it is variety that makes a prospect such as the landscape of Northern Italy so pleasing (*Fam.* 8. 5: cf. *De rem.* 1. 86). All the same, with only a slight shift of emphasis, what appears as diversity, variation, novelty, becomes negative. Variety shades easily into instability of purpose, emotional confusion, intellectual uncertainty, and in general the mutability of the self and the world. A disorder which is calculated and, therefore, in some sense ordered, is not easily distinguished from a disorder which is out of control; and looking for happy chances may just lead to unfortunate accidents. Over and against variety rise the positive virtues of its opposites: tedium and monotony become steadfastness, certainty, clarity, regularity, an overcoming or transcendence of the succession of surfaces that experience and literature present. Of itself variety is not sufficient aesthetically, morally or intellectually: without it something indispensable is lost.

In each of Petrarch's larger works there is some degree of opposition between variety and regularity, order and disorder. All consist of short units, or fragments, assembled over quite long periods of time, with interruptions for work on other projects and with at least some measure of rewriting and rearranging. In the majority, narrative does not structure the whole, though narrative pieces may be included. Instead there are different kinds of loose combination, in which variety seems to be the main criterion – listings under various headings in the *Rerum memorandarum* and the *De viris illustribus*, loose concatenation in the *De vita solitaria* and the *De otio religioso*, free arrangement in the *De remediis* with an overall thematic contrast between its two books. But the urge to go beyond the compendium structure is evident. In the *Africa*, Petrarch's serious attempt at a large-scale poem, the eventual outcome is something incomplete and discontinuous, with damaging consequences for the poem as an epic. In Latin it is only in the collections of letters, conceived and begun at the same time as the *RVF*, that Petrarch manages the arrangement of 'fragments' in a way that satisfies some of the unitary and narrative exigencies evident in the *Africa* and at the same time corresponds to his methods of working and his need for formal freedom. Up to a point the arrangement is chronological (whether invented or not), so that, as Petrarch puts it in the retrospective letter which concludes the *Familiares* (24. 13. 5), 'Thus the reader, if he should be interested, will understand the stages in my progress and the course of my life' ('Ita enim progressus mei seriem, si ea forte cura fuerit, viteque cursum lector intelliget'). But chronology can be readily combined with variety, the more so if more or less fictionalised. Petrarch himself creates the impression in the letter just quoted that he has overstepped the putative dividing line between variety and confusion. He was, he says, prevented from organising the letters as he would have liked, because 'a multitude of things got in the way, including the variety of the material itself and the forcible distraction of my attention onto other matters with only intermittent periods when I could work' ('multitudo rerum obstitit varietasque ipsa et occupati interim intentique aliis animi violenta distractio'). But in fact both the *Familiares* and the later *Seniles* seem, if anything, carefully studied, with amplifications on a particular theme over a number of letters, extended contrasts (such as, for example, the framing of letters on books by political letters in *Fam*. 18), the grouping together of letters to the ancients in *Fam*. 24 or the curious triad of letters, all addressed to Boccaccio, which make up the last book of the *Seniles* – an introductory letter, a longer piece on the need to continue studying in old age, and finally the translation of Boccaccio's story of Griselda, which Petrarch seems to have thought an appropriate conclusion to his correspondence, much as Boccaccio thought the original an appropriate conclusion to the *Decameron*. After all, her constancy is in direct contrast to the variety of both the letters and the collection of stories.

An interplay between narrative, formal patterns and formal freedom seems to be sought in the letters but is only fully achieved in the *RVF*. The solution depends, paradoxically, on the creation of regularities which could not be created in collections of Latin letters and perhaps were impossible in prose in any case. Restricting his metrical forms for most of the work to three (canzone, sonnet and sestina) and making one, the sonnet, overwhelmingly preponderant, narrowing his thematic range, establishing correspondingly narrow limits for the language and style of poetry, Petrarch creates a uniformity in the *RVF* which none of his other works possesses. Within and against that identity or monotony, variation is possible to an almost limitless degree. As in much art and architecture of the time, repetition makes for the cultivation of exceptions and subordinate patterns which have ambiguous structural functions in terms of the whole. The sonnets against the Avignonese Papacy have their place in part as interruptions of regularity. And so too do other thematic and formal exceptions, such as the political and correspondence poems, the canzone to the Virgin, or the double sestina which is the only sestina in Part 2 and the only double sestina in the whole work. Conversely symmetries are made which are themselves exceptional: such as framing the weighty political canzone, *Spirto gentil* (53) between two of the four madrigali in the collection, or making a formal and thematic correspondence between the first and penultimate sestine in Part 1 (22 and 237), or, on a larger scale, repeating in Part 2 much that has appeared in Part 1.

The 'problems' that were outlined in the first section of this chapter are thus aspects of a variation that is constantly and all-pervasively at work. No detail seems to be exempt. There are, for example, no symmetries in either the number or distribution of any of the metrical forms; there is no exact regularity in any of them either, the forms which are not sonnets being continually varied in length, the sonnets themselves deploying several sestet patterns and in some cases departing also in the quatrains from the 'Petrarchan' model (se Chapter 6.6). Correspondingly statements and interpretations of the self, of Laura, and of the world are subject to the same instability, changing, contradicting each other, and, in the midst of it all, repeating themselves. The very representations of Laura as woman and as laurel (see Chapter 5.4) oscillate semantically in a way that can sometimes only be resolved at the cost of the pleasurable uncertainty to which Petrarch gives poetic priority. The words themselves, however much repeated, are repeated in constantly renewed combinations. In a quite non-trivial sense every poem by Petrarch is different.

The risk of formal *divertisement* becoming an end in itself is always a hair's breadth away. If it does not happen, it is in part because of the complexity of the individual units of which the collection is made, in that none of Petrarch's poems are reducible to simple statements or simple emotions, and in part to the problematics of variety discussed above. Whilst these are made thematically explicit with reference to Laura, they also have their formal correlative. What is balance, contrast, variation may also be simultaneously irresolution and incompetence, as is particularly evident in a pair of poems such as *Benedetto sia 'l giorno* (61) and *Padre del ciel* (62), the one praising love, the other asking God for release. From one point of view the two poems complement each other; from another they are an image of psychological disarray. (See also section 4 below on these poems.)

It is in this ambiguous light that the narrative of the collection has to be seen. Narrative development (rather than mere chronological succession) does occur. Familiar elements are combined in new patterns, with substitutions, additions, deletions. Fortunately and unfortunately, time goes by and things happen, most importantly ageing and death. Repetition itself is an action or at least a gesture in time; variation is another movement in the course of an obsession; and exceptions are temporary, perhaps illusory, departures from dominant habits. Thus from a formal arrangement a story emerges – a story which is not limited to the love of Petrarch for Laura in a restrictive sense, but which includes metrical and thematic choices: in other words it is simultaneously and in addition the story of a poet or the story of itself. But the narrative is quite unable to emerge fully: the medium of lyric poetry in Petrarch's hands is too indirect, too allusive, too resistant to the temporal dynamism on which narrative depends. The story sometimes seems to be on the edge of absorbing everything in the collection, but it always turns back towards a formal patterning, which is also never fully achieved, or else dissolves in the shimmering motility of the whole.

Three phases can be distinguished in this emergent story. The third, represented by Part 2, is relatively well-defined, though there are evident bonds with what has preceded. The first two phases, which make up Part 1, are fused inseparably together. All the same, over the central twenty poems of Part 1 (approximately 120–40) a transition takes place from relative diversity to relative uniformity. It is a transition which establishes a degree of formal contrast and balance between the two arms of this first part. At the same time it is a narrative movement in so far as expansion leads to relative restriction.

The beginning of the phase of expansion and diversity is signalled in poem 7 (*La gola e 'l somno*) with the separation of the laurel from Laura. Poetry, it seems, need not adhere to its initial and central inspiration: a certain progression is possible (see Chapter 5.4). The poems that follow (up to poem 140) are of course centred on Laura and on love, and are mostly sonnets, but amongst them are the great majority of the exceptions or deviations from metrical and thematic norms. It is not only the political canzoni (28, 53, 128) and sonnets (27, 103, 104) which appear here, but also the coronation canzone (119), funeral poems (31, 91, 92), the sonnets against the Avignonese Papacy (136–8), poems on various matters addressed to friends (7, 10, 24, 25, 26, 40, 58, 98, 99, 120, 139), and altogether twenty of the twenty-five poems, whether love-poems or not, which have addressees. After poem 140 there remain only two poems in Part 1 which are thematically divergent – 166 (*S'i' fussi stato fermo alla spelunca*), on poetic failure; and 232 (*Vincitore Alexandro l'ira vinse*), a sententious sonnet on anger. There are no similar poems in Part 2, except perhaps for 322 (*Mai non vedranno le mie luci asciutte*), a poem addressed to the dead Giovanni Colonna and again on poetic failure.

Metrical variety is also concentrated in the same area. Petrarch uses five forms altogether, the 317 sonnets making up the norm. The forty-nine poems in other forms comprise twenty-nine canzoni, nine sestine (including the single double one), seven ballate and four madrigali. All the madrigali have appeared by 121, and five of the seven ballate. If Part 1 is divided exactly at 133, the first half includes seventeen canzoni, whilst only three of those left will appear in the remainder of Part 1. Only the sestine are more evenly distributed through Part 1, though in Part 2 there will be no sestine apart from the double *Mia benigna fortuna e 'l viver lieto* (332).

Petrarch makes no explicit correlation between theme and metrical form, other than to assume implicitly, as the whole tradition had assumed, that the weightier the form, the more serious the poem. At one extreme stood the canzone, at the other the madrigale, with the sonnet, ballata and sestina somewhere in

the middle, the last being in scale and origin a special form of
canzone (see Chapter 6.6). But in this first half of Part 1 thematic
and formal deviation overlap. The three major non-erotic poems
are undoubtedly the three political canzoni, each of which appears
in a group that is formally deviant from the norm of amorous
sonnets. There are also three other groups of love-poems in non-
sonnet form, which are interlocked with the three groups just
mentioned. If single cases of deviation and all cases of thematic
deviation in sonnets are left aside as forming subordinate patterns
or as fluctuations in the constant variation, then overall, as the
following chart shows, there is progressive increase in size and
weight from group to group, with a moment of regress after the
fifth.

Number of poems in group	Poems	Theme	Metrical form
2	22	love	se
	23	love	c
3	28	political	c
	29	love	c
	30	love	se
4	52	love	m
	53	political	c
	54	love	m
	55	love	b
4	70	love	c
	71	love	c
	72	love	c
	73	love	c
2	105	love	c
	106	love	m
5	125	love	c
	126	love	c
	127	love	c
	128	political	c
	129	love	c

c = canzone, se = sestina, m = madrigale, b = ballata

In the five canzoni almost at the half-way point of Part 1 the juxtaposition of the erotic and the non-erotic is brought to a head. Petrarch's most powerful public poem, *Italia mia* (128), is set amongst poems in which he is most concerned with issues of love and love-poetry (see Chapter 5.4). This, if anywhere, is the turning-point. The metrical diversions represented by the ballata and madrigale are almost over, the proportion of canzoni is to be seriously reduced. The thematic restriction soon follows. The denunciations of the Papacy are sonnets, not canzoni (136–8), and mark an exodus from the public arena. Noticeably enough two of the few later poems which turn away from Laura are, as already mentioned, about poetic failure (166, 322). As will be discussed in greater detail in Chapter 5.4, a phase that is important for the collection and for Petrarch's view of poetry as a whole has come to an end.

The second half of Part 1, concentrated thematically upon love and Laura and metrically upon the sonnet, gradually moves towards Laura's death, which has been recognised as inevitable since early in the collection (33), but which now becomes a more insistent motif. But it is also here that the most extravagant praise of her appears, interspersed with poems of lassitude, regret and a few on the vanity and moral danger of protracted love. There is thus a complex alternation of themes that are intellectually and emotionally in conflict. And, as earlier, there is a climactic progression: towards the end of Part 1 Laura's death becomes increasingly imminent and the praise of her more intense, reaching its high point with the last poem, *Arbor victoriosa triümphale* (263). The difference from the earlier climactic movement is that the later one is entirely in sonnets. And that signifies a relative weakness. Part 2 will open in strength, countering but not annulling the later phases of Part 1.

I' vo pensando (264) affirms the need for another more serious set of values than those provided by poetry and love, whilst confessing a failure of the will to realise them. It sounds a contrast with most, if not all, of Part 1 and creates a tone which will dominate Part 2 as a whole. It is more doubtful whether there is a contrast of substance. As has often been remarked, this introductory canzone to Part 2 makes a general statement similar to that of the first poem in the whole collection. Whether or not that means that the two poems were composed at about the same time (Wilkins 1951: 152), it is a signal that the new development is also further repetition and variation. There is more concentration and less incident, there are sharper contrasts between past and future, there is the constant shadow of definitive events – loss, death, damnation or final union – but overall Part 2 is a rewriting and re-experiencing of Part 1, particularly its second, more restricted half, in the light of an inescapable need to make an end or to accept one. But only the last four poems will mark a further movement, and even in the canzone to the Virgin the forces working to absorb the poem into familiar patterns are as strong as those signifying change (see Chapter 5.5).

In the shift in tone, the sharper contrasts, the emphasis on death and endings, Petrarch finds compensations for the imbalance between Part 1 and Part 2, rather as he creates compensations between the two unequal parts of a sonnet. One of the factors in the compensating counter-movement is the arrangement of metrical forms in Part 2, which in part contrasts with and in part repeats the arrangement of Part 1. What is thematically a question of endings is formally a structure built on closure.

Part 1 begins with twenty-one poems in minor form (nineteen sonnets and two ballate of sonnet length), followed by a sestina. It ends with a sestina (239) followed by twenty-four sonnets. But, in spite of the relative symmetry, there is openness in the ending, as the last stages of composition indicate (see Chapter 2.2): *Arbor victoriosa* (263) was a replaceable climax, or one that could have been added to. Between the two extremities of Part 1 there are two opposed organisations of poems in non-sonnet form, that dominant in the first half being based upon cumulative groupings, that of the second half tending strongly towards isolation (142 se, 149 b, 206 c, 207 c, 214 se, 237 se, 239 se). Taken together the asymmetrical organisations of the two halves of Part 1 demand the resolution which Part 2 provides.

As had been the case throughout the later phases of its composition, the boundaries of Part 2 are clearly drawn in the opening and closing canzoni. What is more, within those isolated termini non-sonnets are distributed with a greater symmetry than in Part 1:

264 c

268 c
270 c

323 c
324 b
325 c

331 c
332 se (double)

359 c
360 c

366 c

c = canzone, b = ballata, se = sestina

The dominant tendency in each of the groups is towards pairing: first come two triads in which the pairs of canzoni are interrupted, in the first by a sonnet (269), in the second by a ballata (324); then follow two pairs, the second of which at last brings together two canzoni. This final climactic movement is also a thematic culmination, since 359 (*Quando il soave mio fido conforto*) and 360 (*Quel'antiquo mio dolce empio signore*) are not merely bound by the parallel rhetoric of their opening lines but are the last pair of opposed poems in the collection, the first being the last pointer to an unachievable positive (see Chapter 5.5), the second summarising once and for all the aporia that had been first made explicit in *Benedetto sia 'l giorno* (61) and *Padre del ciel* (62). Where Part 1 had proceeded through diversity, Part 2 moves against dispersal towards regularity, though, as always, variation continues. After 360 the narrative progression towards ending can be concluded in the last few poems, in an approximate symmetry with the progression towards death that marked Part 2's beginning.

Again there is a gradated transition, though one which was noticeably absent from the original arrangement of these last poems (see Chapter 2.2). The two sonnets which follow 360 rehearse other moods of Part 2. It is only in 363 (*Morte ha spento quel sol ch'abagliar suolmi*) that a turning to God is projected, and only in the following two last sonnets that prayers are actually made; these in their turn echo other prayers in earlier poems, but they also anticipate the final movement forward of the prayer to the Virgin. It is a movement which has no narrative necessity, beyond the need for a conclusion. But, through his last rearrangement, Petrarch integrates the canzone into a narrative progression, much as he also gave narrative more importance in his final additions to Part 1.

The structure of the collection is largely built on the division between Part 1 and Part 2. If the division is eliminated or moved, then the complex patterns I have been discussing dissolve. It is also clear that it is consonant with the transitions at the end of the collection and in the middle of Part 1 that the division should not be complete. The end of Part 1 looks forwards to Laura's death and the beginning of Part 2 looks on Laura as if she is alive to create bonding between the two parts which in a sense it would be surprising *not* to find.

But there are also reasons of a more serious kind. Petrarch does not make external events the arbiters of literary structure. Though affected by such momentous events as meeting Laura and then her death (at least within the fiction that it creates), poetry is at a certain remove from what it pretends is outside it and is free to rearrange things according to its own order. Dante had already demonstrated in the *Vita nuova*, in his treatment of an analogous transition, that this freedom is not gratuitous. He emphatically declared (24. 1) that the representation that he chose to offer of Beatrice's death was a 'vana imaginazione' ('vain imagining'): the reality was not to be represented. Whilst his explicit justification is puzzling in some ways, it is clear that not only is he (like Petrarch) interlocking the poems of Beatrice's life and poems of her death, but that he is drawing a crucial difference between what was really a departure to a better life and his own inadequate responses. Petrarch's manoeuvre has a similar purpose. The issues that are delineated in *I' vo pensando* (264) are the issues to be faced irrespective of the contingency of Laura's being alive or dead. They are also the issues, as the concluding lines of the poem make plain, which, in contradistinction to Dante, Petrarch cannot or will not resolve. Laura's actual death only confirms the repetitions and variations that have already been inaugurated.

3.4 In the labyrinth

In making a general description of the *RVF* I have repeatedly had to compromise with asymmetries in the emergent order and deviations from the emergent narrative, as well as having to ignore other patterns and regularities of lesser and greater importance. This section tries to counter some of the distortions by moving from the part to the whole, instead of vice versa. It centres on three small groups of sonnets, each quite different from the others, and in some ways from the collection as a whole, yet also representative of Petrarch's constant variation. The preceding section was concerned with finding routes through Petrarch's labyrinth; the present one allows itself to follow side-paths and apparent dead-ends, some of which at least turn out to have their openings too.

Poems 41–3 are three of the earlier poems in the collection to have been written. Within the narrative they spring from an absence of Laura for nine days or more (43. 1–2) that apparently occurred sometime between 1334 (marked in poem 30) and 1336/7 (marked in poem 50).

> Quando dal proprio sito si rimove
> l'arbor ch' amò già Phebo in corpo humano,
> sospira et suda a l'opera Vulcano,
> per rinfrescar l'aspre saette a Giove:
>
> il qual or tona, or nevicha et or piove,
> senza honorar piú Cesare che Giano;
> la terra piange, e 'l sol ci sta lontano,
> che la sua cara amica ved' altrove.
>
> Allor riprende ardir Saturno et Marte,
> crudeli stelle; et Orïone armato
> spezza a' tristi nocchier' governi et sarte;
>
> Eolo a Neptuno et a Giunon turbato
> fa sentire, et a noi, come si parte
> il bel viso dagli angeli aspettato.

(When from its own setting there departs / the tree that Phoebus once loved in human form, / Vulcan sighs and sweats at his work, / to reinvigorate Jove's fierce arrows. / He [Jove] now thunders, now sends snow, now rain, / without honouring Caesar any more than Janus; / the earth weeps, and the sun stays far from us, / seeing his dear friend in another place. / Then Saturn and Mars, / the cruel stars, recover their boldness; and Orion in arms, / smashes the unhappy sailors' helms and shrouds. / Aeolus makes his turmoil felt by Neptune [the sea] and Juno [the air], / and by us, as the lovely face / awaited by the angels takes her leave.)

> Ma poi che 'l dolce riso humile et piano
> piú non asconde sue bellezze nove,
> le braccia a la fucina indarno move
> l'antiquissimo fabbro ciciliano,
>
> ch' a Giove tolte son l'arme di mano
> temprate in Mongibello a tutte prove,
> et sua sorella par che si rinove
> nel bel guardo d'Apollo a mano a mano.
>
> Del lito occidental si move un fiato,
> che fa securo il navigar senza arte,
> et desta i fior' tra l'erba in ciascun prato.
>
> Stelle noiose fuggon d'ogni parte,
> disperse dal bel viso inamorato,
> per cui lagrime molte son già sparte.

(But when the sweet, unpresuming, gentle, smiling face / no longer hides her extraordinary beauties, / the ancient Sicilian smith [Vulcan] / vainly strains his arms at his furnace, / since the weapons are taken from the hands of Jove / that were tempered to the utmost in Mongibello [Etna], / and his sister [Juno, the air] seems to be renewed / steadily in Apollo's beauteous gaze. / A breeze blows from the western shore, / that makes careless voyaging secure, / and wakens the flowers in every meadow. / Noxious stars flee in every direction, / scattered by the beautiful face that is at one with love, / for which many tears are already shed.)

Il figliuol di Latona avea già nove
volte guardato dal balcon sovrano,
per quella ch' alcun tempo mosse invano
i suoi sospir, et or gli altrui commove.

Poi che cercando stanco non seppe ove
s'albergasse, da presso o di lontano,
mostrossi a noi qual huom di doglia insano,
che molto amata cosa non ritrove.

Et cosí tristo standosi in disparte,
tornar non vide il viso, che laudato
sarà s'io vivo in piú di mille carte;

et pietà lui medesmo avea cangiato,
sí che' begli occhi lagrimavan parte:
però l'aere ritenne il primo stato.

(The son of Latona [Apollo] had already nine / times looked
from his balcony on high / for her who once vainly caused / his
sighs, and now stirs those of others. / When, wearily looking, he
could not discover where / she was staying, whether it was near
or far, / he showed himself to us like a man driven mad with
pain, / who cannot find something dearly cherished. / And
remaining withdrawn in this sorry state, / he did not see that
face return, which will be praised, / if I live, in more than a
thousand pages; / and pitiful suffering had changed the sun
himself, / so that his fair eyes wept meanwhile: / hence the air
retained its previous condition.)

As a miniature story telling of her departure, absence and return,
the three sonnets complement poems 37–9: those three poems (a
canzone and two sonnets) allude to a journey or journeys which
Petrarch made away from Laura, whilst the second three spring
from a journey she makes away from him. Between these two
triads, narratively complementary though otherwise quite distinct,
there is poem 40, a correspondence poem like poem 38, which is
addressed to Orso dell'Anguillara, but of a different kind. It is a
request to a friend for a book needed to finish some project that
Petrarch is working on. The friend may have been Giovanni
Colonna, the project the *Rerum memorandarum*. Whatever the

historical circumstances, the poem talks of bonding 'l'un coll'altro vero' ('the one truth with the other'), that is, the truth of pre-Christian antiquity with Christian truth, and making 'un mio lavor sí doppio / tra lo stil de' moderni e 'l sermon prisco / che, paventosamente a dirlo ardisco, / infin a Roma n'udirai lo scoppio' ('a work of mine so double [that is, an ambivalent, but also synthesising work] / between the style of the moderns and the ancient language / that, I dare nervously to say, / you will hear the commotion as far away as Rome'). The three poems which follow are not at all grand, but on a small scale they bring about precisely the fusion that Petrarch has said he is aiming at. Classical mythology, of which there had been none in the poems immediately preceding, is here integrated with the modes of vernacular poetry, the fusion between this classicism and Christian thought being made explicit in the first poem (41. 12–14). It then reappears in a different guise in 44 (also a relatively early poem), which builds its first quatrain around the tears of the pagan Pompey and its second around the biblical David. But 44 is also bonded in other ways to 43: this poem makes rain into Apollo's tears at Laura's absence, and 44, in contrast, regrets Laura's failure to shed tears of sympathy, some important phrasing of the two poems in their sestets being similar (43. 12 = 44. 9, 43. 13–14 = 44. 13–14). The continuity extends still further: in a reflexive movement, the eyes which had come to be the centre of attention in these poems and particularly in their two concluding tercets, reappear as the centre of the following poem (45). Whenever the poems 37–45 were originally composed, they have been arranged in such a way as to create a series of linkages of different kinds that succeed each other and merge with each other, cutting across the apparently inviolable barriers between one poem and another.

That the triad 41–3 should be deeply embedded in its immediate context is typical of most of the poems in the collection, whether they form similarly identifiable groups or not. But as a unit the three poems combine narrative and formal features in an unusual way. They tell a (minimal) story and their rhymes are repeated. For this there are only loose parallels. Amongst sonnets, 100 and 101 have identical rhymes and together make up a reflective, though not narrative, pair, the first on the desire to weep, the second on the vanity of doing so, whilst other groups of poems also tell miniature stories without being connected by repeated rhymes – such as the poems on Laura's eye-illness (231 and 233) and on her lost glove (199–201). Although there are obvious differences, the closest comparable grouping is on a much larger scale: it is the three canzoni on Laura's eyes (71–3) with their attendant sonnets (74–5) (see Chapter 5.5). Thus, though 41–3 do not seem to announce themselves as being exceptional in the manner of most of the thematic and formal exceptions discussed in the previous section, looked at a little more closely they too prove to have anomalous features. The regularity that is fundamental to the order is a matter of perspective – though, for all that, no more to be discounted than the figures in a pointillist painting which at close range dissolve into dots.

Another part of the overall order is narrative sequence. This too is disturbed within the three poems. Laura's departure, with ensuing bad weather and the predominance of the planets of violence and gloom, occupies the first poem. In the second she returns, restoring calm to the elements and defeating malign astral influences. But the third poem, in which the sun is overcast because he does not know whether Laura has returned or not, is ambiguous. Depending on how line 10 is interpreted, either Laura has returned, but the bad weather has recurred or continued, or she is still absent and the meteorological benefits detailed in the second poem are still to come. On the first interpretation the second poem is nullified by the third; on the second the poems are out of temporal order. But the story is clearly secondary here to the thematic contrasts between the poems and, even more, to the formal structure of the group. The rhymes of 41 and 43 are in identical order; the same rhymes are inverted in 42. The two outer poems thus embrace the inner one, creating a poetic order in the midst of narrative confusion.

The other two groups in Part 1 which I mentioned above show a similar unwillingness to allow narrative to dominate poetry. The two sonnets on Laura's eye infection, which then affects Petrarch's right eye (231 and 233), are interrupted by a sententious, rather erudite sonnet on anger, unconnected with the events alluded to in the other two poems. But there is a connection of another kind. The theme of the diseased eye reappears in a quite different context: one of the examples of famous victims of anger is the

Roman general Sulla: 'l'ira cieco del tutto, non pur lippo, / fatto
avea Silla: a l'ultimo l'extinse' ('anger had made Sulla completely
blind, not merely blear-eyed: / in the end it killed him': 232. 7–8).
Conversely in the glove-group (199–201) it is the narrative
perspective which changes. The sequence begins, in a sense, half-
way through the story, with the obligation, presented as one in
force at the time of writing, to return a glove 'stolen' from Laura
(199), and continues, at apparently a short distance in time, with
her hand putting on again the now restored glove (200). But then
there is a shift in the third sonnet which looks back from some
later time to the one single day in which he gained and lost the
glove (201. 5–6). The pseudo-dramatic representation of the two
moments in the first two poems and the longer perspective of the
third do not together subvert time (as in 41–3) nor are they just
variation. Here narrated time is stretched and then compressed,
even if the expected sequence of events is preserved.

It is arguable that there is some measure of play in most,
perhaps all, of these sonnets, which contributes to their temporal
instability and their varying formal patterns. They are after all
remarkably hyperbolic, and self-consciously so. But some of the
same features, and some further ones, appear in 61 and 62, two
poems which are usually reckoned amongst the most serious
which Petrarch wrote.

> Benedette le voci tante ch'io
> et la stagione, e 'l tempo, et l'ora, e 'l punto,
> e 'l bel paese, e 'l loco ov'io fui giunto
> da' duo begli occhi che legato m'ànno;
>
> et benedetto il primo dolce affanno
> ch'i' ebbi ad esser con Amor congiunto,
> et l'arco, et le saette ond'i' fui punto,
> et le piaghe che 'nfin al cor mi vanno.
>
> Benedette le voci tante ch'io
> chiamando il nome de mia donna ò sparte,
> e i sospiri, et le lagrime, e 'l desio;
>
> et benedette sian tutte le carte
> ov'io fama l'acquisto, e 'l pensier mio,
> ch'è sol di lei, sí ch' altra non v'à parte.

(Blessed be the day, and the month, and the year, / and the season, and the time, and the hour, and the moment, / and the fair country, and the place where I was caught / by two lovely eyes that have bound me fast; / and blessed be the first sweet tribulation / that I bore on being joined with love, / and his bow, and the arrows by which I was pierced, / and the wounds that penetrate to my heart. / Blessed be the many cries which I / have spread abroad calling the name of my lady, / and the sighs, and the tears, and the desire: / and blessed be all the writings / with which I bring renown to her, and my thoughts / which are solely of her, so that no other has any place in them.)

> Padre del ciel, dopo i perduti giorni,
> dopo le notti vaneggiando spese,
> con quel fero desio ch'al cor s'accese,
> mirando gli atti per mio mal sí adorni,
>
> piacciati omai col Tuo lume ch'io torni
> ad altra vita et a piú belle imprese,
> sí ch'avendo le reti indarno tese,
> il mio duro adversario se ne scorni.
>
> Or volge, Signor mio, l'undecimo anno
> ch'i' fui sommesso al dispietato giogo
> che sopra i piú soggetti è piú feroce.
>
> *Miserere* del mio non degno affanno;
> reduci i pensier' vaghi a miglior luogo;
> ramenta lor come oggi fusti in croce.

(Father of heaven, after the wasted days, / after the nights spent raving, / with that wild desire that flared in my heart, / on seeing conduct which, to my misfortune, was so beauteous, / may it please you now with Your light to have me return / to another life and to finer enterprises, / so that, having stretched his nets for me in vain, / my unrelenting adversary may be frustrated. / It is now the eleventh year which is in course, my Lord, / since I was subjected to the pitiless yoke / that is most cruel to the most susceptible. / Show pity for my undignified tribulation; / redirect my errant thoughts to a better place; / remind them how you were crucified today.)

The two poems are in strong contrast, even in contradiction, the one celebrating love as a good, the other asking God for release from the pain and waste. They are not the only pair of contrasting sonnets (cf. 85–6, 229–30), but they are two of the most notable. The oscillation between negative and positive assessments of love, which had been intimated almost from the beginning of the story (3, 5, 6), is here explicitly articulated for the first time. From now onwards it will recur throughout the *RVF* in various formulations, not all of them antithetical, its final and fullest articulation being the last pair of canzoni (359, 360). If the positive survives even in both these late poems, the accent repeatedly falls on the negative, in part because from 62 onwards there is no comparable ascending pair in which there is a move from rejection to celebration of love. But also, in *Padre del ciel*, as in other poems which it anticipates (142, 364, 365, 366), the strength of the negative is reinforced by adopting the rhetoric of prayers of repentance. Orthodoxy cannot but outweigh the fragile ethos of conventional love-poetry.

But, though 61 and 62 are important in the general evolution of the collection, they, like the triad of poems just discussed, are also firmly embedded in their immediate context. Poem 59, a ballata, is a complaint at being prevented from seeing Laura, ending with a commitment to love whatever its consequences; 60 is the strongest condemnation in the collection of the laurel, that is, of Laura herself or of her tree; then comes the positive of 61 and the negative of 62, which is followed in turn by 63, another ballata, in which her greeting and her angelic voice bring him life and self-knowledge and, as in the previous ballata, Petrarch is ready to receive anything from her, for good or ill. The circle is not, however, allowed to rest completed: 64 returns to the threatening imagery of 60, with a sharp injunction to Laura not to abuse her power over him. Thus 61 and 62 are the point at which the antithetical movement between positive and negative alternatives, created in surrounding poems, assumes its most direct and most moral form.

Again the symmetry proves more intricate, more like variation, the more we look at the two poems. It is not simply that their rhetoric and organisation are different, the repetition of the blessing finding only a partial echo in the requests of the second poem. There is none of the malediction that we would expect if the two poems were to be evenly balanced against each other. If there are maledictions in the air surrounding 62, they are in 60, or, more remotely, in poems by others, in particular a sonnet by Cecco Angiolieri (51), the opening of which may well have been the starting-point for 61:

> Maledetta sie l'or' e 'l punt' e 'l giorno
> e la semana e 'l mese e tutto l'anno, . . .

(Cursed be the hour and the point and the day / and the week and the month and the whole year. . .)

In *Padre del ciel* Petrarch avoids such an easy opposition, preferring to work out the negative in more subtle ways: love has been a period of wasted time, not something springing from a moment that he wishes always to bless; the risks it involves are risks of damnation (assuming that the adversary of line 8 is the devil); fame, poetry and the complaints of love are irrelevant; what counts now on this Good Friday, the anniversary of his falling in love, is to pray. Concentration on the significance of the crucifixion (62. 13) replaces uncoordinated reiteration of the name of the beloved (61. 10) and obsessive thinking of her (61. 14). Rather than simply issuing a writ of condemnation, the second poem covers all the points made in the first, but also any other positives that could be discovered in love. Where the first poem had opened itself to a potentially endless series through its repetitions, the second attempts through rhetorical diversity to achieve closure and definition.

The absorption of 61 into 62 has also another aspect with more general implications. A striking number of words appear in both poems: 'giorno' (61. 1), 'giorni' (62. 1); 'anno' in rhyme with 'affanno' (61. 1 and 5; 62. 9 and 12); 'loco' (61. 3), 'luogo' (62. 13); 'desio' (61. 11; 62. 3); 'pensier' (sing. in 61. 13; plural in 62.13). Lexical repetitions of this kind are frequent. It is particularly common for a word occurring near the end of one poem to be picked up near the beginning of the next, in what Santagata (1979: 33ff) believes may be a development from the Provençal technique of linking stanzas within a single poem (*coblas capfinidas*), as when 124 ends ' . . . et tutti miei *penser* romper nel mezzo' ('. . . and breaks all my *thoughts* in their midst') and 125 begins 'Se 'l *pensier* che mi strugge . . .' ('If the *thought* that destroys me . . .'), or, more subtly, 250 ends '. . . non sperar di *vedermi* in terra mai' ('Do not hope ever to see me on earth') and 251 begins 'O misera et horribil *visione!* ('O wretched and horrible *vision*'). As Santagata points out, the repetitions need not be so close together: for example, the opening of 53, 'Spirto gentil, che quelle membra reggi / dentro a le qua' *peregrinando* alberga . . .' ('Noble spirit, who guide those limbs / within which *on pilgrimage* there dwells . . .') is paralleled in the opening of the following madrigale: 'Perch'al viso d'Amor portava insegna / mosse una *pellegrina* il mio cor vano . . .' ('Because she bore the emblem of love in her features / a *pilgrim* stirred my heart . . .') (for another example see 306. 1 and 307. 1). But it may also be that, as in 61 and 62, the repeated words are much more densely spread (for other examples see 43–4, 153–4).

Such repetitions show how pervasive is the play of variation in Petrarch's poetry. In all the examples quoted the repeated words change their reference or their associations, most strikingly in the transition from seeing Laura alive in 250 to a vision of her death in 251. An unstable network of correspondences is created between poems but also a play of difference. Working no doubt subliminally for most readers, though almost certainly consciously developed by Petrarch, the constant repatterning brings a strangely fluctuating, uncertain quality to a poetry that from some other points of view impresses with its clarity. (See Chapter 6.5.)

In at least one series of poems the process of repetition and variation becomes a more prominent organisational principle through its being focused in openings. Four sonnets appear close together, all opening with the familiar pun on Laura's name, followed by an adjective, and then, in three of the poems, a relative clause:

L'aura gentil, che rasserena i poggi 194
(The noble breeze, that restores calm to the hills)

L'aura serena, che fra verdi fronde 196
(The calm breeze, that amongst green leaves)

L'aura celeste che 'n quel verde lauro 197
(The heavenly breeze, that in that green laurel)

> L'aura soave al sole spiega et vibra   198
> (The pleasing breeze displays and makes tremble)

The four sonnets form a distinct group, characteristically interrupted at 195 by a sonnet with a quite different opening ('Di dí in
dí vo cangiando il viso e 'l pelo'), though connected in other ways
with the poems in its vicinity.

   There are only three other examples of poems beginning
'L'aura . . .' (146, 327, 356), and no other example in the
collection of an opening which is so prominently repeated. Again
Petrarch has made an anomalous minor pattern within the
structure of the whole. It also seems that two of the poems were
inserted at a very late stage in the collection's development (see
Chapter 2.3). But in making the insertions, Petrarch in fact merely
heightened a tendency to repetition and variation in openings
which was already at work in this area of the collection.

   Perhaps surprisingly there are only seventeen poems in all which
begin 'Amor . . .' Four appear close together not long before the
'L'aura' poems:

> Amor mi sprona in un tempo et affrena   178
> (Love simultaneously spurs me on and reins me in)

> Amor fra l'erbe una leggiadra rete   181
> (Love amongst the grass a charming net)

> Amor, che 'ncende il cor d'ardente zelo   182
> (Love, which fires the heart with burning zeal)

> Amor, Natura, et la bella alma umile   184
> (Love, Nature and the beautiful humble soul)

The repetition would be banal if it were not that there is no
comparable concentration of 'Amor' openings elsewhere. If we
integrate this set of openings with the 'L'aura' openings which
they prelude, we can easily arrive at a functional explanation. This
is a point in the *RVF* when the centrality of Love and Laura is
most affirmed. The repetitions reinforce the importance of both:
the transition from the weaker 'Amor' openings to the stronger
'L'aura' ones is the stylised representation of an increasing
urgency of desire, which finds expression and satisfaction not only

in the openings of the 'L'aura' poems but also in the repetition, variation and substitution of her name that extends into the body of all the poems from 194 to 198.

As always such an absorption of the structuring of the collection into the story cannot be fully carried through. The organisation retains always some element which is irrevocably formal. Leaving aside the obvious formal element in the openings already mentioned in this part of the *RVF*, there are two other openings which interrupt the 'Amor' series which it is impossible to assimilate to any narrative purpose:

> Geri, quando talor meco s'adira   179
> (Geri, when sometimes she is angry with me)

> Po, ben puo' tu portartene la scorza   180
> (Po, you may well carry away the outer shell)

There are only six other poems which begin with a proper name in this Roman fashion (34, 38, 98, 112, 128, 287). Here, as in the series already discussed, Petrarch has made an unusual pairing of two poems with this kind of beginning, and once again at a late stage in the composition of the collection. Poem 179 was an poem already written in the 1330s, which Petrarch only inserted (with patent indifference to the historical order of composition) sometime after 1367 (see Chapter 2.2). The new insertion fits well enough: it connects through the word 'forza' (line 8) with the preceding poem (178. 12), and in its imagery of flying (line 4) with the poem that follows (line 7–8), 12–14): its Medusa imagery (line 10–11) even looks forward, in the final version, to 197. 5–8. At the same time it was also unnecessary, since there is a stronger continuity of lexicon and imagery between 178 and 180 than between 179 and either of these. However, 179 does create a break and a new, perceptible pattern. Instead of the same word, the same vocative structure is repeated, once with a human addressee, once with a river or river-god. Difference and similarity meet, once again in a unique fashion.

It would obviously be wrong to look for repetition and variation of this kind in openings throughout the collection. Even within this segment there are clear movements in other directions in poems 185–93. Elsewhere the connections between poems and the patterns created take other forms and have other effects, which in their turn invite exploration as structural elements. That the variation is all-pervasive, constant and permanently exceptional suggests that the process of exploring the labyrinth is potentially endless.

4

The tradition

4.1 The self and the past

The *RVF* proposes that the genesis of the poems lies in the self who speaks in and through them. They express a response to internal pressures to complain or to celebrate, to release emotion or to plead for help. They may bring immortal fame to Laura, and even to their writer, but they may also be inadequate to do justice to her, or have only personal value, or, more negatively still, they may represent wasted time, the only consequence of which are notoriety and pain. In this fictional perspective there is little continuity with a preceding tradition. If the self is the source of what is being written, if what is being written is of ambiguous value, then there is no place for proclaiming debts to poetic fathers in the manner of thirteenth-century poets. Where Guinizzelli had found paternity in Guittone, and Dante in Guinizzelli, Petrarch claims no progenitors.

Those connecting lines which are suggested seem to be undermined even as they are being drawn. Other poets, classical and vernacular, are mentioned, as friends, as points of comparison, or even as predecessors, but there is a sense of separation, not only from distant Homer and Virgil, but from figures much closer in time. When Cino da Pistoia, the last survivor of the original *stilnovisti*, dies in 1336 or 1337, he does not receive from Petrarch the kind of fullsome tribute which he, in his turn, had paid to Dante. The sonnet (92) is perfunctory: Cino the love-poet is dead, says the poem, and it asks in turn ladies, love, lovers and Pistoia (which exiled him) to weep for him. And that is all. The much less

78

significant figure of Sennuccio del Bene (see Chapter 1.4), who is the addressee of several poems, receives on his death a much more impressive sonnet than the one for Cino (287). It is in this poem, and the canzone *Lasso me* (70), that poetic predecessors are most explicitly evoked, the latter proposing a line that runs from Arnaut Daniel, through Cavalcanti, Dante and Cino to the young Petrarch of *Nel dolce tempo* (23). But it is implied that the line is broken: Petrarch cannot compose poetry as he and they once did. As so often with Laura herself, it is traces and memories which are left.

Something fundamental has been lost, but the traces of the past are massively present. The significant choices of forms, language, style and themes assert continuity with the tradition of the lyric from the Sicilians to Cino at its most canonical. From the very first poem it is clear that there is to be no truck with alternative traditions – the didactic poetry of the North, the *laude* of Umbria, the narrative poetry of Boccaccio (already in existence in the early 1330s) – or even with the various adjuncts and extensions to the central core of the lyric tradition itself. There is no comic verse, no parody; there is no everyday language, no interference, in spite of Petrarch's protracted residence in the North, from Northern dialects. The canzone and sonnet are the favoured forms, and in their canonical guises. The canzoni look back to the *stil novo*, Dante and Provence. The sonnets are free from the additional lines or internal rhymes which had been introduced by the Guittonians, just as they are from the extensions which had flowered in the fourteenth century. Of those forms which had developed later only the madrigale is admitted and then in tiny quantities. Whatever the professions of uncertainty, Petrarch makes a major investment in establishing his connections with the past at the expense of the present. If little by little textual interactions with his contemporaries have come to light, they are far outnumbered and outweighed by the links with his predecessors.

There is of course much more involved than continuity, or the reaffirmation of a tradition that was in danger of dispersal or even dissolution (see Chapter 1.2). The range of texts towards which pointers are offered extends far beyond the Tuscan lyric tradition and the Provençal tradition on which the Tuscans, like the Sicilians before them, had themselves regularly drawn. Whether artfully concealed or inadvertently retained, whether repressed or secretly acknowledged, there are continual traces of Petrarch's vast reading in Latin poetry and prose (classical, biblical, patristic, medieval and early humanist), traces of other Tuscan literature than lyric poetry, especially Dante's prose and the *Divina commedia*, and traces too of Petrarch himself, whether as echoes of other poems in the collection or as echoes of his own Latin writing in both verse and prose. Perhaps more than any other European poetry, the *RVF* has drawn its readers into a complex, sometimes speculative game of exploring for parallels and sources in the nooks and crannies of Petrarch's reading, and often beyond it. Petrarch may not have known Homer, but, in poem 35, a reformulation of a fragment of Cicero's translation can lead back to the fountain-head. Correspondingly, in a way that Petrarch may have been unable to foresee but which the encyclopaedical nature of his enterprise catered for, the very choice of the *RVF* as a model in the Renaissance multiplies the forward-looking relations to infinity.

A mode of writing which is so dense with literary resonances obviously runs counter to a notion of self-expression which emphasises originality, that is, the rejection of the past. Since the Renaissance charges have been levelled at Petrarch that he borrows too much or is over-literary. After all even his professions of attending to a personal inspiration have their antecedents (e.g. 127. 5–8; cf. *Purg.* 24. 52–4), not to mention his images, turns of phrase, rhymes, his very lexicon. But, whether we call them debts, borrowings, or thefts, these traces of past literature are not signs of weakness or hypocrisy. It is in and from the ambiguous encounter with the past that the self emerges, assuming definition through its power simultaneously to absorb what it wishes from the past and to reject what threatens its own autonomy. A new poetry is created, and also a new history of poetry. Before Petrarch, Italian lyric poetry found its terminus in the *Divina commedia*. After him the *Commedia* was excluded: lyric poetry led to Petrarch himself, though only to be metamorphosed in its moment of arrival.

4.2 The Latin self

At various points in his letters Petrarch comes close to a theoretical discussion of his relationship with the past in what he has to say about imitation, that is, primarily stylistic imitation. He confronts what will become a topos of Renaissance literary debates – whether a single great author should be taken as a model or whether the models should be multiple. In spite of admiration for Cicero and Virgil, he declares himself against the first possibility. Such figures are admired friends, not masters. They are to be learned from at one's own discretion. As he says with contradictory irony, discussing how elusive truth can be:

> Hoc apud Marcum Tullium, hoc apud ipsum patrem August-
> inum didici, quod ipse apud eundem Tullium se didicisse non
> negat; nam apud Horatium Flaccum nullius iurare in verba
> magistri puer valde didiceram. (*Fam.* 4. 16)

> (I learnt this from reading Cicero and father Augustine himself
> too, it being something which he himself does not deny having
> learnt from that same Cicero. Yes, as a boy I had well learnt
> from reading Horace not to swear by the words of any master.
> (Horace, *Epistles*, 1. 1. 14))

Imitation of specific figures is admitted in the apprentice stage of an author's career, but even then there is to be no aping: the likeness should be more that between father and son, the particular resemblances being ones that are gradually recognised by a third party and not such as to threaten the individuality of the later writer (*Fam.* 23. 19). They are a possible source of additional pleasure, not a confirmation of status or value. But Petrarch's emphasis is much more on the alternative and more difficult procedure. The image to which he returns is the Horatian one of the bee (*Carm.* 4. 2. 27–32), which takes pollen from many flowers but makes its own special honey (*Fam.* 1. 8, 22. 2, 23. 19). Individuality is all, though, of course, since that is the general rule, he can only speak in terms of his own personal preferences:

> Nolo ducem qui me vinciat sed precedat: sint cum duce oculi,
> sit iudicium, sit libertas; non prohibear ubi velim pedem ponere
> vel preterire aliqua et inaccessa tentare; et breviorem sive ita fert
> animus, planiorem callem sequi et properare et subsistere et
> divertere liceat et reverti. (*Fam.* 22. 2)

> (I do not want a leader who binds me, but precedes me. Let the

leader have the eyes, the judgment, the freedom to choose. Let me not be prevented from putting my foot where I will, from going past him to some degree and trying unexplored regions. And let me be allowed, if I have the impulse, to follow a shorter path or a smoother one, and to hurry on or to stop a while or to turn aside or to turn back on my tracks.)

The individual voice has to be more than gathering of other men's flowers (*flosculos, Fam.* 4. 15). It must assimilate, not just borrow. If there are to be quotations, they must be explicit. Inadvertent citation is to be corrected, as Petrarch demonstrates by his own example in the letters cited and elsewhere.

Absolute principles are no more authoritative than particular authors. The doctrine of the three styles, treated as axiomatic in the generation before Petrarch, is reduced to a guideline, whose utility is once again to be determined by the writer himself (*Fam.* 13. 5; *Sen.* 2.1). For his own part Petrarch feels the attraction of a style which is not over-refined (*incomptius*, literally 'rather uncombed', *Fam.* 18. 7) rather than one which satisfies official or academic prescriptions, but which he can feel is somehow true to himself. The restrictions, other than this awkward concept of not going against the self, are metrical and grammatical rules, derived from classical usage, which are seen as almost inflexible (*Fam.* 12. 17; *Ep. met.* 2. 3, 3. 26), though humanist predilections also dictate that generally the pollen from which honey is to be made will be classical.

Style was not just a literary or personal question. It also had moral and religious dimensions, which cast a shadow over the solutions which Petrarch was drawn towards. Though he insisted that poetry should contain truth of some kind under its attractive outer veil of words (*Af.* 9. 90–105), he was also aware that literary texts are open to multiple interpretations (*Sen.* 4. 5). But there was also a serious possibility that his whole emphasis was mistaken. Metrical and grammatical punctiliousness may not matter all that much (*Fam.* 16. 4): the truth – or an approximation to the real truth of Christianity – is perhaps best stated in some other language and style than one which makes an individual synthesis of classical precedents (*De rem.* 1. 9). God chose to spread his word amongst illiterates in a non-literary language (*Fam.* 7. 2; *Ot. rel.* 808). It may be that the model is the

Bible, if, that is, there is anything to be said for the disease of writing at all (*Fam.* 13. 7). At one point in the *De remediis* (1. 44) Reason proposes that writing is just another form of melancholia, whilst allowing, contradictorily, that it may be also its cure:

> Melancholiae species infinitas ferunt: alii lapides iactant, alii libros scribunt, huic scribere furoris initium est, huic exitus.

> (People suffer infinite kinds of melancholia. Some throw stones about, others write books. For one man writing is the beginning of insanity, for another the way out of it.)

In sum, in characteristic fashion Petrarch takes up a number of positions towards the relationship between the self and writing, which are not easily reconciled amongst themselves except as a series of possibilities and problems, or as different aspects of a self which is drawn at one time or another in all these directions. In practice the consistency of the self in the Latin works is entrusted to constant stylistic proficiency and decorum, and to the recurrence in different guises of certain preoccupations, such as the function of study and writing, the relationship between antiquity and the present, and the very inconsistency and debility of the self. But it is a precondition of the diversity and abundance of Petrarch's work that the self should continually adapt its voice to the specific context in which it is speaking. The epic mode of the *Africa* is quite different from the pastoral one of the *Bucolicum carmen*, though both are, in different senses, Virgilian. The polemical rhetoric of the *Invective* is different both from the poems and from the pared-down sententiousness of the *De remediis*, where, as in the *Psalmi penitentiales*, there is a movement towards the anti-style which conscience declared was necessary. Up to a point Petrarch is willing to risk a dispersal of himself by speaking with many voices.

All the same for much of the letters and the treatises, and, to some degree, in the poetry too, a characteristic mode of writing is evident which partly accords with the self-imposed prescription that honey should be made from the pollen of different flowers, though it does not quite resolve some of the formidable difficulties involved. As Petrarch himself was aware, and the next generation of humanists even more so, the basic framework within which he chose to work was not fully mastered. In spite of his stylistic and linguistic sensitivity and the immense pains he took, by classical standards his Latin still showed a measure of grammatical uncertainty and stylistic awkwardness. Particularly in his narrative writing he still made some use of rhythmical patternings and the *cursus*, which had developed in the medieval period. In poetry he could still make mistakes of scansion. In general the phrases or words from which he made his own style sometimes betray their origin, demonstrating the immense breadth and depth of his reading but not quite cohering into the distinct stylistic self he claimed he wished to create. Similarly the frequent citations from other authors and references to them (as in the short passage quoted near the beginning of this section) mark his work as a dialogue with earlier literature or affirm the presence of others in himself, rather than indicating a triumph of the self in which precedents have been fully absorbed into an autonomous whole.

4.3 Assimilating the past

The programme of assimilation which Petrarch sketches out in his letters and which could only have partial success in Latin was fully actualisable within the limits which Petrarch established for himself in Italian. Here the pollen from different flowers could really be made into honey. Naturally the dilemmas and uncertainties remained. In one sense they were strengthened by the theoretical indefensibility of the project of writing Italian poetry at all. But in Italian the self could be manifested, or created, stylistically to an outstanding degree and could maintain through its various changes a constancy that ran counter to all admissions of multiplicity and liability. In other words Petrarch found a voice which could adapt to diversity but in some way would remain the same.

One of the reasons why this was possible was that he was totally in command of the rules and, to an important extent, was able to adjust them to his requirements. There was no authority, personal or impersonal, to dictate the configuration of pauses in Italian verse, to declare that this or that grammatical rule was to be followed. At most there was Dante's *De vulgari eloquentia*, which in all probability Petrarch did not know, and which, in any case, his resistance to Dantesque thinking would almost certainly have excluded from consideration. So he was at liberty to draw on his predecessors as he wished, to exemplify his own rules in his practice, and, by his own excellence, to validate them.

But the making of honey was also eased in Italian precisely for the reason that it was a different language from Latin, and with a different kind of verse. Citation ceased to be citation by the mere fact of translation and by the more difficult feat of integration into a different context: it became variation, allusion, echo, but always assimilation, not dispersal. If it was dialogue, it was dialogue on Petrarch's terms. So, for example, a famous line and a half spoken by Medea in the *Metamorphoses* can appear almost word for word as the introduction to the sixth stanza of *I' vo pensando* (264):

> Quel ch'io fo veggio, e non m'inganna il vero
> mal conosciuto, anzi mi sforza Amore.
>
> (91–2)

(I see what I do, and misapprehension of the truth / does not deceive me, no, love forces me.)

> Quid faciam video, nec me ignorantia veri
> decipiet, sed amor.
>
> (*Met.* 7. 92–3)

(I see what I do, and ignorance of the truth will not / deceive me, but love.)

This is one of the relatively few places where Petrarch remains close to his original to the extent of maintaining its phrasing and pauses, but the effect is not of an insertion into the canzone or a departure from its tone. The bleakly dramatic assertion of impotent self-awareness is a continuation and reinforcement of what has been the poem's rhetoric from its very beginning. The likeness to the parent-text appears fleetingly here, more as shadow or suggestion, as Petrarch had said was permissible, than as homage or authorisation. The otherness of the original is no longer a threat.

It is primarily authoritative texts which keep even this shadowy form. The conclusions of poems in particular are often reformulations of classical or biblical tags. *I' vo pensando* concludes with another Ovidian reference, and this time a particularly famous one. Here the original is triumphantly made into an epigram which epitomises not only the thrust of the poem which it brings to an end but a cluster of dilemmas that figure in poem after poem. Again the original speaker was Medea, who, in the middle of her deliberative soliloquy on whether to submit to her passion for Jason, had asserted:

> Video meliora proboque,
> deteriora sequor.
> (*Met.* 7. 20–1)

(I see the better [alternative] and approve, / I follow the worse.)

Petrarch, appropriating Ovid for the conclusion of his equally deliberative poem, makes what appears minimal alterations:

> et veggio 'l meglio, et al peggior m'appiglio.
> (264. 136)

(I see the better, and adhere to the worse.)

But he has created a much stronger dilemmatic structure, in which the two almost equal parts of the line are thematically in tension with each other and yet bound together not only by the chiasmus (which is in Ovid) but also by the complex, and quite emphatic, system of sound repetitions. (See also Chapter 6.3.)

There are poems which seem to develop from a single precedent. *Ponmi ove 'l sole occide i fiori et l'erba* (145), for instance, reworks the latter part of Horace's Lalage poem (*Carm.* 1. 22). But noticeably enough the famous conclusion of the original appears in a different poem, again as the conclusion. Horace had written: 'dulce ridentem Lalagen amabo, / dulce loquentem' ('I shall love Lalage sweetly laughing, / sweetly speaking'). And Petrarch (*In qual parte del ciel*):

> non sa come Amor sana, et come ancide,
> chi non sa come dolce ella sospira,
> et come dolce parla, et dolce ride.
> (159. 12–14)

(he does not know how love heals, and how he kills, / who does not know how she sweetly sighs, / and how she sweetly speaks, and sweetly laughs.)

The adverbial use of 'dulce', already a deviation from standard Latin in Horace, is maintained and elegantly incorporated into a fairly elaborate pattern of inversions and repetitions. So the parent text is fragmented, and reconstituted in two different contexts, perhaps in both instances being the original impulse to the poem rather than an insertion that came happily to hand.

But Petrarch's poetry would not be so dense with cultural resonances if this were his only procedure or his principal one. It is far more common for individual poems to bring together echoes of many texts of different kinds and different epochs. Whilst on the whole Latin texts furnish epigrams or transformed citations of the kind just exemplified, preceding vernacular poetry tends to be more thoroughly fragmented. Speaking in broad terms, we might say that the preceding lyric provides the basic conventional material from which Petrarch makes his own style. But there are hints that the process seems to have been far more textual. A copy of a note to *Aspro core et selvaggio* (265) says that the poem was composed after reading another poem by Arnaut Daniel:

MCCCL. septembris 21. martis hora 3. die Mathei apostoli; propter unum quod leggi [*sic*] Padue in cantilena Arnaldi Danielis *Aman prians safranca cor uffecs*. (Quoted Zingarelli 1935: 392)

(1350, September 21, Tuesday at the third hour, on the day of St Matthew the Apostle, on account of something I read in Padua in a poem of Arnaut Daniel, *By loving and begging, a haughty heart is made gentle*.)

The line of Arnaut (*Amors e iois e liocs e tems*, 40) is in fact re-formed towards the end of the sonnet:

> Vivo sol di speranza, rimembrando
> che poco humor già per continua prova
> consumar vidi marmi et pietre salde.
>
> Non è sí duro cor che, lagrimando,
> *pregando, amando*, talor non si smova,
> né sí freddo voler, che non si scalda.

(I live solely on hope, remembering / that I have in the past seen a little moisture through unrelenting effort / wear away marble and solid stones. / There is no heart so hard that, by weeping, / *begging*, *loving*, it will not sometime be moved, / nor desire so cold it will not be warmed.)

The original has been reduced to a quite insignificant phrase. If a source were to be proposed for these lines in ignorance of the note, it might well be St Augustine, who is cited by Carducci and Ferrari in their notes to the poem: 'Nihil est tamen tam durum atque ferreum quod non amoris igne vincatur' (*De mor. eccl. cath.* c. xli) ('However nothing is so hard and ironlike that it cannot be overcome with the fire of love'), whilst the image of water wearing away stone could stem from Bernart de Ventadorn or Chiaro Davanzati (see Zingarelli 1935: 392). It may well be that various texts, both vernacular and Latin, did blend in composition, even if Arnaut Daniel was the actual trigger.

Some idea of how broad a range of texts may contribute to a single poem and how thorough the pulverisation has been, can be gained from looking at a single example (133), which I have chosen because it shows Petrarch, even at his most playful, creating a poem which none of his predecessors could have written:

Amor m'à posto come segno a strale,
come al sol neve, come cera al foco,
et come nebbia al vento; et son già roco,
donna, mercé chiamando, et voi non cale.

Dagli occhi vostri uscío 'l colpo mortale,
contra cui non mi val tempo né loco;
da voi sola procede, et parvi un gioco,
il sole e 'l foco e 'l vento ond'io son tale.

I pensier' son saette, e 'l viso un sole,
e 'l desir foco: e 'nseme con quest'arme
mi punge Amor, m'abbaglia et mi distrugge;

et l'angelico canto et le parole,
col dolce spirto ond'io non posso aitarme,
son l'aura inanzi a cui mia vita fugge.

(Love has set me as an arrow's target, / as snow in the sun, as wax in the fire, / and as mist in the wind: and I am already hoarse, / lady, calling for mercy, and you do not care. / The mortal blow came from your eyes, / against which I find no time or place an adequate defence; / from you alone come – and it seems to you play / – the sunlight and the fire and the wind which make me so. / My thoughts are arrows, her face a sun, / and my desire fire: and with these weapons together, / Love pierces me, dazzles me, destroys me: / and the angelic song and words, / with the sweet spirit against which I have no protection, / are the breeze before which my life is fleeing.)

The poem opens with a citation from Jeremiah (Lamentations 3: 12): 'posuit me quasi signum ad sagittam'. But the second and third images have appeared in vernacular poetry: Dante, *Da che convien*, 37: 'Ben conosco che va *la neve al sole*'; and Guido delle Colonne, *La mia vit'è*, 3 : 'anzi distrug/g/o *come al foco cera*'. Although the following image, of the mist in the wind, is no more striking than the others, it seems to be unprecedented. The phrase 'mercé chiamando' (l.4) seems commonplace, though it appears in precisely this form in Lapo Giani (13.83) and in Dante (*Così nel mio parlar*, 38). Dante's *Amor tu vedi ben* has phrases very close to two of the phrases in lines 5 and 6: '*Da li occhi suoi* mi ven la dolce luce' (43) and 'solo per lei servire, *e luogo e tempo*' (47). Line 7 resembles Cino, 110. 7–8: 'sí che la mia pesanza / non *paresse* a lei sollazzo e *gioco*'. Line 11 takes up an image from *Purg.* 8. 5 '. . . lo novo peregrin d'amore / punge'. And line 13, 'dolce spirto', had appeared at least in Cavalcanti (28. 10). In line 14 the pun on Laura–*l'aura*, which appears in many other places in the *RVF*, stems in all probability from Arnaut Daniel. Even some of the rhyming has clear precedents: 'distrugge: fugge' had been used by Dante (*Se vedi li occhi miei*, 2:3) and by Monte Andrea (*Ahi, misero tapino*, 66:67) and 'arme: aitarme' also by Dante (*Così nel mio parlar*, 12:13). Both pairs are also used elsewhere by Petrarch.

The poem which has emerged from this combination of fragments is anything but fragmentary, anything but pastiche. Each of the images in the opening quatrain is integrated with the others through the repetition of the syntagmatic structure; each is then taken up in the triplets of lines 8 and 10–11, before the final triplet, which becomes more clearly a figuration of Laura. In any case, from first to last word, the poem asserts itself as being Petrarchan. Its rhythms, images, turns of phrase, its particular music, all declare it to be related to other poems, to belong to the same voice. Nothing here is unique except the actual combination achieved. The remarkable thing is that elements which are so much Petrarch's stock in trade emerge from such diverse sources, and create such a wide network of possible references for this one poem.

Up to a point none of this is distinctive. It was the practice of Italian poets before Petrarch, as of any poets working within a tradition, to draw on the language and imagery of their predecessors, just as they followed more general conventions of the psychology and sociology of love. In the preceding century Bonagiunta da Lucca had even been criticised by Chiaro Davanzati for too direct and blatant borrowing from Giacomo da Lentini, the father of Italian poetry (*Poeti* 1,430). But imitation of one or more masters had been the norm. Provençal had repeatedly provided the models and the sources for innovations in Italian, from the bestiary *canso* of Rigaut de Barbezieux, which had supplied Stefano Protonotaro with the imagery of his *Pir meu cori alligrari*, to Arnaut Daniel, from whom Dante had taken the sestina form and the harsh style of his *rime petrose*. In the earlier part of the fourteenth century Dante himself had been plundered to a remarkable extent by Cino, who from early in his career had woven into verse Dantesque phrases at first from the lyrics and later from the *Commedia*, just as lesser-known contemporaries of Petrarch were also to do (see Chapter 1.2).

But the air of continuity, even of repetition, is deceptive. Petrarch's poetic of the self is rigorously maintained, and the changes which it brings about are radical. The degree to which he was able to fragment and to resynthesise the texts on which he drew was unprecedented. The Tuscan poets of the thirteenth century had frequently tried out different styles, but the assumption, as strong in Italian practice as in contemporary Latin theory, that different styles were appropriate to different subjects, worked to fragment the self. A notorious case is Rustico Filippi, a poet who belonged to the generation before that of Dante. Though the exact numerical equivalence is mere coincidence, it so happens that of the fifty-six sonnets of Rustico which have survived, half are in the comic style – conversational, humorous, sarcastic and in some instances grossly obscene – and the other half adopt a median version of the familiar courtly style, which, in comparison, is elevated in tone, language and theme. There is no convincing way of bringing the two halves together as the production of the same personality, except perhaps of one who was interested in stylistic and thematic diversity. Nor is Rustico alone. The *stilnovisti* also wrote one or two poems in the comic style that were a great deal more concrete and earthy than their more well-known verse (Guinizzelli 17 and 18, Cavalcanti 51). Dante himself in the ambiguous *tenzone* with Forese Donati, makes a foray into vulgarity, which is at odds with his more familiar elevated mode. Whilst Dante's other experiments in different styles in his lyrics remain, broadly speaking, within the courtly idiom, they are marked by a discontinuity that can only be sealed over by a narrative external to the poems, as occurs in the *Vita nuova*. Only in the *Commedia* will he achieve the fusion of all possible modes.

Amongst the *Rime disperse*, there are poems which do not seem characteristically Petrarchan (see Chapter 1.4), and there could well be others, equally genuine, amongst the many poems attributed to Petrarch but taken from him purely on stylistic grounds. But within the *RVF* the only marked departures from the Petrarchan mode as Petrarch has created it are perhaps the three sonnets against the Avignonese court. When Petrarch makes poems which historically fall within a sub-section of traditional practice, he inevitably recuperates them. In 134 (*Pace non trovo*) he takes up the nonsense mode which went back to the troubadour Guilhem IX of Aquitaine (*Farai un vers de dreyt nïen*) and which in Italy had found an indifferent realisation in Ruggieri Apugliese's *Umile sono e orgoglioso* (*Poeti* 1, 885). If there is an element of wit in Petrarch's poem, there is no vulgarity or inelegance. The mode has been refashioned. Noticeably it will be as Petrarchist that this type of verse will become known. In 154 he comes close to a particular kind of *stilnovismo* (see particularly Cavalcanti 4), but without the transcendentalism. *Se 'l pensier che mi strugge* (125) and *Chiare, fresche et dolci acque* (126) reshape the *rime petrose* of Dante, which he echoes in both poems. But Dante had been deliberately and explicitly harsh. The first of Petrarch's two poems takes up Dante's rhetoric of harshness, without exactly achieving the same effects; the second still uses some of the same devices (especially rhyme-words and sounds), but eradicates harshness altogether. (See also Chapter 5.3.)

Petrarch's use of a single style or register (*monolinguismo*) has often been contrasted with the stylistic and linguistic diversity (*plurilinguismo*) of Dante. As Contini, the originator of the contrast, pointed out (1951), there is in fact a kind of *plurilinguismo* in Petrarch too, precisely because there are in the collection moves towards such diverse styles. But the internal limits are clear, and the voice is constant through its infinite changes.

4.4 Viewing the tradition

The preceding sections may have suggested that Petrarch's is an all-embracing encyclopaedia of earlier poetry. In fact it is highly selective. Rather than attempting to absorb all the practices of vernacular poetry, it assesses, interprets, excludes, supplements; it is a critical reading of the tradition, not just its reaffirmation.

Unlike Dante, Petrarch has little to say about Italian poetry beyond what he says in the poetry itself. Such comments as he makes in his Latin writing focus on the problems of its 'vulgarity', and, except for some jeers at the dreamy incompetence of the *Roman de la Rose* (*Ep. met.* 3. 20) in comparison with modern Italian poetry and, much later, an ambiguous assessment of Dante (see below), give no hint of which poems or poets he valued, or what views he held about the history of the lyric. They do not even suggest what anthologies of poetry or what other vernacular texts he read or owned. Nor is the question clarified by external evidence: whereas the growth and contents of Petrarch's Latin library are known in some detail, of his Italian library nothing is known beyond the fact that a manuscript of the *Commedia* was sent to him by Boccaccio in 1353. However, in his Italian poetry he continues his predecessors' practice of commenting on other poets and evaluating them. Characteristically this occurs in a way that, in comparison with Dante and other earlier poets, seems particularly allusive and unemphatic. Yet there is a coherence in his position, and what he says in part reflects his practice, though it does not account for its complexity.

His explicit allusions to earlier vernacular poets occur only in four places – the sonnets on the deaths of Cino (92) and

Sennuccio (287), the canzone *Lasso me* (70), in which each of the stanzas ends with the direct citation of the opening line of a famous poem, and the fourth section of the *Triumphus Cupidinis*, in which Petrarch imagines meeting a succession of love-poets, first the ancients, then the Italians and finally the Provençals. From these artfully casual listings, an assessment emerges of earlier poetry which is rather different from that of Dante, and, in some ways, from modern orthodoxies of Dantesque derivation.

First of all Provençal poetry is downgraded in relation to Italian. Only Arnaut Daniel is singled out: the *Triumph* designates him the 'gran maestro d'amor, ch'a la sua terra / ancor fa onor col suo dir strano e bello' ('the great master of love, who to his land / still brings honour with beautiful unconventional poetry': *Tr. Cup.* 4. 41–2), and it is from a poem that Petrarch almost certainly thought was by him that *Lasso me* draws its first citation (though it is actually either anonymous or by Guilhem de Saint-Gregori). The rest of the troubadours, ranging from Jaufré Rudel to Peire Vidal, whom Petrarch chooses to mention in the *Triumph* are bundled together in a group that seems to have no historical or evaluative order to it and is noticeable only for its exclusions: there is no mention here of Bertran de Born, whom Dante rated a force to be reckoned with in the *De vulgari eloquentia* (2. 2. 9), or of the later generation of troubadours, including Guilhem de Montanhagol and Giraut Riquier, whose spiritualisations of the love ethos anticipated and may even have influenced the *stilnovisti*, or of the Italians, such as Sordello (see *Purg.* 6), who wrote in Provençal.

If Arnaut is the only Provençal poet who seems to come close to the Italians, amongst the Italians themselves *Lasso me* suggests that the high points are, in sequence, Cavalcanti, Dante (as a lyric poet), Cino and Petrarch himself with *Nel dolce tempo* (*RVF* 23). The Sicilians, at least some of whome Dante considered to have written important poems, have fallen away. This aesthetic devaluation (on which modern criticism tends to agree with Petrarch) does not discount their historical significance: the *Triumph* pointedly put them last in the procession, after having been first in time ('che fur giàl primi e quivi eran da sezzo': 1. 36). But Petrarch's revision of Dante's schema does not stop there. Dante's *bête noire* had been the leading poet of the previous generation, Guittone d'Arezzo, over whom ever since has hung a cloud of critical disapproval which various half-hearted reassessments have failed to lift. Petrarch upgrades Guittone in the *Triumph* and in the sonnet for Sennuccio, suggesting in both that, contrary to the implications of *Lasso me*, the first three Italian poets are, in order, Dante, Cino and Guittone, thus putting Guittone and, as is also surprising, Cino, above Cavalcanti and Guinizzelli, the two poets who loom much larger than either in Dantesque as in modern historiography. Neither Cavalcanti nor Guinizzelli is mentioned in the sonnet, and in the *Triumph* they appear just in front of the never very prominent Onesto Bolognese and the Sicilians. And whereas Dante had written of both with affection, in both Petrarchan texts the affection is reserved for Petrarch's real friends, Sennuccio and Franceschino degli Albizzi, acknowledged implicitly as minor poets, but celebrated as intimates.

This view of the vernacular tradition – personal, not fully worked out, not articulated in terms of principles and programmes, but with a definite historical sense and undoubtedly aware of disturbing the Dantesque system – points away from giving too much importance to the *stil novo* and to the troubadours in the *RVF*. Certainly there are echoes of both in plenty, as charted respectively by Suitner (1977) and, much earlier, by Scarano (1900); and there are some poems which are reworkings of *stil novo* or troubadour topoi. But, if Dante is left aside, it is Arnaut and Guittone who seem particularly prominent presences, although it may well be that quantitatively the number of echoes is not especially large. Arnaut is the begetter of the sestina, an early explorer of the possibilities of the word *aura*, and the expert in a virtuoso harsh style which Petrarch only follows closely in *RVF* 29, but which he regularly mixes with the sweet to make his own music. Noticeably it is Arnaut, not any other poet in Provençal or Italian, who is twice strongly echoed in the way Petrarch normally reserves for Latin authors (212. 8 and 239. 36).

Guittone, who himself looks to the harsh and deliberately difficult style of the *trobar clus* for some of his effects, might be thought too wayward or simply too unpoetic to carry much weight with Petrarch. Arnaut's poetry was easily judged unconventional but beautiful; that of Guittone could well have seemed merely bizarre. Certainly in the fourteenth century generally he was no longer the necessary point of reference that he had been in the thirteenth. But there is a noteworthy foreshadowing of the narrative of the *RVF* in Guittone. His poems suggest a story of looking for someone to love, eventually having success, and then remaining in love for some time before a moment of reconsideration arrives; then Guittone becomes Fra Guittone, denouncer of carnal love and defender of reason, but still a writer of poems, as he proclaims in the programme for his second phase, *Ora parrà s'eo saverò cantare*, a poem which is what Petrarch's *I' vo pensando* should have been, if he were actually going to reform his desires and yet continue writing poetry. And there are more technical anticipations too. If there is any earlier poet who can shape his sonnets to a climactic final line or who knows how to exploit trochaic rhythms, as Petrarch does, it is not any of the *stilnoisti* or even Dante, at least in his lyrics, but once again Guittone. The discrepancies between the sonnet and the *Triumph* suggest that Petrarch hesitated over quite where to put him in any table of poets, but he clearly had no doubts that it was near the top. The generational hostility that led Dante and Cavalcanti to underestimate just how much affected they themselves were by Guittone has disappeared. Guittone can be accepted without subterfuges.

But neither Guittone nor Arnaut nor any other single poet is as important for the *RVF* as Dante. It is an importance which it would be wrong to limit to his lyric poems on the grounds that the *Divina commedia* and the *RVF* belong to different genres. Echoes of the lyric poems are present in the *RVF* in abundance, particularly of the *rime petrose* (e.g. in *Amor m'à posto*: see section 3 above). But it is plain that Petrarch, like other poets of the fourteenth century (see Chapter 1.2), had also to deal with the *Commedia*, the immensely powerful exception to all the rules, which overshadowed all forms of poetic writing and threatened to invade and annul them all.

Retrospectively the two writers might appear simply to be different from each other, or to represent two different historical moments. Emerging from the proto-humanist culture of Avignon and soon dominating it, Petrarch committed himself to a path that diverged radically from that of Dante – classicising and elitist, not divulgative; politically relativist, not imperialist; Augustinian, not Thomist; philological, moral and historical where Dante was syllogistic, metaphysical and meta-historical; self-obsessed where

Dante was directed outwards. And so on: at every turn there are striking differences, which are barely mitigated by the so-called humanism of Dante (as suggested in the *Convivio* or in the Ulysses episode of the *Inferno*), or by the regressive asceticism prospected in some of Petrarch's writings. So different are they that, if a watershed is to be found between the Middle Ages and the Renaissance, it could well be in the space between them – the one linguistically progressive but summing up the past, the other apparently conservative but drawing the lines for major changes in the future.

But clearly Dante posed serious problems for Petrarch historically. He probably first read the *Commedia* not long after it was first released. Given the close ties between the Italians of Avignon and literary circles in Northern Italy, the work must have been known in Provence in the 1320s. In any case he spent several periods in Bologna as a student between 1320 and 1326. A marginal note in the fairly early *Rerum memorandarum* taking issue with a point Dante makes in the *Paradiso* (Billanovich 1965: 39) suggests that Petrarch knew the text well, as seems to be confirmed by echoes scattered throughout his works. However, until 1359 he makes no public mention of Dante in any of his discussions of literature. And when he does eventually do so his embarrassment is plain.

In 1353 Boccaccio sent Petrarch a copy of the *Commedia*, together with an accompanying poem praising Dante to the skies and urging Petrarch to read and admire him. The reply which Petrarch eventually wrote, at least six years later, takes the form of a defence against charges made by certain members of the *vulgus* – in all probability, Florentine enthusiasts of Dante's work – that he hates, despises and envies Dante. He professes nothing but admiration for a fellow-citizen and friend of his father, who, he claims (with a slight adjustment of the facts), was exiled on the very same day and thereafter devoted himself to poetry. In his work Dante was 'popularis quidem quod ad stilum attinet, quod ad rem haud dubie nobilis poete' ('of the people admittedly as regards style, but as regards matter indubitably a noble poet': *Fam.* 21. 15), yet his writing was 'in suo genere optimus' ('excellent in its kind'), so that he deserves 'vulgaris eloquentie palmam' ('the palm of vernacular eloquence'). Petrarch claims that, as a young man, he never read Dante's work, because he himself was then thinking of composing a large-scale work in the vernacular and was frightened of being excessively influenced in spite of efforts to the contrary. He then goes on to say that any resemblances that might be found between his own work and Dante's are the result of chance or because their minds think in a similar way ('vel casu fortuito vel similitudine ingeniorum'). Throughout the letter, his discomfort is apparent. He refuses to name Dante directly, referring to him always as 'ille' ('that man'), as if, in spite of his protestations, the name is too explicit an acknowledgment of Dante's worth. On the other hand he clearly echoes Dante's phrasing at various points, most obviously when, in commending his commitment to poetry, he draws on the famous speech of Ulysses: 'non amor coniugis, non natorum pietas ab arrepto semel calle distraxerit' ('not love of his wife, not proper feelings for his children distracted him from the path once he had taken to it': cf. *Inf.*: 26. 94–6), when it seems that he is indirectly acknowledging the power of an influence which he is also drawn to deny.

This letter, which, understandably, has often been judged hypocritical, ungenerous and egotistic, is not the whole story. A few years later, in 1366/7, Petrarch wrote a far more balanced letter to Boccaccio (*Sen.* 5.3), in which he is far more appreciative of 'ille nostri eloquii dux vulgaris' ('our leader in vernacular eloquence'), as he is of the positive, creative openings offered by vernacular writing. But this second letter was written at a time when Petrarch was apparently much more sure of his position. By then the composition of the *RVF* was well advanced, and, thanks to Boccaccio, a version of it had already been made which was coupled in the original manuscript with the *Commedia* and other works of Dante (see Chapter 2.2). It is the ambiguities of the first letter which reveal how difficult it was to deal with the mixture of admiration, hostility, frustration and envy generated by this poetic father whose dominance threatened any kind of writing that followed in his wake.

The differences between Petrarch and Dante are from this point of view not atemporal nor simply the indicators of a general shift in European culture. They represent a reorientation of intellectual and literary activity on Petrarch's part away from Dante's influence and a correction of his position, the particular point of abrasion between the two being the vernacular. Petrarch's overall solution was to remove from Italian and to a large extent from poetry explicit discussion of most of the areas of intellectual concern which had figured prominently in the *Commedia*. Politics, religion, philosophy, knowledge in its widest sense, were all both reshaped and declared once again to be the province of the literate language of the whole of Europe, not of a local vernacular. In its turn the vernacular was restricted, drastically, to what had been its core before Dante had blown it open – the love-lyric, free from explicit narrative or continuity, with at most excursions into other areas such as politics, morality and religion. But it was in the vernacular that major problems had to be solved. Petrarch could not simply cut back towards a centre. The centre itself had to be reshaped because Dante himself had reshaped it. Elsewhere Petrarch could almost pass over or round Dante; here he had to face him directly, and on something more than a stylistic level.

Dante's own reshaping lay in Beatrice. Loving her meant finding a rationale for love and for poetry, any one of the three terms justifying and informing the others; it meant finding a continuity between one poem and another, because poet, lover and reader could progress through the text (whether it was the *Vita nuova* or the *Commedia*), gaining in understanding of everything the text presupposed and gradually brought to light. Everything else assumed a sense in virtue of its relationship to her, including deviations from her, all of which have to be experienced and transcended in a progressively stronger affirmation of truth. And yet there is no idolatry: Beatrice herself will only be transcended high in Paradise, but from the beginning of the *Vita nuova* it is made plain that loving her leads to the godhead. She is not instrumentalised, but she is an instrument.

There was no precedent for such a narrative in Italian poetry or even in Provençal. Such romantic stories as were attached to the names of poets were barely apparent in the poetry itself, which consisted for the most part of lyrics almost devoid of a narrative context. The majority of the stories that could be constructed, from Bernart de Ventadorn and Sordello to Cavalcanti, were in any case stories of change, of infidelity, the endings of which are hazy. To judge from the few samples of laments for dead *donne* which survive in Italian, death was a conclusion, not the beginning of a second, more important phase (see *Poeti* 1, 126, 146, 390). If there was an expected narrative pattern, it was that exemplified in

Italian only in the progression of Guittone d'Arezzo from lover to moralising friar. (See also Chapter 5.2.)

Dante's love-story had to be reinterpreted by any major writer who followed him, and from many points of view it is this reinterpretation which the *RVF* undertakes. The very act of making an arrangement of Italian poems meant facing questions of narrative already raised by Dante. Focusing upon a single *donna* meant encountering all the problems of transcendence, reason, morality and truth in both love and poetry which Dante had apparently resolved. Without Beatrice the dead Laura would not have continued to obsess Petrarch poetically, but even during her life the implicit point of reference is Dante's experience of a single justified love. The previous chapter (3.3) has discussed the ambiguous combination of narrative and formal organisation which Petrarch substitutes for Dantesque progression; the following chapter (5) will examine his remaking of the love-story as such and his reinterpretation of the figure of the *donna*. Here it is sufficient to stress that at every point Dante is dominated and denied. The fragmentation of the synthesis is triumphantly, if painfully, carried through, as Petrarch returns again and again to the fundamental questions which must be those of any post-medieval reader of Dante. What remains when the structures of thought upon which Dante's poetry appears to rest have irrevocably collapsed? What is left from that experience of wholeness, except perhaps literature? And what in the end is that?

If in one sense Petrarch's reply is that emotionally and imaginatively much does remain and that the loss is itself indelible, in other ways his response to Dante is to level the *Commedia* to another text which he allows to emerge into the *RVF* only in fragmentary form. The Purgatorial dawn had had a 'dolce color d'oriental zaffiro' ('sweet colour of oriental sapphire': *Purg.* 1. 13); Laura's fingers, or perhaps even fingernails, have 'di cinque perle oriental colore' ('the orient colour of five pearls': *RVF* 199. 5). Dante had wanted to say to Virgil as Beatrice appeared that 'Men che dramma / di sangue m'è rimaso che non tremi: / conosco i segni dell'antica fiamma' ('Less than a dram / of blood do I have left that does not tremble: / I recognise the signs of a flame belonging to the past': *Purg.* 30. 45–8). Petrarch picks up the rhyme and the sense for something much lighter: Laura 'non lascia in me dramma / che non sia foco et fiamma' ('She

leaves less than a dram in me / that is not fire and flame': 125.
12–13). The reminiscences are surprisingly frequent, with particular attention as Trovato (1979) has charted in some detail, to
Inferno 5, *Purgatorio 6–8*, and the Earthly Paradise canti.

Petrarch was not alone amongst fourteenth-century poets in
reappropriating Dante in fragmentary form (see Chapter 1.2); but
he was unique in his ability to integrate his appropriations into his
own work. That he was able to do so is linked with his literary
self-confidence: for all the links which he establishes between
himself and the past, Petrarch refuses to be bound by his
predecessors. The following section discusses his reform of some
basic features of the tradition.

4.5   Anti-medievalism

The forces of rupture at work in the *RVF* are at least as strong as
those working for continuity. One major difference from earlier
poetry is the textuality of the collection (see Chapter 2.1), but at
least as important is the radical refusal of the dominant cast of
thought of his predecessors and the styles of writing associated
with it.

In his polemical treatises Petrarch was openly hostile to
fourteenth-century Aristotelianism, though he proclaimed a certain respect for Aristotle himself. His prime target was medicine,
but he dismissed any intellectual enterprise concerned with
investigating and classifying natural phenomena. His position is
not merely polemical: it is one that he abides by throughout his
writing. He refuses constantly to define his terms, to construct
propositions which lay claim to absolute validity, or to have any
truck with analytic and syllogistic argument. When, exceptionally,
he allows himself to be driven to a definition of nobility by a
correspondent, his response is to proceed by exclusion, saying
what nobility is not, never what it is (*Fam.* 11. 16). When he
reflects on the significance of gold, he does so by looking at
examples of how gold has been used and how it has been
described (*Fam.* 6. 8). When he is asked for his view of human
life, he strings together image after image in a rhetorical
concatenation, not a logical one (*Sen.* 11. 11). Discourse which
pretends to mirror metaphysical structures simply does not
appear, since truth of a more than human kind is beyond our
understanding. As he says of the island of Thule, drawing an

explicit analogy with the concept of truth, the learned have the name available for discussion, but not the thing (*Fam.* 3. 1 and 2). This is not to say that words may not somehow allude to truth, but the method is indirect and the truth in question will be textual, moral or historical, or else it will regard the self.

The mode of thought is inseparable from a mode of writing which also goes against medieval practice. In Latin the rupture is patent, at least in intention. The lexicon of medieval Latin is excluded almost in its entirety: its 'corrupt' grammar is rejected. Instead there is the attempt to return to the grammar, syntax and vocabulary of antiquity, and, to some extent, to its literary genres. The direction is certain, though the realisation may not always be fully assured.

In Italian the regeneration is carried through. From its beginnings in Sicily, thirteenth-century poetry had been drawn towards analysing love as a phenomenon or as an objective entity. Giacomo da Lentini, for instance, in the course of one of the earliest *tenzoni*, produced a definition-poem which fairly neatly encapsulated commonplaces of contemporary psycho-physiological thinking within the confines of a sonnet (*Poeti* 1, 90). The urge to define, to analyse, to find an intellectual systemisation, which reached heights of virtuosity with Caval-canti's *Donna me prega*, was particularly prevalent in the *stil novo*, the *Vita nuova* being the most complex and dynamic fusion of intellection, love and poetry. But even poetry which is not so overtly intellectual often takes the form of an argument, such as the sequence 'If . . . therefore . . . but . . .', which lent itself easily to the sonnet structure. As Contini pointed out (1951), a remarkably well-articulated form of discourse, far different from the loose arrangement of stanzas in Provençal poetry, became almost the norm.

Petrarch eliminates scholastic thought and terminology. There are no technical terms in the *RVF* in the sense that there are no terms implying specialised scientific or philosophical knowledge. There is no definition of any term that might control or restrict meaning: what controls there are, are established by other means than argument. There is no interest in the mechanics of love-psychology as such. That love comes through the eyes is simply accepted as self-evident; that the heart, mind and soul are also affected is also taken as given, though the relationships between these terms are not fixed. Love itself is neither a substance nor an accident but something undefinable, because, as becomes almost a game in a poem such as *S'amor non è* (132) (see Chapter 6.5), only contradictory things can be said of it. Words such as 'amore', 'umile', 'beltà', 'salute', 'virtù', which had been favoured by the *stil novo*, reappear without their intellectual resonances, though with resonance as words which had been used by the *stil novo*. The associations are prevalently literary and extend into all areas of Petrarch's reading. So 'virtù', for example, may be classical or Christian, narrowly sexual, or indicate 'power' or 'strength' (e.g. of the self in 2. 5 or of the stars in 9. 3); what it does not have is a place in a psychological or philosophical system. For good or ill a certain conceptual precision has been abandoned and in its place has come a richness of literary allusion and evocation, whose limits are not specified. Whilst syntactic lucidity is augmented (see Chapter 6.5), in general metaphorical and associative aspects of language dominate rational and analytic ones. What remains is a concern with truth and with the inadequacies, from this point of view, of a poetry which knows that it lacks the metaphysical underpinning which would validate its own existence.

Up to a point, the process of discarding preceding systems of thought and remaking the techniques of rhetoric into something more flexible, more adherent to the self's requirements, is affected by Petrarch's work in Latin. Classicising rhetoric is at its strongest in the political canzoni and in the polemical sonnets, although other poems too may edge towards the classical in particular citations, such as those from Horace mentioned in section 3 above, or in their exploitation of devices, such as chiasmus or antithesis, which had previously been relatively little used. Generally it is not so much the case that overtly classical rhetoric is introduced as that the rhetoric of preceding poetry is modified in order to make it more able to express the self who is the ghostly regulator of the poems. I shall examine in Chapter 6 how some features are entirely discarded, whilst others are recast down to their finest details to create a poetry which is denser, more flowing and more musical than anything that had been written before.

To a very large degree the sixteenth century was justified in finding Petrarch a model realisation of its ideas of what poetry should be and in making him a new beginning, not, as he also is, a conclusion. In this perspective Petrarch is as much a herald of the Renaissance in Italian as he is in Latin.

5

Themes

5.1 The introduction

The poem which introduces the *RVF* is extraordinary. It has no precedent in medieval poetry, since of course there were no comparable collections of poems to be introduced. And it is quite unlike classical poems (such as those by Catullus (1) and Horace (*Odes* 1. 1)) which had a similar introductory function and which may have provided a precedent, just as it is also different from later poems introducing collections based on Petrarch's own, even when they take it as a model. Considered solely in terms of its meaning or meanings, Petrarch's poem is the opposite of an invitation: in effect it enjoins us to close the book we have just opened and to do something better than read what is to be shamefully exposed to us. But at the same time it overrides its own injunctions, drawing us into what is to follow – the labyrinths, woods, uncharted paths of the collection. If we now choose to enter this ambiguous region, it is because, thanks to this poem, we think we will like it, not for any other reason. We go forward on our own responsibility, not Petrarch's.

> Voi ch'ascoltate in rime sparse il suono
> di quei sospiri ond'io nudriva 'l core
> in sul mio primo giovenile errore
> quand'era in parte altr' uom da quel ch'i' sono,
>
> del vario stile in ch'io piango et ragiono
> fra le vane speranze e 'l van dolore,
> ove sia chi per prova intend' amore,
> spero trovar pietà, nonché perdono.

Ma ben veggio or sí come al popol tutto
favola fui gran tempo, onde sovente
di me medesmo meco mi vergogno;

et del mio vaneggiar vergogna è 'l frutto,
e 'l pentersi, e 'l conoscer chiaramente
che quanto piace al mondo è breve sogno.

(You who hear in scattered rhymes the sound / of those sighs on which I fed my heart / at the time of my first youthful erring, / when I was different in part from the man I am, / for the varied style in which I weep and discourse / amidst vain hopes and vain pain. / – should there be any [amongst you] who understand love through direct experience, / I hope to find pity, not only pardon. / But I see well now how for the whole populace / I was long a scandal, for which reason often / I brood with myself on the shame which I feel for myself. / And the fruit of my vain words and behaviour is shame, / and repentance, and knowing clearly / that all that pleases in the world is a brief dream.)

The reader is effectively advised that the following poems are defective in literary, moral, social and ontological terms. They form a loose collection of 'scattered rhymes', by implication inferior to any collection which is organised and unworthy of the name of poetry. Like this poem itself, they are not separable from the 'youthful erring' and its related emotions; they are not therefore a proper moral assessment of them. The possibility that there could be any amongst the readers who might be sympathetic, is raised, only to be forgotten or discounted in the transition to the sestet. Petrarch is alone: the cognoscenti are absorbed in the generality, unforgiving but not wrong to be so. The result now is a highly self-absorbed shame for himself as he is and was, repentance, and a recognition of the illusoriness of all earthly attractions (including, presumably, poetry as well as love or beauty). Everything said here is negative, unless shame, regret and the knowledge of vanity are positive. If so, the path forwards should lead to something more substantial, but we know from the beginning of this poem that it in fact leads into the vanity itself. If the reader accepts what the poem says, he or she will agree with the populace as a whole, leave Petrarch to his shame, and go away.

Two later poets, introducing collections of poems on the Petrarchan model, say much more what we might expect. Gaspara Stampa, writing in the mid-sixteenth century, follows Petrarch's poem closely but also strongly resists it:

> Voi, ch' ascoltate in queste meste rime,
> in questi mesti, in questi oscuri accenti
> il suon degli amorosi miei lamenti
> e de le pene mie tra l'altre prime,
>
> ove fia chi valor apprezzi e stime,
> gloria, non che perdon, de' miei lamenti
> spero trovar fra le ben nate genti,
> poi che la lor cagione è sí sublime.
>
> E spero ancor che debba dir qualcuna:
> – Felicissima lei, da che sostenne
> per sí chiara cagion danno sí chiaro!
>
> Deh, perché tant' amor, tanta fortuna
> per sí nobil signor a me non venne,
> ch'anch'io n'andrei con tanta donna a paro?
>
> (ed. Ceriello 1954: 13)

(You who hear in these sad rhymes, / in these sad, in these obscure accents, / the sound of my amorous laments / and of my pains that were first amongst all others, / should there be any who appreciate and value true worth, / it is glory for my laments, not merely pardon, / which I hope to find amongst people nobly born, / since their cause is so sublime. / And I hope further that some lady may have to say, / 'Most happy is she, since she bore / so splendid sufferings for so splendid a cause! / O why did so great love, so great fortune / for so noble a lord not come to me, / that I might be equal with such a lady?')

By Petrarchan standards this is a very flawed poem, which relies on indiscriminate repetition to fill out its parts to the correct size, and to create simple, though peculiar, musical effects (especially in line 2). But the statement which it makes is precisely the opposite to that made by Petrarch's poem: Gaspara Stampa expects to win glory from her poems amongst the noble. Whatever their limitations, whatever pain they may reveal, the poems will make others aware, even jealous, of the sublime passion which inspired them. There is every reason for proceeding further, at least if we give priority to the argument of the poem: any pain, any defects which the following poems will reveal are only the necessary accompaniments of an excellence that cannot fail to impress itself upon us. Or so she would have us believe.

Some eighty years before, that is, in the early 1470s, Matteo Maria Boiardo composed his *Amorum libri*, introducing them with a poem which establishes a little more distance between itself and Petrarch's introductory poem.

> Amor, che me scaldava al suo bel sole
> nel dolce tempo de mia età fiorita,
> a ripensare ancora oggi me invita
> quel che allora mi piacque, ora mi dole.
>
> Cosí racolto ho ciò che 'l pensier fole
> meco parlava a l'amorosa vita,
> quando, con voce or leta or sbigotita,
> formava sospirando le parole.
>
> Ora de amara fede e dolci inganni
> l'alma mia consumata, non che lassa,
> fuge sdegnosa il puerile errore.
>
> Ma, certo, chi nel fior de' soi primi anni
> sanza caldo de amore il tempo passa,
> se in vista è vivo, vivo è sanza core.
>   (ed. Scaglione 1966: 45)

(Love that warmed me in its fair sun / in the sweet time of my flowering years, / again today invites me to think back / on what then pleased me and now gives me pain. / So I have gathered what my crazed thoughts / said to me during my life of love, / when, in tones that were at times joyful and at others dismayed, / I shaped words as I sighed. / Now my soul, wasted, not merely weary, / flees in disdain the puerile mistake / of bitter fidelity and sweet deceits. / But, certainly, he who in the flower of his

early years, / spends his time without the heat of love, / if in
appearance he is alive, is alive without a heart.)

Like Petrarch, Boiardo looks back to a time when he was young
and foolish, though from a vantage-point of more clearly defined
disavowal, and, in the concluding lines, with a strong inversion.
Granted that love and love-poetry were a waste of spirit, youth
without love is not life at all. The paradox is energetically
formulated in Boiardo's half Petrarchan, half local language,
though needing a certain padding in the second quatrain and first
tercet. It assures us that the poems we are about to read are a
reflection of the necessary vitality of youth, part of whose positive
value is that we should outgrow it.

Petrarch is nothing like so simple as either Stampa or Boiardo.
The explicit meaning of his introductory poem, itself much denser
than is the case with the two later poems, is only part of its
complex rhetoric, and not the most important one in terms of
effects, which depend less on what is being said than on the
relations created between speaker and reader. As rhetoric the
poem is a particular adaptation of the subtle exordium (*insinuatio*)
which the *Rhetorica ad Herennium* (1. 6. 9) advises as appropriate
when the cause is discreditable and the speaker himself is
displeased with what his opponents judge 'unworthy or criminal
acts' ('indigna aut nefaria'). Here the reader is placed in four
positions in succession – as one of the listeners, as one of the
special group who have experience of love, as one of the generality
who have no time for the speaker, and as someone who cannot
fail to agree with the final statement, whilst the speaker himself
moves from an appeal (echoing a similar appeal in *Vita nuova* 7
and a passage in Jeremiah (Lamentations 1) on which it was
explicitly based) to an imagined intimacy and then into painful
isolation, which, in the last line, becomes participation in
universally shared knowledge. The effect is to cast the reader into
uncertainty over his own eventual position, whilst feeling that
either a disclosure or a dramatic display is enacted before him.
Though it is an invitation which the reader can refuse, he is
invited to participate in the emotional performance, to enter the
subjective world of the speaker, suspending the judgment which
he is also invited to make.

All this, if disquieting, is potentially pleasurable to the literate reader, the more so since nothing explicitly grievous, sinful or indecorous is associated with the error and the vanity. Instead the lexicon, the balance of the phrasing, the control and yet flow of the syntax, the varied distribution of the pauses, all have a subtlety and decorum comparable to those of classical poetry. This may be vernacular poetry, but, in spite of what it implies, it is not vulgar. Above all there is the music of the poem, running through everything else in it, threatening to dominate meanings which in any case (particularly at certain points, such as line 2) can easily become more evanescent the more we look at them. Almost irrespective of what it is saying, the poem demands to be read and offers its music, its rhetoric, its decorum, its very uncertainties as a sample of what is to be expected. In a word, the poem offers and promises pleasure, conscious of its vanity being part of its particular appeal.

For ease of exposition I have divided the exploration of this ambiguous poetic pleasure into two parts. I have postponed to Chapter 6 discussion of language, rhythm, style, form – that is, the features of Petrarch's art as a poet, which are essential to each and every poem. In the present chapter I shall discuss a number of themes to which the poetry constantly returns – individual experience, whether real or invented (section 2), sensual desire (3), words themselves, whether seen as having little or no meaning or as capable of affirming more public, humanist values (4), and transcendent reality (5). Any one of them might be the source or object of poetry: all are subsumed in what we actually read. The divisions are again for reasons of convenience. In the collection itself one issue merges with another or emerges from it both within and across poems, although, in accordance with the emergent, if never fully defined, narrative described in Chapter 3, one issue or another comes into prominence at different moments, and one at least – the possibility of Apollonian poetry – is eventually discarded.

5.2 History

The history of Petrarch's love for Laura is elusive and enticing. At various times since the fourteenth century the facts have seemed quite secure, if hard to come by. At others everything has dissolved in mist, in invention. We first hear of serious doubts about the reality of it all from Petrarch himself in a letter (*Fam.* 2. 9) to his friend Giacomo Colonna, who, like Boccaccio and other humanists of the following century, apparently wanted to believe that Laura was simply an allegory of the poetic laurel. Petrarch disabused him: Laura was a woman and his passion was anything but feigned. An apparently private note in Petrarch's treasured manuscript of Virgil seems to confirm the letter and to provide some hard information: Petrarch first saw Laura at matins in the church of St Clare in Avignon on 6 April 1327; she died twenty-one years later on 6 April 1348 at the same time of day. *RVF* 211 and 336 reiterate the same dates and times, as does the *Triumphus Mortis* (1. 133). It also emerges from other poems (3, 62) that the first day was Good Friday. Beyond the bare and, I shall argue, deceitful security of the dates, the 'facts' are meagre indeed. Laura was born in a small town or lived in one (*RVF* 4), though she may also have lived in Avignon (*Ep. met.* 1. 7. 100); she belonged to the established nobility, since Petrarch says that she was 'renowned for her ancient lineage' ('sanguine nota vetusto': ibid. l. 38); and she was almost certainly married, as was to be expected and seems to be confirmed by poems hinting at marital jealousy (especially *RVF* 196, 206, 222). She was of course chaste and beautiful, with golden ringlets or curls and dark eyes.

We can integrate these facts, if facts they are, with much else in the poems. There are continual allusions to journeys, illnesses, visits, meetings and other incidents of this kind, and there might also be a psychological and intellectual evolution discernible in the poems over the years. The external events and incidents, the inner story of the writer, appear to lie behind the poems, to be what called them into existence: they are, we say, their inspiration, though all we know of them has come from the very texts which they seem to have inspired. If we accept the invitation, certainly extended by the collection, to read it in this way, then we can make a résumé of the love-affair and of the narrative progress of the collection itself much as we might do with a diary or an autobiographical notebook. We can read the poems as a kind of history, perhaps fragmented and disordered for poetic reasons, but recuperable into solid prose, on more or less the following lines.

Petrarch saw Laura and fell in love with her on Good Friday (3), 6 April 1327 (211). It was a love with sensual aspects (e.g. 22), though by no means entirely sensual and certainly capable of elevated moments (e.g. 72). Laura resisted Petrarch's sensual advances from motives that combined innate morality and concern for her good name. Perhaps she also took pleasure in teasing him, or, as he saw it, torturing him (45, 46, 87). Sometime between 1334 (signalled in 30, the first of the 'anniversary poems') and 1337 (50) she fell ill, but recovered (33, 34). In the same period Petrarch had a portrait painted of her by Simone Martini (77, 78). A little later he thought for a time that he had freed himself from his passion, but relapsed even more strongly (55). He would have similar delusions again (80), by which time he realised, or thought he realised, that Laura too was in love (88). There were separations of course: she had been away at some time (41–43), he travelled through the Ardennes in 1333 (176, 177) on a journey he also wrote about in a letter (*Fam.* 1. 5), and made visits to Italy (129, 180), returning once by way of the Rhône (208). But neither distance nor time made any difference. The first prayer for release was on Good Friday 1338 (62). There would be other prayers and temporary renunciations, but from now on there would be no escape, whether Petrarch proclaimed his happiness and celebrated Laura, or complained and blamed himself, or her, or his fate. If anything, there would be an intensification bordering on monomania. Where Petrarch had attempted other kinds of poetry on occasion, the early 1340s saw the last of the political canzoni (128). There was a final outburst in the sonnets denouncing the Avignonese court (136–8). After that there was only the personal world of love, with even poems of friendship diminishing almost to nothing. So the years went by, their passage marked in other anniversary poems: 1340 (79), 1341 (101, 107), 1342 (145), 1343 (118), 1344 (122), 1345 (266), 1347 (212, 221).

But the 1340s were relatively rich in incidents, not all of them unpleasant. Laura leaves a glove in Petrarch's house, which, to his regret, she then recovers (199–201). She is offended by a remark which he is reported to have made, but he insists the report is a falsification (206). She is one of a group of twelve beautiful women who sail along the Rhône and then ride together in a carriage (225). She is selected for the special and quite unusual favour of a kiss from an important visitor whom Petrarch does not identify (238). An older man sees Laura and Petrarch together, compliments them as a unique pair of lovers and presents them with a bunch of roses (245).

But the relative calm was to be disrupted. Ageing meant weariness and regret. It meant also becoming increasingly aware of Laura's mortality. Petrarch had foreseen as early as poem 12 that Laura's eyes would some day lose their sparkle. In 90 he registered that this had happened. Though 127 has him celebrating her emergence into womanhood as the perfection of her beauty, they were growing old together (168). At some point in the 1340s she suffered a serious eye infection, which Petrarch himself caught (231, 233). Soon after he realised that she was sick, possibly mortally so (248–255), ironically at a time when she seemed more responsive (257–9), though, as he proclaimed in the last three poems of Part 1, she was still as chaste as she was beautiful.

Her death in 1348, coinciding with that of Petrarch's friend Giovanni Colonna (269), was of course painful (267, 268). But then (270) it also seemed a release from a passion which he analysed in the introductory canzone to Part 2, written before Laura's death, as something paralysing his will and endangering his soul. However, the release was as illusory as those which had preceded it years before. He was tempted by another love, who conveniently died (271), and then he was drawn back to Laura. He was unable to forget her as she had been, or as he liked to imagine her, but he also repeatedly imagined her as she must be in heaven, and sometimes had dreams or visions in which her spirit visited him, consoling him and encouraging him to think of his salvation. But he could neither abandon his memories nor follow where Laura seemed to be leading, nor forget the whole business. Again the years were passing in irresolution, though only two more were marked in the poems, 1351 (278) and 1358 (364), the latter signalling the end of the affair and of the collection. In the last poems Petrarch attempts renunciation and makes two final, culminating pleas, to God (365) and to the Virgin (366), to rescue him and to grant him peace.

I argued in Chapter 2.1 that the narrative only partially corresponds to the actual time of composition, since, in the *RVF* as elsewhere, Pertrarch wove history and fiction about his own life inextricably together. In fact some poems have had to be forced into the account I have just given. Some, including ones that can be dated externally, are not in their rightful place. Poems 176 and 177, for example, on the journey through the Ardennes that

Petrarch actually made in 1333, look as if they belong to the 1340s. Many can be given some kind of historical location only because they happen to come between two poems which mark the passage of the years. Again and again what seems firmly grounded in life has increasingly appeared grounded in literature. An apparently innocuous instance such as the poem on Laura sailing on the Rhône and then riding in a carriage with some other ladies (225) has an uncomfortable resemblance to some early poetry of Boccaccio (especially *Rime* 6). Other incidents, such as the loss of a glove, or an illness, have the air of literary commonplaces, even if a precise source is not always identifiable. Some anniversary references have analogies in Provençal poetry (Scarano 1900: 333). Others (see Chapter 2.3) are late insertions. Of course almost everything, from Laura's name and golden hair to Petrarch's internal debates, may be true in some sense. As Petrarch said in the *Africa*, the poet must base his work in history: 'he who invents whatever he recounts, does not deserve the honour of being called a great or serious poet, but only the name of liar' ('Que fingit quodcumque refert, non ille poete / nomine censendus, nec vatis honore, sed uno / nomine mendacis': 9. 103–5). But such a formulation allowed for as much leeway as was needed poetically in the *Africa* itself or in any other kind of poetry.

We know nothing of a historical Laura, as Ernesto Carrara made plain as long ago as 1934. Luigi Peruzzi, writing between 1439 and 1449, made her a member of a family called Di Salso from the village of Thor. In his introduction to his 1525 edition of Petrarch's Italian poems, Alessandro Vellutello gives an exact account, supplemented by a detailed map of the area, of the first meeting between Petrarch and Laura Chabau of Cabrières, born in 1314 as his researches demonstrate. Other equally plausible candidates were suggested in the course of the sixteenth century, but it was not until the 1760s that the most detailed version of Laura was constructed. The Abbé P.A. de Sade, a member of the same family as the Marquis, revealed that she was the daughter of Audibert de Noves and wife of Hugh de Sade, by whom she had eleven children. The documents on which the Abbé based his revelations have not been found. In all probability, according to Carrara (1959: 104–5), his main concern was to buttress the prestige and power of his family by claiming an illustrious ancestor, though attempts have been made recently to revive his identification (Jones 1984b).

The veil is and has always been impenetrable. After all, if we are to believe Petrarch, a close friend, Giacomo Colonna, suspected that Laura was a fiction. And the anonymous fourteenth-century commentator on *Bucolicum carmen* 3, who may have known Petrarch personally, produces as naively romantic a version of the story as could be imagined. Laura's beauty, he says, was recognised by many ('multis placuit'), but she was so virtuous that she rejected all her suitors ('in tantum honestissima fuit, quod omnes respuit'). She was rich, the poet poor but devoted to study ('pauper sed studiosus'). He eventually won fame and was courteously and honourably loved by her ('curialiter et honeste amatus'). We are only a step away from the fifteenth-century tales of the Pope offering special dispensation for Petrarch and Laura to marry, only to be refused by Petrarch on the grounds that marriage would destroy his inspiration. But we are no nearer the truth with any other version of what happened.

We cannot even be sure of her name. 'Laura' is a *senhal*, a code-name like Beatrice or Cino's Selvaggia. It is a name rich in associations and double-meanings which the poems continually exploit (see section 4 below), and which may have descended ultimately from Arnaut Daniel or from Bernart de Ventadorn, perhaps via the early Boccaccio (see Contini 1957). There is no reason for thinking that it is the name of a woman who actually existed, or for preferring it to the two variants that Petrarch also uses – 'Laureta', found only in *RVF* 5, where it is fragmented into its constituent syllables, and 'Laurea', the form which Petrarch uses in Latin and which also probably appears in *RVF* 225. There is also 'Aurora', another *senhal* which appears in various poems, and which he also uses in a note to *RVF* 268 in his rough manuscript (see Chapter 2.3). With the name we are as firmly in the world of literature as we more obviously are with the blonde hair and such other characteristics and features as are ascribed to the Laura of the poems.

Then there are the dates. Apart from the remarkable coincidence between the moment of first meeting and the moment of Laura's death, they contain an important factual error, as already pointed out in Chapter 3.2: 6 April 1327 was not Good Friday, which that year fell on 10 April. The discrepancy would be trivial if this were one date among many. Given that it is the crucial moment, on which all other dates mentioned in the *RVF* depend, and that no other day of the month is identified in the poems, the error is gross. Of course, from another point of view, it is not an error at all, but a literary manoeuvre, and an important one.

Almost any love-lyric presupposes a minimal narrative, however schematic and formulaic: a poem of absence presupposes a parting or a meeting, a poem of desire a time when desire will be satisfied or when it did not exist, or merely that desire will continue for ever. And so on. As I noted in Chapter 4.4, Italian poetry of the thirteenth century had minimalised narrative possibilities. The husband and the *lauzengers* (malicious gossips) who had given the barest and most formalised of contexts to Provençal poetry fade away. The *donna* tends to lose even the coded specificity of a *senhal* much as she loses most of her bodily features. The emphasis falls instead on the problematics of love, whether or not the issue is confronted directly as a problem of definition. The work of almost all poets – the notable exception being Guittone d'Arezzo – refuses to take narrative shape. Even otherwise well-defined figures such as Cavalcanti or Cino seem to write for a confused series of *donne* or for no one in particular. And literary culture seems to have been attuned to this situation. No biographies of poets of the Provençal type are known to have existed: it is as if no need was felt to fill in the gaps, however fantastically.

Dante, Petrarch and Boccaccio all create autobiographical love-stories. Though the formulations and ends are different, all three stories are allusive and elusive, always open to elaboration and completion by readers. For some time the biographical reality of Bice Portinari has been a minor issue in Dante studies, whilst Boccaccio's circumstantial references to his own romantic birth and upbringing and to his unhappy love for Fiammetta, that is, the noble, if illegitimate, Maria d'Aquino, have been shown to be complete fabrication. It would appear that all three writers are drawing on a literary expectation or convention, the sense of which has been partly lost to us. Whilst it is a mistake to look for reliable documentation in what clearly excludes it, the rhetorical functions of the device are obvious. It strengthens the credibility and power of the literary work, lending it mystery, stimulating the reader's imagination and intelligence to supply what they cannot know; it makes for participation and belief. In a general sense, which applies to all three writers, it makes personal and historical what could have been abstract or fantastic. As far as Petrarch is concerned, it was impossible for him to have replied to Giacomo Colonna in any other way than he did in his letter without threatening the viability of his poetry, though the fact that his assertion of sincerity comes in a letter otherwise concerned with jokes and irony indicates that we should read this part too with a certain sophistication.

But in Petrarch the historical force of the fiction is much stronger than in Dante and Boccaccio. The detail with which he invests it reflects his general redirection of literary and intellectual activity away from any scholastic predilection for the meta-physical and the speculative, towards a more human realm and the problems that ensue. Dating poems, putting them in a chronological sequence (fictive or not), locates them not merely in time but in the life of their author. They gain a dimension that is specific to the life of an individual. They enter historical time as determined events springing from other determined events, even if from other perspectives they are in some ways generalisable. In this respect there is once again a marked break with Dante.

From the arrangement of poems in sequence in the *Vita nuova* and their accompanying prose commentary, there emerges the story of Dante's love for Beatrice up to and beyond her death, which is simultaneously the story of Dante's moral, intellectual and poetic education. Contingency is resisted as much as possible. Such times, places, and events as are admitted are signs, which when interpreted correctly and with the necessary hindsight, point to the coherence of being: analogy is not subjective association, but a way to the truth. The city that can seem like Jerusalem, the years or events that somehow are manifestations of the number 9, are on a par with Cavalcanti's *donna* preceding Beatrice as John the Baptist preceded Christ, or the Platonic reverberations of Beatrice's beauty, virtue and humility. With the *Divina commedia* the elements of forcing and uncertainty that are perceptible in the *Vita nuova* vanish. In its very conception a journey beginning on Good Friday 1300 and passing in three days through Hell, Purgatory and Paradise is an analogue of Christ's death and resurrection. And Dante integrates the basic schema with other symbolic systems. Everything signifies. If Dante affirms also the force of individual identity and individual experience, as he does with particular force at the climactic moment of losing Virgil and finding Beatrice (*Purg.* 30), he has the confidence that in some powerful way they coexist with the system of the whole and are part of it.

Petrarch refuses to eliminate contingency: if time has significance it is in a human, or even private sense. In his specifically historical writings (*De viris illustribus, Africa*) he makes his accounts as accurate as possible: he sets to rights the text of Livy, his principal source for ancient history, and to a degree he collates it with other sources; the result is an ordering and distinguishing of historical matters that had been confused for centuries. But though ancient times may have been glorious and the intervening centuries a period of darkness, time itself is just sequence, cut by the Incarnation into a before and after, but without the shape that it unquestionably has for Dante. Something similar is perceptible in Petrarch's treatment of his own time. In his letters and notes, he dates as obsessively as any modern bureaucrat. Of course he sometimes looks further. At some point he drew up a list of dates which seem to have had secret meaning for him (De Nolhac 1907: 2. 288–9), and in his letters on the climacteric he voices the old fear that the sixty-third year is a time of particular risk (*Sen.* 8. 1 and 8). But only one date looms large: 6 April is not only the date of falling in love with Laura and of her death. According to the letter addressed to posterity (*Posteritati*), it was on 6 April 1338 that there was the first inspiration for the *Africa*. And it was on 6 April 1341 (which was a Good Friday) that Petrarch arrived in Rome prior to his coronation on Easter Sunday. It may just be, as Calcaterra (1942b) suggested, that 6 April was to be understood as the date of the creation of man, of his fall and of the original crucifixion, though it has been doubted (Martinelli 1973). In any case the implications of such mighty connotations remain obscure and contradictory for any eventual interpretation of the *RVF*. All we know is that Petrarch returns to the date as one that is powerful, but whose power is indeterminate. The two poems which are crucial for any historicisation of the *RVF* make dates their climax, but within each poem the date is significant precisely because Petrarch makes it the climax, drawing out the pathos of its lack of meaning, except for himself, and of the utter irrevocability of the contingent moment to which it points, except in these quite empty words.

> Mille trecento ventisette, a punto
> sull'ora prima, il dí sesto d'aprile,
> nel laberinto intrai, né veggio ond'esca.
>   (211. 12–14)

(In 1327, precisely / at the first hour on the sixth day of April / I entered the labyrinth, and cannot see how to leave.)

> Sai che 'n mille trecento quarantotto,
> il dí sesto d'aprile, in l'ora prima,
> del corpo uscío quell'anima beata.
>   (336. 12–14)

(You know that in 1348 / on the sixth day of April, at the first hour, / that blessed soul left her body.)

(For the composition of these poems see Chapter 2.3.)

So too with all the time-markers in the *RVF*: 1327, 1348 and the other years form no system, point to no transcendent truth. They are important because they have power for the poet-lover and can be made to function poetically. Recurrence of sacred time in the Good Friday which is also the anniversary day, is outweighed by historical succession. It is the failure to respond to the holy day which counts and which continues through, and in spite of, the passage of the years. As in the writing of more formal history, there is a painful recognition that time has the value that humanity gives it and that its passage is implacable.

There is no dynamic return, as there is in Dante. But it is also uncertain whether there is progress or development. Where Dante had projected a triple movement of love, poetry and understanding towards the point from which the text took its origin, Petrarch minimises movement forward. In creating a narrative he simultaneously undermines it.

Immediately after the introductory poem he raises a string of contradictory possibilities. Poem 2 establishes the main fact: he was stricken by love after prolonged resistance. Poem 3 takes up the negative implications: he fell in love on the day of Christ's crucifixion. A corresponding positive follows in poem 4: God has exalted an insignificant township by selecting it as Laura's birthplace, just as he chose incarnation in Judaea, not Rome. Poem 5 turns to the laurel: to speak of Laura is to speak of the laurel and hence to risk offending Apollo whose tree it is. In poem 6 the identity becomes the transformation which, in narrative terms, should have preceded poem 5: the crazed sexual pursuit of the woman leads only to the gathering of bitter fruit from the tree into which she has turned. Then the significance of the loss of the woman is inverted: in 7 there is no Laura, only the laurel, which now, together with the myrtle, the symbol of Venus, is associated with some humanist enterprise that a friend is encouraged to pursue in spite of the difficulties involved. But this is obviously no terminus: with poems 8 and 9 we are back with the female Laura, though with a change of perspective.

The possibilities presented so incoherently (from the point of view of narrative progression) are those of the collection as a whole and of the story. Time will see them not so much unfold as interweave, criss-cross, recur: they will be amplified and varied, but inconsequentially. Time passes and Laura dies, but ageing and death are met by repetition and variation. The obsession is unrelenting, even if it seems possible in an earlier phase to redirect it towards Apollonian poetry, and at a later stage towards prayer. If history is change, development, progression, there is little history in the *RVF*, unless it is the history of failure. But, by the same tokens of narrative incoherence and psychological impotence, there is an ambiguous success. Every failure, every repetition and variation, is also a poem or emerges from a poem. In the consistency of the poetry from beginning to end, in its material density (see Chapter 6.2 and 3), in the complex arrangement of the poems, in which narrative is not the only element (see Chapter 3.3), time, disorder and destruction are circumvented or dissolved in the very act of invoking them. It is always implied that the poetic solution is ultimately inadequate, though of course in poetry there is no other.

5.3 The senses

Twice, towards the end of a sestina, Petrarch puts his desires in patently erotic terms:

Con lei foss'io da che si parte il sole
et non ci vedess' altri che le stelle,
sol una nocte, et mai non fosse l'alba;
et non se transformasse in verde selva
per uscirmi di braccia, come il giorno
ch'Apollo la seguia qua giú per terra.
(22. 31–6)

(Would I were with her from the moment the sun leaves / and no one were to see us but the stars, / for only one night, and there were never dawn: / and she did not transform herself into green wood / to escape from my arms, as on the day / when Apollo was pursuing her here below on earth.)

Deh or foss'io col vago della luna
adormentato in qua'che verdi boschi,
et questa ch'anzi vespro a me fa sera,
con essa et con Amor in quella piaggia
sola venisse a starsi ivi una notte;
e 'l dí si stesse e 'l sol sempre ne l'onde.
(237.31–6)

(Oh would I were now with the moon's lover [Endymion] / asleep in no matter what green woods, / and would she who brings my life to its evening before vespers [i.e. before its time], / came with her [i.e. the moon] and Love to that spot / alone to stay there for one night: / and the day and the sun stopped for ever below the waves.)

The two sestina stanzas, identically placed in their respective poems and so similar to each other in imagery and phrasing, frame the great majority of poems in Part 1, strengthening the suspicion that there may be nothing in them but disturbed and displaced sexuality. Mercy, hope, fear, cruelty, anguish – the traditional vocabulary of love-poetry may be only euphemisms, and the trembling and confusion, the burning, freezing, crying all clear indicators of the real nature of desire. On this account, poetry is a way of wooing the beloved, or a compensation for frustration. It is therefore inevitably tainted. Poem after poem is nothing more than a testimonial to a sinfulness which is made worse through being concealed or prettified.

The worry that such a reduction can be carried through, constantly surfaces in the *RVF*, from the 'folle mi' desio' ('my crazed desire': 6. 1) to the recognition in the canzone to the Virgin that, if Laura had responded as Petrarch wished, the result would have been 'a me morte, et a lei fama rea' ('death for myself and for her a ruined name': 366. 97). It is a bass note, only half-hidden, against which everything else is measured and which partly accounts for the insistence on shame and guilt in the opening poem and many others that follow it. So much of life should not have been spent on something of so little worth, something which, prolonged into maturity, became a threat both to personal dignity and to the ultimate fate of the soul.

One counter to such bleak implications could have been derived from the *stilnovisti*. In their poetry the senses were radically purified and the contemplative intellect given pride of place. Only sight was privileged: according to contemporary ideas, it was the noblest sense, since it was the least physical and seemed to offer a direct window on to and from the soul. Seeing the beloved, looking into her eyes or at them, was a pleasure in itself, but, following the common metaphorical identification of seeing with understanding, sight was blurred with insight into the qualities present in her or to which she alluded. Other parts of the *donna*, which a literal-minded observer might say could also be seen, were deleted. Characteristically she is all eyes and abstractions: even if she performs human actions such as giving a greeting or walking, she has neither hands nor feet.

Like his predecessors, Petrarch looks repeatedly to Laura's eyes, in some ways surpassing the *stil novo*. No one, except, perhaps, Dante in some parts of the *Paradiso*, had written anything comparable to the three linked canzoni (71–3) on the very inexhaustibility of the theme. The word 'occhi' (eyes) appears more than 250 times in the collection, a little less than half the instances referring to Petrarch's own eyes and slightly more than half to those of Laura. And that is to leave out of account metaphors such as 'lumi' (lights), 'stelle' (stars), 'sole/i' (sun/s), as well as verbs and nouns of all kinds that suggest or presuppose acts of seeing. But not only does Petrarch not have the insight of the *stilnovisti*, he cannot delete the physical body to the same degree, nor does he wish to do so. It is Laura's hair which is most particularised: for Laura has blond hair (habitually metaphorised as gold) that falls in ringlets, or may be tightly curled. She has other parts to her body too. In one poem or another her head, brow, cheek, mouth, neck, breast, shoulders, arms, hands, fingers and feet are all mentioned, though some more frequently than others. She is accordingly better equipped for human behaviour than her predecessors: she sits, sings, walks, talks, weeps, wears clothes (green according to 29), a veil, a necklace, gloves, just as she also falls ill and dies. The emphasis has shifted towards presenting a being with a material existence, a being who can be loved within the terms of the story which the collection creates.

The location of Laura within the sphere of the human, risks confirming that the desire is simply sensual. However, the Laura of the poems is a human being who has been transformed or, alternatively, fragmented. She is obviously not specific: she has more in common with stereotypes of female beauty that appear throughout medieval and Renaissance literature than she has with any particular individual. All the same Petrarch is highly selective even by contemporary standards. Laura is always decorous and laudable in her behaviour, whatever pain she seems to cause and whatever reproaches are levelled at her for her cruelty. She is also decorous and laudable in her person. Physical features that a woman undoubtedly has and which to some degree appeared in descriptions of ideal beauty in medieval literature are eliminated. Nothing in Laura suggests comedy, aggression, irregularity or an obtrusive sexuality. Elbows, ears, a nose, even legs have no place in the *RVF*. On the few occasions when Petrarch mentions Laura's breast, he uses the more Latinate 'petto' or 'seno' which can easily take on a metaphorical sense rather than the patently physical 'mamille' or 'tette' that were certainly available to him. What is more, his evocations of Laura's person are less descriptions than incantatory listings in which a few of the items listed above are unsystematically mingled with other features of her personality. In these lines, for example, there is none of the beginning at the top and working downwards (*effictio*), as was standard practice in poems and prose detailing a beautiful woman (see, for example, the poem by Brizio Visconti discussed in Chapter 1.2):

> Et per pianger anchor con piú diletto,
> le man' bianche sottili,

et le braccia gentili,
e gli atti suoi soavemente alteri,
e i dolci sdegni altermente humili,
e 'l bel giovanil petto,
torre d'alto intellecto,
mi celan questi luoghi alpestri et feri:
                                   (37.97–104)

(And, to weep further with increased enjoyment, / the slender white hands, / and the noble arms, / and her pleasingly haughty behaviour, / and her sweet moments of disdain, which are haughtily humble / and her lovely youthful breast, / a tower of high intellect, – / these untamed, mountainous regions hide them from me.)

The *donna* has become a human ideal which corresponds to specifically human desires. In her the abstract and the material, the angelic and the physical, come together without it being possible to say that she belongs entirely to either the lower or the higher category. But any representation of her has to be contradictory, partial and indeterminate. For the most part she is absent, and it is only traces of her which can be recovered through the action of memory. She is like poetry itself – something fragmented, the fragments of which are cherished in a way that is psychologically and morally questionable from many points of view, but which are constantly reconstituted. Again like poetry, both the absent whole and the fragments which are remade are inevitably found to be aesthetically pleasing. Whatever the doubts about her status or meaning, Laura is always beautiful, as Petrarch constantly reiterates in his insistent application of 'bello' and its cognate nouns to her and to every part and aspect of her from beginning to end of the collection.

In general terms Laura's beauty takes on positive associations through being evoked in images which suggest light or brightness. Characteristically she enlightens, clarifies, illumines. She is a star, though the second of the two sestine quoted above is exceptional in associating her with the moon. Much more frequently she is like the sun, or is the sun, or is brighter than the sun. The Christian potentialities of light imagery are self-evident. There are also humanist ones. Even prior to her transformation into the laurel, rhetorically and poetically she belongs to the realm of the sun-god, Apollo, who is also the god of poetry. Laura and the poetry about her are by implication on the side of things virtuous and serious, at least on humanist reckoning.

But sublimation into such realms is often resisted in favour of something more ambiguous, in which the sensual elements are not denied, although they may be modified. Brightness may dazzle or blind as well as illumine. Here is one of Petrarch's most visual poems:

> Quel sempre acerbo et honorato giorno
> mandò sí al cor l'imagine sua viva
> che 'ngegno o stil non fia mai che 'l descriva,
> ma spesso a lui co la memoria torno.
>
> L'atto d'ogni gentil pietate adorno,
> e 'l dolce amaro lamentar ch'i' udiva,
> facean dubbiar, se mortal donna o diva
> fosse che 'l ciel rasserenava intorno.
>
> La testa òr fino, et calda neve il volto,
> hebeno i cigli, et gli occhi eran due stelle,
> onde Amor l'arco non tendeva in fallo;
>
> perle et rose vermiglie, ove l'accolto
> dolor formava ardenti voci et belle;
> fiamma i sospir', le lagrime cristallo.
>
> (157)

(That ever bitter and honoured day / sent its living image so into my heart / that there will never be wit or style that can describe it, / but often I return to it in memory. / Her demeanour, made more lovely by a noble distress, / and the bitter-sweet moaning which I heard / made me wonder whether it were a mortal *donna* or a goddess / who was bringing calm to the heavens around. / Her head was fine gold, her face snow warm with life, / her brows ebony, her eyes two stars, / from which Love did not stretch his bow in vain. / There were pearls and red roses [her teeth and lips], where concentrated / pain formed beautiful, ardent words. / Her sighs were flame, her tears crystal.)

The sight of Laura weeping is cast as a memory which the sonnet recovers and reproduces, gradually substituting for remembering a representation of Laura as she was on that day, though a representation which concentrates on metaphorical transformations rather than depiction. For all the brightness and colour of the imagery the experience is not purified. Pity and dismay complicate the aesthetic pleasure. However, rather than weakening the effect of the experience or the memory of it, they seem to make it more overwhelming, if less acceptable. The experience of beauty here involves something like sadism, if only the sadism of looking. Brightness does not point to transcendence but to something fearfully fascinating, morally ambiguous, but also quite irreducible to frustrated sexual desire. Nothing further is wanted: the questionable event is sufficient in itself, at least within the single poem.

There is a further problem. The poem is hyperbolic throughout, and the sense of some of its images hard to determine (above all lines 7–8 and 14). As an artefact it pretends to register subjective experience and gives force to its semantically indeterminate images through the positive power of its rhetorical organisation, its music, and its form. But it is easy enough to say that all there is here is words, a bubble that may be aesthetically pleasing in a perhaps disturbing way but which bursts as soon as we stand back from it. The images become commonplace, the artifice a trick.

The status of the pleasure or beauty of a poem such as 157 is fundamentally unstable. Morally something more complex than mere looking is involved, something more interesting, if also suspect. Ontologically there is a question surrounding the very nature of the thing that is read. Nor can it be otherwise: Petrarch has accepted fully the consequences of his rejection of any system of thought that pretends to objectivity, to designate what is real. The subjectivity of the experience alluded to and the subjectivity of the poem go hand in hand, the reader being put into a position of having to decide whether anything worth the name happened at all. The senses are not excluded, but we are inside a special area that can only be thought of as the poetic, though Petrarch can never designate it as such.

Hence poems praising Laura's beauty may incorporate phrasing and terminology of the *stil novo* into their complicated hyperboles, but almost always with an undermining of the significance which they had in the earlier poets. In the same sequence as *Quel sempre acerbo* there is a poem focused on the discovery of the incredible in the trivial, in which the traditional language of praise is only just this side of the language of the hyperbolic compliment.

> Amor et io sí pien' di meraviglia
> come chi mai cosa incredibil vide,
> miriam costei quand'ella parla o ride
> che sol se stessa, et nulla altra, simiglia.
>
> Dal bel seren de le tranquille ciglia
> sfavillan sí le mie due stelle fide,
> ch'altro lume non è ch'infiammi et guide
> chi d'amar altamente si consiglia.
>
> Qual miracolo è quel, quando tra l'erba
> quasi un fior siede, over quand'ella preme
> col suo candido seno un verde cespo!
>
> Qual dolcezza è ne la stagione acerba
> vederla ir sola coi pensier' suoi inseme,
> tessendo un cerchio a l'oro terso et crespo!
>
> (160)

(Love and I as full of wonder / as anyone who ever saw something beyond belief, / gaze, when she speaks or laughs, at her / who resembles only herself and no other. / From the beautiful serene of her tranquil brows / my two trusty stars sparkle so, / that there is no other light that can inflame and guide / one who purposes to love sublimely. / What miracle is that, when in the grass / she takes her seat like a flower, or when she presses / against a green bush with her [pure] white breast! / What sweetness is it in the unripe season [i.e. spring] / to see her walk alone with her thoughts, / weaving a garland for the polished, curled gold [of her hair].)

Though Laura performs normal actions which in themselves are insignificant, she is beyond belief, a unique object of contemplation. Her eyes are guiding stars, as the Virgin was traditionally said to be: she is a miracle, rather as Beatrice had been said to have come to earth to show a miracle (*Vita nuova* 26). But the potential significance of such analogies is never realised: they serve only to impress the power of what it is to see Laura. Any transcendentalism is denied in the images of the tercets, climactically arranged but literally down to earth, particularly in the concluding image. It is the impossibility of finding correlatives or replacements for her which the poem reiterates. Laura is said initially to be unique, and the poem culminates with the image of a self-absorbed human figure weaving a garland for her hair. In a sense it too has woven a circle. Abstract uniqueness and physical solitude are aspects of the same thing, Laura being not completely absorbed into one or the other but absorbing both.

The subjectivism implicit in 157 and 160 commonly comes more strongly to the fore. Petrarch normally interposes reflections on the significance of what is seen or otherwise perceived, on the act of perceiving, and on his own fluctuating responses, ranging over the past and future as well as over the present which had been the dominant time in much earlier poetry, moving between memories and imaginings with an almost startling rapidity. Uncertainty surrounds any such reflections of course, in view of Petrarch's epistemological positions, but, by the same token, the psychological and poetic texture is denser, more self-sufficient. Psychologically more complex mental processes are intimated to be at work than in previous poetry, with a remarkably lucid self-awareness accompanying their action but not directing them. External values may be registered and may even threaten what occurs, but the poems insist on pursuing a path which is their own.

There are two linked canzoni in which a combination of memory, contemplation and anticipation work to defeat a sensualism that the two poems also suggest, whilst also defeating any prospects of a transcendental solution. They are *Se 'l pensier che mi strugge* (125) and *Chiare, fresche et dolci acque* (126), two of Petrarchs most famous, not to say notorious poems. The first of the two is Petrarch's major encounter with the harsh mode as developed in the *rime petrose* by Dante, who, elaborating on his model, Arnaut Daniel, had posited a circular equation between linguistic harshness, sexual obsession and irreducible resistance in the beloved, all three elements finding their emblem in the word 'petra' (stone). Harshness, in its materiality and negativity, was at the opposite pole to 'dolcezza' (sweetness), which was associated with the impulse to transcendent values and realities. Not surprisingly the harsh style would be the basis for the poetry of Lower Hell (see *Inf.* 32. 1–9). Petrarch's poem proclaims its own harshness and corroborates the proclamation by using some of the harsh rhymes which Dante had used in the *rime petrose*:

> Però ch'Amor mi sforza
> et di saver mi spoglia,
> parlo in rime aspre, et di dolcezza ignude:
> (125. 14–16: cf *Cosí nel mio parlar*, 8
> and 26)

(Since Love exerts force on me / and strips me of my wits, / I speak in rhymes that are harsh and bared of sweetness.)

In fact Petrarch dissolves Dante's equation. Even in these lines the regularity of the rhythm, the habitual refusal to dwell on the rhyme-words, and the balance of the antithesis, set the verse within the range of Petrarch's customary musicality. Where Dante had been deliberately heavy, Petrarch is light. The short lines bring the rhymes round rapidly with an effect more of harmony than harshness. Thematically too the poem turns away from harshness, or rather it incorporates sweetness as well as harshness into its development. The harshness is on the outside, in a language that does not correspond to inner feelings (lines 16–26). As the poem progresses, it turns more and more to the problem of expressing the sweetness that is felt, eventually finding a way of externalising it. By addressing the landscape, and imagining it to bear traces of the beloved from her passage through it at some previous time, some uncertain, illusory satisfaction can be found:

> Ben sai che sí bel piede
> non tocchò terra unquancho
> come quel di che già segnata fosti;
> onde 'l cor lasso riede
> col tormentoso fiancho
> a partir teco i lor pensier' nascosti.
> Cosí avestú riposti

> de' be' vestigi sparsi
> anchor tra' fiori et l'erba,
> che la mia vita acerba,
> lagrimando, trovasse ove acquetarsi!
> Ma come pò s'appaga
> l'alma dubbiosa et vaga.
> >   (125. 53–65)

(You know well that so beautiful a foot / never touched the
earth / as that by which you were once marked. / Hence my
weary heart returns / with my tormented body / to share their
hidden thoughts with you. / Would you had similarly preserved
/ some lovely scattered traces / still amongst the flowers and the
grass, / that my embittered existence / could find, in the midst of
its tears, some place in which to rest. / But my doubting,
unstable soul / finds satisfaction as best it can.)

But the uncertainty is essential for the imagination to work: it is
precisely through not having secure knowledge that the positive
effects occur.

> Cosí nulla se 'n perde,
> et piú certezza averne fôra il peggio.
> Spirto beato, quale
> se', quando altrui fai tale?
> >   (125. 75–8)

(So nothing is lost, / and to have more certainty about it would
be the worst [thing]. / Blessed spirit, what / are you, when you
make a man like this?)

Se 'l pensier brings sweetness and harshness together in a way
that undermines the implications of either mode in their
Dantesque forms: subjectivity finds pleasure in itself, if at the risk
of fetishising elements in the landscape because of their presumed
contact with the beloved. *Chiare, fresche et dolci acque* moves
forward from the conquests of the preceding poem into areas of
riskier sexuality, taking as its starting-point an analogous address
to the landscape.

Chiare, fresche et dolci acque,
ove le belle membra
pose colei che sola a me par donna;
gentil ramo ove piacque
(con sospir' mi rimembra)
a lei di fare al bel fiancho colonna;
herba et fior' che la gonna
leggiadra ricoverse
co l'angelico seno;
aere sacro, sereno,
ove Amor co' begli occhi il cor m'aperse:
date udïenzia insieme
a le dolenti mie parole extreme.

(126. 1–13)

(Clear, fresh and sweet waters, / where she who alone appears
to me to be *donna* placed / her beautiful limbs; / noble branch
where she chose / (I remember it sighing) / to make a support
for her lovely body; / grass and flowers which covered / her
delicate dress / and angelic breast [or (perhaps) its white folds];
sacred, serene air, / where Love opened my heart with her lovely
eyes: / together give hearing / to my last painful words.)

The 'harsh' rhymes are taken up again, but now only with the
lightest of allusions in the conjunction of 'dolci' with the 'harsh'
'acque'. A memory is evoked of Laura having bathed or at least
having stood by a stream or pool. Though quite what occurred is
duly vague, it is clear that Laura and the landscape are intimately
bound together in the memory and imagination. So too for the
future: Laura absent, the place substitutes for her. Contact with it
is imagined bringing peace at the moment of death in a way that
carries connotations of a substitute sexual fulfilment, though there
is no sense that the substitution should ideally be replaced by real
congress.

S'egli è pur mio destino,
e 'l cielo in ciò s'adopra.
ch'Amor quest'occhi lagrimando chiuda,
qualche gratia il meschino
corpo fra voi ricopra.

e torni l'alma al proprio albergo ignuda.
La morte fia men cruda
se questa spene porto
a quel dubbioso passo:
ché lo spirito lasso
non poria mai in piú riposato porto
né in piú tranquilla fossa
fuggir la carne travagliata et l'ossa.

(lines 14–26)

(If it is finally my destiny, / and heaven works to this effect, / so that Love closes these eyes in tears, / may some grace find a covering for my wretched / body amongst you, / and may my soul return naked to its own resting place. / Death will be less cruel / if I carry this hope / to that fearsome transit. / My weary spirit / could never in a more restful harbour / or more tranquil hollow / flee from my exhausted flesh and bones.)

This leads to a further imagining: it may be that she will return and, finding him dead, sigh and weep so sweetly that heaven will grant him mercy. Beauty of this particular kind, disturbed as in 157, apparently trivial as in 160, might overwhelm heaven, not just himself.

Tempo verrà anchor forse
ch'a l'usato soggiorno
torni la fera bella et mansüeta,
et là 'v' ella mio scorse
nel benedetto giorno,
volga la vista disïosa et lieta,
cercandomi: et, o pieta!,
già terra in fra le pietre
vedendo, Amor l'inspiri
in guisa che sospiri
sí dolcemente che mercé m'impetre,
et faccia forza al cielo,
asciugandosi gli occhi col bel velo.

(lines 27–39)

(The time may yet come / when to its customary haunt / the

wild creature comes back beauteous and gentle, / and where she
espied me on that blessed day, / turns her eyes full of desire and
joy, / seeking me, and (the pity of it!), / when she sees [me]
turned to dust amongst the stones, / Love may inspire her / to
sigh / so sweetly that she wins [divine] mercy for me, / and takes
heaven by force, / as she dries her eyes with her lovely veil.)

But can that overwhelming occur? With the next stanza there is a
transition that is more abrupt than any other in the *RVF*: the
poem moves from an imagined future to a past that seems to be
the same as the one evoked in the opening stanza, though it may
or may not be. But there is a connection with what has come
before. Here is Laura at her most overwhelming, in a rain of
flowers that echoes those that fell on Beatrice as she appeared to
Dante in the Earthly Paradise (*Purg.* 30. 28–33):

> Da' be' rami scendea
> (dolce ne la memoria)
> una pioggia di fior' sovra 'l suo grembo;
> et ella si sedea
> humile in tanta gloria,
> coverta già de l'amoroso nembo.
> Qual fior cadea sul lembo,
> qual su le treccie bionde,
> ch'oro forbito et perle
> eran quel dí a vederle;
> qual si posava in terra, et qual su l'onde;
> qual con un vago errore
> girando parea dir: Qui regna Amore.
>
> (lines 40–52)

(From the lovely branches fell / (sweet to remember) / a rain of
flowers on her lap; / and she sat humbly / in such great glory, /
soon covered by the amorous cloud. / One flower would fall on
her hem, / another on her blonde tresses, / which were
burnished gold and pearls / to see that day; / and another came
to rest on the ground, another on the water, / whilst another
turning with a light, uncertain motion / seemed to say: Here it is
Love who rules.)

Whilst it is clearly enough recognised that this is not Paradise, though it may be a bower of bliss, the knowledge that such an interpretation was self-delusion makes no difference to the power of the memory and to the attachment to the place now that she is no longer present:

> Quante volte diss'io
> allor pien di spavento:
> Costei per fermo nacque in paradiso.
> Cosí carco d'oblio
> il divin portamento
> e 'l volto et le parole e 'l dolce riso
> m'aveano, et sí diviso
>
> da l'imagine vera,
> ch'i' dicea sospirando:
> Qui come venn'io, o quando ?;
> credendo esser in ciel, non là dov'era.
> Da indi in qua mi piace
> questa herba sí, ch'altrove non ò pace.
>
> Se tu avessi ornamenti quant'ài voglia,
> poresti arditamente
> uscir del boscho, et gir in fra la gente.
>
> (lines 53–68)

(How many times did I say / then full of fear: / Surely she was born in Paradise. / So heavy with oblivion / had her divine bearing / and her face and words and sweet smile / made me, and so divorced / from the true image, / that I said sighing: / How did I come here, or when?; / believing myself to be in heaven, not there where I was. / From then until now this grass pleases me / so, that elsewhere I have no peace. / If you [my song] had all the ornaments you wish, / you could boldly / leave the wood, and go amongst people.)

The *congedo* concedes that this has not been a poem in the high style; it does not have the necessary poetic 'ornaments'. In that sense, like 125, it acknowledges its failure. But, as has been the case from poem 1, failure in one sense is tacitly proposed as success in another. The poem is to be read, if only by those who also remain in its ambiguous wood.

From the metamorphosis of categorisations of what is sensual in experience and in poetry, something else, specifically not divine, has emerged, something of uncertain status between the imaginary and the imaginative, something that refuses absolutes or ultimate definitions of any kind. Loving and writing poetry about love belongs neither to beasts nor to angels: it is in the middle. But the poetry which comes to a head in *Chiare, fresche et dolci acque* is not caught in a fearful avoidance of extremes or excess, either poetically or experientially. The centre is immensely strong: it takes from extremes what it needs in order to create itself as something free from strain, that is, in literary terms, without pastiche, and, in ontological or moral terms, able to confront its own doubts without denying their force.

In *Chiare, fresche et dolci acque*, as in other poems discussed in this section, place and the natural world are almost as prominent as Laura. Petrarch repeatedly sketches a rural setting, with rivers, hills, mountains, woods, streams, with birds, flowers, trees and other flora and fauna which are wild or untamed, though not exotic. It is a setting well away from the city, largely unpeopled, offering the solitude and tranquillity which Petrarch repeatedly declared outside the *RVF* (notably in the *De vita solitaria*) to be necessary for introspection and writing. Historically the place is, of course, Vaucluse, where Petrarch had his villa from 1336 until he finally left Provence for Italy in 1353, and the river is the Sorgue, or the Rhône, or the Durence, the city in the background Avignon. Earlier Italian poetry had given less emphasis and focus to the setting. When there was spatial location, it was at least for the *stil novo* as likely to be urban as rural. Petrarch's relative insistence upon a setting is another aspect of his making poetry more historical and earthly, although once again within limits. In spite of his identification of place the actual passages of description, if such they can be called, are quite unspecific. The same generic elements recur in continuously varied combinations, or, it may be, in isolation. In other words the landscape and natural world are treated much like Laura, fragmented, beautiful, open to constant metamorphosis of the same constituent features. Though the immediate source for the elements of his landscape was primarily the *rime petrose* of Dante, it was possible to integrate these with Virgil (see particularly 50) or Ovid (23) or to reduce them to isolated emblems. The landscape resembles Laura in taking many forms whilst remaining the same. It also merges with her: it evokes her, substitutes for her, marks her absence, sometimes, as in *Chiare, fresche et dolci acque* performing all three functions in barely separable succession.

Since the natural world is so charged, then reference to it in Laura's absence can be a way of giving voice to, and finding pleasure in, psychological states that can only be crudely categorised as melancholia or frustrated desire. The landscape provides what might be called objective correlatives, though ones which are less symbolic points of reference than uncertain indicators which might at any moment prove to have no reference beyond the words themselves.

This set of ambiguities, intimately bound to Laura, but also different from her, is at the centre of a poem such as 35, in which a withdrawal into uninhabited country for reasons of shame leads to a sense that the landscape knows, if people do not, what his condition is.

> sí ch'io mi credo omai che monti et piagge
> et fiumi et selve sappian di che tempre
> sia la mia vita, ch'è celata altrui.
>
> Ma pur sí aspre vie né sí selvagge
> cercar non so ch'Amor non venga sempre
> ragionando con meco, et io col lui.
>   (35. 9–14)

(so that I now believe that mountains and slopes / and rivers and woods know of what temper / is my life, which is concealed from others. / And yet I cannot seek out such harsh or savage paths / unless Love always comes / talking with me, and I with him.)

A post-Romantic reader might think of the pathetic fallacy, but, as always, Petrarch's projection is conscious: the subjective element is acknowledged, and a mood is created under the direction of desire which combines unhappiness, loneliness, pleasure, secrecy and indiscretion, which might also be mere pretence, mere hyperbole. As in the other poems discussed in this section, it is hard, perhaps impossible, to arrive at a clear moral or epistemological assessment of what occurs; again something dense and complicated has been created, which might suddenly dissolve.

The poetry of landscape and the poetry of Laura as discussed in this section merge with other kinds of poetry to be found in the *RVF*. It is against them that not only the threat of sensuality but also the search for serious values is to be seen. But the problems will be no more eliminated in the second case than in the first. The moral negatives may be partially eroded by poetry; the positives undergo a similar, perhaps more disturbing erosion.

5.4 Laura and the laurel

The fascination which words held for Petrarch finds a focus in and around the two syllables of Laura's name. Laura is a *senhal* like Beatrice ('she who blesses') or Cino's Selvaggia ('the wild one') or Boccaccio's Fiammetta ('small flame'), but all of these are in comparison mere ciphers with only secondary parts to play. Though half-concealed as a name, *Laura* is at the centre of the *RVF*. Its sound has talismanic power. It sets the key for the collection: its very combination of liquid consonants and dark vowels, the two syllables repeating and yet varying each other, epitomises the music of Petrarch's poetry. Other important words are derivable from it by addition and substitution of syllables, almost like variations on a musical phrase. But it is also rich in complex, often divergent meanings, which play against each other and against and through the repetition of its syllables.

The name is an exact homophone of 'l'aura' (breeze, breath), something transient, invisible, intangible, and, therefore, insubstantial, and empty, or, alternatively, something cooling, consoling, or even vital when it becomes the breath of life or inspiration. It merges also with 'aurora' (dawn), which Petrarch used occasionally as an alternative *senhal* (see Chapter 5.2). Then there is 'auro' (gold) or its less Latin form 'oro' (and the related adjectives 'aurato' (gilded) and 'aureo' (golden)), which is the

colour of Laura's hair, though it may also symbolise the material
wealth that she and everything connected with her are above
(263. 10) or the qualities of the Golden Age (137. 14). Most
important of all, there is 'lauro', formally the masculine of 'l'aura',
and its complement, since it echoes in its final vowel the aspect of
the stressed diphthong which the feminine form ignores: 'lauro'
or, at a slight remove, its alternative form 'alloro', the laurel,
suggests poetry, fame, classical studies and achievement, the other
aspect of Petrarch's culture, in many ways opposed to poetry
associated with the *donna*. And other words hover at Laura's
borders – 'ora' (time, the fleeting present), the possible confusion
of which with Laura is directly played on only in a sonnet
excluded from the *RVF* (*RD* 17: see Chapter 1.3), or 'lode'
(praise) and its associated verbs 'lodare' or 'laudare', the Latin
'laus' having been connected with 'laurus' in a false etymology of
the word by Isidore of Seville (17. 7. 2); and then there are all
those others which rhyme with Laura or contain anagrams of its
sounds. In the extreme a line can be almost a babble around the
central word: 'Là ver' l'aurora, che sí dolce l'aura' (239. 1).
('There towards the dawn, that so sweet the breeze. . . ') has traces
of Laura even in its opening two words, an adverb and a
preposition, before the more common 'aurora' and 'aura' (cf.
especially 194, 196–8, 327).

If we wish, we can call this punning, though it is plain that
Petrarch is not primarily concerned to impress with novelty or wit.
As always, he prefers exploring the implications of repetition and
variation to linguistic adventures. In the movements towards and
away from the name Laura he focuses on much that occupies him
more explicitly in other moments. Here the fascination of change
and instability appears in a specifically linguistic guise.

The instability begins with the name and the basic homophone.
From the Renaissance onwards editions of the *RVF* have normally
printed the name 'Laura' only at four points (239. 7 and 23;
291. 4 and 332. 50), allowing also the form which Petrarch used
in Latin, 'Laurea', in one other poem (225. 10). Elsewhere the
same sounds are printed as 'l'aura'. This is in fact a resolution of
an ambiguity in the original manuscript: Petrarch did not have
apostrophes and always wrote 'laura', which allows both the
associations of the *donna* and those connected with 'l'aura' to
emerge at its every appearance. The variation comes in the

changing interplay, depending on context, between the two sets of associations, each of which is also unstable within itself.

Sometimes the double meaning is patent. *Non al suo amante piú Dïana piacque* (52), the most elegant of Petrarch's madrigals, contains an image of a shepherdess dipping a veil in a stream or pool:

> . . . la pastorella alpestra et cruda
> posta a bagnar un leggiadretto velo,
> ch'a l'aura il vago et biondo capel chiuda, . . .
>
> (4–6)

meaning '. . . the cruel mountain shepherdess / stooped to bathe a delicate veil / that will bind her loose, blonde hair *against the* wind' and also '. . . that will bind *Laura's* loose, blonde hair'. Elsewhere the metaphorical senses of 'aura' can be more powerful:

> Ne l'età sua piú bella et piú fiorita,
> quando aver suol Amor in noi piú forza,
> lasciando in terra la terrena scorza,
> è l'aura mia vital da me partita,
>
> et viva et bella et nuda al ciel salita:
>
> (278. 1–5)

'In her most beautiful and blossoming years, / when Love has customarily most force within us, / leaving on earth her earthly covering, / my vital *breath* has left me / and risen alive and beautiful and naked to heaven . . . ' Or alternatively: '. . . my vital *Laura* has left me, etc.'. In the poems where convention prints the proper name, the other connotations are still present, perhaps most strikingly in 225. 10, where 'Laurea' is also 'l'aurea' (the golden one), to be set against the Golden Fleece, which has been mentioned earlier in the poem. But often the double meaning will flicker over the surface of the text and vanish, as if it is a sense that appears only to be denied, or as if what appears at one moment to be identity has at others to be affirmed as difference. In the sestina *Là ver l'aurora* (239), whose very first line, as already remarked, evokes Laura so insistently but without allowing any coherent sense to emerge from this repetition of the sounds of her

name, 'Laura/l'aura' continues to appear throughout the poem as
one of the rhyme-words. At each appearance the relationship
between the two aspects changes. First there is an equivalence, a
spring breeze that vivifies as Laura vivifies; in stanza 2 Laura, the
donna, is uppermost; in stanza 3 there is a separation of the two,
Laura resisting as a harsh mountain resists the gentle breeze; then
in stanza 4 there is a stronger equivalence than in stanza 1, as she
will not be made to 'trarre o di vita o di martir quest'alma' ('draw
this soul from life or pain'), nor will inspiration or empty breath;
the equivalence is continued in a different way in stanza 5, as
Petrarch urges himself to continue writing 'mentre fra noi di vita
alberga l'aura' ('so long as the breath of life dwells amongst us'),
that is, so long as he is alive, or she is alive, or both; and finally in
the last stanza, there is the remodelling of Arnaut Daniel 'et col
bue zoppo andrem cacciando l'aura' ('and with the lame ox we
shall go hunting the wind': cf. Arnaut, *En cest sonet coind' e leri*,
43–5), in which, as in the *congedo*, the accent falls on the
elusiveness of both breeze and Laura. It is the appropriate
conclusion: the word has stayed the same throughout, its meaning
has not, though the play of possible meanings has been carefully
channeled throughout this poem as elsewhere. The indeterminacy
is infinite within lines that have been firmly drawn.

Laura is 'l'aura'; she is also 'lauro', the laurel. Into the change
of vowel Petrarch has compressed a complex reworking of the
myth of Daphne. The story was known to him as it was to all
post-classical writers, primarily from Ovid's *Metamorphoses*
(1. 450–567). Ovid's account was a straightforward narrative
which explained the association between the laurel tree and the
god Apollo. Daphne (the Greek for 'laurel' or 'bay') was a nymph
devoted to chastity for whom the god conceived an irresistible
passion. She escaped rape at the last moment through being
transformed into a laurel tree by her father, the river Peneus, at
which Apollo adopted the laurel tree as his emblem. Its leaves, he
says, will always adorn his lyre and his hair and will accompany
victorious generals and triumphal processions in Rome. The tree
itself will stand outside the temple of Augustus and be always
green, just as his own hair is always that of a young man (lines
557–65). Like many other stories in the *Metamorphoses*, the story
was obviously rich with possible significances which Ovid himself
does not make explicit, and which Christian writers would

interpret in various, not always bizarre ways.

Like many of his predecessors and contemporaries, Petrarch was able to see Apollo as Christ (*Eclogue* 1; perhaps *RVF* 188), but for the most part he interpreted the myth in the terms of secular humanism. Finding what support he could elsewhere in ancient literature, he explained in his coronation oration (*Collatio laureationis*) that the laurel signified everything connected with Apollo – triumph, glory, prophecy, healing, learning. Above all, since Apollo was the god of poetry, it signified poetic glory and immortality, and so poetry itself. He was thinking in grand terms. Apollonian poetry was less lyric than epic, less intimate than public. The poet's life and work were amongst the great, as was symbolised in the friendship between Ennius and Scipio in the *Africa*. Greatness needed poetry in order to be duly recognised by future generations; poetry needed greatness in order to have the worthwhile material which made it worthwhile as poetry.

On this account the thwarted pursuit of the nymph could obviously have various symbolic meanings, loosely connected with each other, such as necessary renunciation or frustration of sensual desire in poetry, the transformation of life into art, or, more specifically, the sublimation of love-poetry into something comparable with poetry written in Latin. Whatever version might be chosen, the fundamental before and after of the Ovidian story would be maintained. This Petrarch does not generally do. Whilst he maintains the narrative on occasion, it is more characteristic of him to subvert it, confusing and separating the before and after as it suits him.

His reworking of the myth is only fully carried through in the *RVF*, although it is suggested in the conflation of female and arboreal figures in *Eclogues* 3 and 10. The first few poems define the possible relations between the two terms, Laura and 'lauro', almost in their entirety. Laura may be distinct from the laurel (2, 3, 4). She may be the laurel (5), or change into the laurel (6). The laurel may be distinct from her (7), or it may change into her (as occurs in the transition from 7 to 8).

These alternatives, which are combined, varied and elaborated in the course of the *RVF*, cannot be reduced once and for all to one of their terms. Early humanists, from Giacomo Colonna onwards, were eager to make Laura an allegory of the laurel. Apart from Petrarch's explicit denial that this was her exclusive significance (*Fam.* 2. 2. 9: see section 2 above), it is plain that in poem after poem the human figure is differentiated from the laurel. However, the connections between the two are more pervasive than might appear.

Up to a point Laura as a human figure is also Daphne, a figure of myth as well as a figure in the historical world. Like Ovid's Daphne, Laura is beautiful, chaste, elusive and changeful. Again like Daphne, she is associated with the countryside (always posited as necessary for study, writing and contemplation by Petrarch, as already mentioned in the previous section), and with rivers, the Sorgue, Durence, Rhône taking the place of the Peneus. Apart from her eyes, the feature of her which is most emphasised is her hair. It is her one physical attribute about which Petrarch is at all specific. From the point of view of the story we have to say that Laura had remarkably beautiful, blonde hair, normally let down in ringlets or curls for the breeze to play with, which fascinated Petrarch. But uncombed hair, loose in the wind, is also the one feature of Daphne which Ovid emphasises too (lines 477, 497–8, 529, 541–2, 550), in words which are very close to Petrarch's (see 90, 127, 83–4, 143. 9–10, 227. 1–4). Ovid's narrative reason for putting so much stress (relatively speaking) on Daphne's hair was made plain in his story: the hair became the leaves of the laurel, when the arms became the branches. It was from the leaves that laurel-crowns would be woven.

Laura's hair cannot be directly equated with the leaves of the laurel, any more than any other part of her or anything associated with her can be presumed directly to signify the laurel, although it may do so. But in her hair, and in other features of her, Petrarch creates a potentiality for the laurel, the source from which a more serious poetry might spring. Hair blowing in the wind in the *RVF* repeatedly suggests an ever-changing, unordered beauty which his own poetry re-creates through the action of memory, but which it does not and cannot transform into something else. Whatever moral or other doubts there may be, poetically the fascination of the hair itself is enough:

> Erano i capei d'oro a l'aura sparsi
> che 'n mille dolci nodi gli avolgea,
> e 'l vago lume oltra misura ardea
> di quei begli occhi, ch'or ne son sí scarsi.
>
> (90. 1–4)

(Her golden hair was loose in the breeze [implying also: Laura's golden hair was loose] / which wound it in a thousand sweet tangles, / and the bewitching light burned beyond measure / in those beautiful eyes, which now are so scantly illumined.)

There are points at which the potentiality is more developed, as, for example, at the end of the early *Apollo, s'anchor vive il bel desio*, where Laura is represented as both woman and tree.

> sí vedrem poi per meraviglia inseme
> seder la donna nostra sopra l'erba,
> et far de le sue braccia a se stessa ombra.
> (34. 12–14)

(so we shall see in wonder together / our *donna* sit upon the grass / and make shade for herself with her arms.)

But customarily Petrarch prefers to juxtapose the two words or emblems, 'Laura/l'aura' and 'lauro', in a way which unites them in the texture of the verse and suggests a blurring of them together, and at the same time implies a separation: how can a woman and a tree be identified? how can the disordered beauty of love-poetry and the grandeur of Latin come together? Yet mysteriously or nonsensically they do, though once again it may be in a poetry of potentiality rather than one which is fully articulate, or else in a poetry about a poetic vision which, for the present, it may be impossible to realise.

Chapter 4 examined Petrarch's way of composing his own poems by working from the poems of others, or from his own. It is poetry ('lauro') which is the inspiration ('l'aura'). Petrarch is self-reflexive enough to represent the process. A poem such as *Giovene donna sotto un verde lauro* (30), which is decorative persiflage as a poem praising a purely human figure, becomes powerful in a way that corresponds to its actual intuitive impact, when seen as a poem about the perception of novelty in the old, which it is the poet's desire to make actual, to realise in his own poetry:

> Giovene donna sotto un verde lauro
> vidi piú biancha et piú fredda che neve
> non percossa dal sol molti et molt'anni;

> e 'l suo parlare, e 'l bel viso, et le chiome
> mi piacquen sí ch'i' l'ò dinanzi agli occhi,
> ed avrò sempre, ov'io sia, in poggio o 'n riva.
>
> (lines 1–6)

(I saw a young *donna* beneath a green laurel / whiter and colder
than snow / not stricken by the sunlight for many, many years. /
And her speech, and her lovely face, and her hair / so pleased
me that I have her before my eyes, / and always will have,
wherever I am, whether on high ground or on low.)

Similarly a sonnet such as the following, which also might seem
extravagant praise of the human *donna*, acquires significance
when seen in the context of the laurel:

> Se Virgilio et Homero avessin visto
> quel sole il qual vegg'io con gli occhi miei,
> tutte lor forze in dar fama a costei
> avrian posto, et l'un stil coll'altro misto:
>
> di che sarebbe Enea turbato et tristo,
> Achille, Ulixe et gli altri semidei,
> et quel che resse anni cinquantasei
> sí bene il mondo, et quel ch'ancise Egisto.
>
> Quel fior anticho di vertuti et d'arme
> come sembiante stella ebbe con questo
> novo fior d'onestate et di bellezze!
>
> Ennio di quel cantò ruvido carme,
> di quest'altro io: et oh pur non molesto
> gli sia il mio ingegno, e 'l mio lodar non sprezze.
>
> (186)

(If Virgil and Homer had seen / that sun which I see with my
eyes / they would have put all their efforts into bringing fame to
her, / and mixed the one style with the other: / at which Aeneas
would be distraught and disconsolate, / so too Achilles, Ulysses
and the other demigods, / both he [Augustus] who ruled the
world for fifty-six years / so well, and he [Agamemnon] whom
Aegisthus killed. / That ancient paragon of virtue and arms

[Scipio Africanus] / – how similar was his star to that of this /
new paragon of virtuousness and beauty [Laura]. / Ennius sang
a roughly made poem about the former, / I [sing similarly]
about the latter. Oh may she not find my power of invention
merely distasteful, / and not scorn my praise.)

There was nothing comparable for such exorbitant comparisons
between the *donna* and classical heroes in earlier poetry. But,
following the etymology of Isidore, mentioned above, which
Petrarch certainly knew, the very act of praise was itself a
constituent feature of the name. Poem 5, which has resemblances
with *Se Virgilio*, had made 'laudare' into one of the words
amongst which Laura's name is fragmented: here again the verb
'to praise' reappears (line 14). But the laurel implies praise which
draws Laura into the area of humanist culture, or rather the latter
into the area of the former. Poetry for and about the vernacular
donna is imagined merging with a poetry which characteristically
celebrates heroes and which by implication has permanence,
status, moral virtue.

Poems such as *Giovene donna* and *Se Virgilio* allude to a
problem of integration, which generally was only to be solved by
juxtaposition. The two aspects diverged or conflicted intellectually, even if they might be made to harmonise aesthetically.
Inevitably one is dominant in the *RVF*. 'Laura / l'aura', unstable,
elusive, free of definite meanings, but perpetually enticing,
perpetually refreshing with the breath of its words, absorbs
'lauro', even if it is changed by it. In the *RVF*, in other words,
Latin culture is absorbed by the vernacular, even if the vernacular
acquires some of its features. As *Se Virgilio* implies, a poetry of
the 'lauro' necessarily belongs elsewhere and to another time, to
epics written long ago or perhaps writeable in some distant future
(see *Africa* 9. 456–77). Rather than attaining Apollonian enuncia-
tion, there is a constant return to the processes of enunciating, to
the fascinating pleasurability of words themselves, with all the
moral and sexual ambiguities which they evoke.

However, there are poems in the first half of Part 1 which seem
to depart from Laura. In the three political canzoni, in particular,
Petrarch changes theme and, up to a point, changes voice, acting,
it seems, on the hopes for poetic renewal which poems such as
Giovene donna (30) allude to. In fact from the start the

manoeuvre has recognition of its own failure written into it, even
if, from another point of view, the lost laurel leads to a certain
kind of poetic success.

The occasions of the three canzoni are as veiled as those behind
the love-poems, suggesting, as always, that what provoked a poem
is only poetically significant for Petrarch in so far as the reader can
be made to believe that something in the real world did provoke
it. *O aspectata in ciel* (28), which perhaps stemmed from a
Crusade projected by Philip VI of France in 1333, and
traditionally thought to be addressed to Giovanni Colonna,
projects the hope of restoring ancient virtue in a Christian
context: the campaign against the unbelievers will repeat the
triumphs of the Romans and Greeks in the face of Eastern threats,
deriving additional strength from the Christian religion and in
turn reinforcing it by drawing on ancient examples. But the
distance of the poem from the event and from direct intervention
is evident: it is addressed not to a pope, emperor or king, but to
an intermediary, who will awaken the necessary energies with his
learning and eloquence (esp. in lines 64ff). The *congedo* confesses
its author's limitations. He is detained by love, though he willingly
recognises that love can rise beyond the love of women:

> Tu vedrai Italia et l'onorata riva,
> canzon, ch'agli occhi miei cela et contende
> non mar, non poggio o fiume,
> ma solo Amor che del suo altero lume
> piú m'invaghisce dove piú m'incende:
> né Natura può star contra 'l costume.
> Or movi, non smarrir l'altre compagne,
> ché non pur sotto bende
> alberga Amor, per cui si ride et piagne.
>
> (28. 106–14)

(You, my song, will see Italy and the honoured shore, / which is
concealed and grudged to my eyes / not by the sea, not by hill or
river, / but only by Love, who with his haughty light / most
entrances me where most he burns: / nor can Nature stand firm
against habit. / Now go, do not stray from your companions
[i.e. other poems], / since it is not only under bands [i.e. in
women] / that Love dwells, through whom one laughs and cries.)

For all its self-confessed limitations, *O aspectata in ciel* is the most optimistic projection of the humanist dream of renewal in the *RVF*. The other two poems are marked by increasing uncertainty. *Spirto gentil* (53) is addressed to an unidentified figure, recently appointed to the Roman senate (and, therefore, probably not Cola di Rienzo, who was a tribune), whom Petrarch admits in the *congedo* to knowing only by report. Again the classical and the Christian come together: the great dead of Republican Rome (the Scipios, Junius Brutus, the consul Fabricius) rejoice below at the possibilities for restoration of lost glory, the blessed above call for reform of the Church, whilst the victims of current disorder in Rome itself beg for protection against the barbarous, unprincipled holders of power. But the accent is recurrently negative: it falls on decadence, inertia, conflict, destruction, impotence. Instead of confident incitement the tone becomes that of a plea. And when, in the final stanza, the glory attainable by the new senator is summarised, it is the glory of rescuing an aged *donna* from death:

> Quanta gloria ti fia
> dir: Gli altri l'aitâr giovene et forte;
> questi in vecchiezza la scampò da morte.
> (lines 96–8)

(How great a glory will it be for you / to say: The others helped her when she [Rome] was young and strong; / this man saved her from death in old age.)

The third poem, the only one of the three to speak directly to figures in power, is also the bleakest. *Italia mia* (28) may have been written near Parma in the winter of 1344–5, when Petrarch was under the protection of Azzo da Correggio, the ruler of Parma and one of the protagonists in a messy little war fought mostly by mercenaries on behalf of the several Northern Italian states in conflict with each other. It begins with the rhetorical ploy appropriate to a desperate situation; eloquence is vain in the circumstances (1–3). None the less the poem attempts to speak: against disunity, falsity of vision and unjustifiable violence amongst the princes, and treachery, greed and bestial fury amongst the mercenaries, it sets a vision of Italian and Roman *virtus* that could be made reality if only the princes would respond:

> . . . et pur che voi mostriate
> segno alcun di pietate,
> vertú contra furore
> prenderà l'arme, et fia 'l combatter corto:
> ché l'antiquo valore
> ne l'italici cor' non è anchor morto.
>
> > (lines 91–6)

(. . . and if you only show / some sign of pity, / [Roman] virtue will take arms against [bestial] fury / and the battle will be brief: / for the valour of old / is not yet dead in Italian hearts.)

The princes themselves are invited to think of the fate of their immortal souls and to spend their time on the kind of honourable and peaceful pursuits that are appropriate to their position:

> Al passar questa valle
> piacciavi porre giú l'odio et lo sdegno,
> vènti contrari a la vita serena;
> et quel ch' in altrui pena
> tempo si spende, in qualche acto piú degno
> o di mano o d'ingegno,
> in qualche bella lode,
> in qualche honesto studio si converta:
> cosí qua giú si gode,
> et la strada del ciel si trova aperto.
>
> > (103–12)

(As you pass through this vale [of life] / may it please you to lay down your hatred and scorn, / winds [of passion] contrary to a life of calm; / let the time now spent on others' harm, / be redirected to some worthier exploit / of might or mind, / to some laudable enterprise, / to some honourable effort: / thus pleasure is had here below, / and the road to heaven is found open.)

The two passages just quoted suggest Renaissance ideals. But

the dismay is evident: the lines formulate an appeal for peace in a
state of war with little confidence that it will happen. And rightly:
political realities were against it, as they were against any crusade
or restoration of ancient institutions in Rome, as the example of
Cola di Rienzo (irrespective of whether he was the original
addressee of *Spirto gentil*) proved to Petrarch's horror. Any
contemporary greatness that Petrarch could measure against
antiquity had to seem second-rate: what was Robert d'Anjou
compared to Augustus? Or Niccolò Acciaiuoli compared to Scipio
Africanus? But there were also internal reasons why Apollonian
poetry should not develop. The three canzoni are themselves
incomplete movements away from the poetry of Laura. A more
pronouncedly humanist ideology appears in them than in other
poems, and their rhetoric is correspondingly more elevated. No
other poems have such Ciceronian moments as the aposiopesis in
the middle of *Italia mia* (lines 48ff), or the anaphoric questions a
little later in the same poem (lines 81ff); none have such a grand
array of interwoven metaphor as the opening stanza of *O
aspectata in ciel* (for which see Chapter 6.5). But it is a rhetoric
which in many ways lacks poetic conviction, and which repeatedly
gives way to passages which reshape in a more public context
motifs, imagery, phrases and cadences from other poems. When,
for example, Petrarch reproaches the Italian princes for their lack
of forethought, he resorts the darker tones of his more personal
reflections on the passing of time and the imminence of death:

> Signor', mirate come 'l tempo vola,
> et sí come la vita
> fugge, et la morte n'è sovra le spalle.
> Voi siete or qui: pensate a la partita:
> ché l'alma ignuda et sola
> conven ch' arrive a quel dubbioso calle.
> > (128. 97–102: cf. 91. 12–14;
> > > 272. 1–4)

(My lords, watch how time flies, / and how life / is fleeing, and
death is at our back. / You are now here: think of your
departure: / for the soul must arrive naked and alone / on that
fearful road.)

And when, at the end of the same poem, he appeals for peace in Italy (lines 112–22), he does so in words that anticipate his own plea for peace after death that concludes the poem to the Virgin (366. 131–7).

The positioning of the poems, as well as their sparseness in the great mass of love-poems, signals a recognition that the humanist transformation is a qualified one. Only the first canzone is prepared for at all, being anticipated by a sonnet on the same subject (27). The others are isolated, *Italia mia* strikingly so, since it is placed amongst four of the most erotic canzoni in what is more a variation or another demonstration of uncertainty than a progression. Indeed, it marks an end. After it there would be no more Apollonian poetry in major form, only the three sonnets (136–8) vituperating the Avignonese church in a way that echoes Petrarch's letters *Sine nomine*, and these would rapidly modulate back into the more personal manner via another sonnet (139). Poem 166 (*S'i' fussi stato fermo alla spelunca*) will mark a recognition of poetic inadequacy which reaches out to the *Africa* but also embraces poetry in Italian. *Se Virgilio* (186), which was discussed above, seems to confirm these doubts.

Yet historically Petrarch has performed a task of consolidation and restoration. In the sixteenth century the political canzoni and the other poems on various subjects scattered through the first half of Part 1 (see Chapter 3.3) indicate the possibilities for another kind of poetry than love-poetry and show the extent to which it can absorb humanist values and culture. Not surprisingly the political canzoni will be favourite poems of the humanists of the next century. And Machiavelli will make lines 93–6 of *Italia mia*, which are quoted above, the conclusion of his *Prince*. But Petrarch has declared limits that accord with poetic practice in Italy up to and including the early work of Dante: this more patently humanist poetry is to be considered an out-growth of the love-lyric, but not able to absorb its parent. The inclusion of such poems confirms their right to exist, but only in a subordinate place within the encyclopaedia of poetic possibilities.

The failure or refusal to transform Laura totally into the laurel halfway through Part 1 does not mean abandoning their alternate merging and separation. After various further reprises, it is the theme which Petrarch chooses to make the climax and conclusion of Part 1. Poems 260–2 are apparently centred on the human

Laura. They stress her unique combination of beauty, sweetness
and chastity: this gives her glory, albeit an appallingly transient
one (260), points the way to heaven (261), and surpasses (in the
priority which Laura herself gives to chastity over everything else)
everything that philosophers have said on the topic (262). But
obviously much of this applies also to poetic achievement, which,
as Petrarch imagined it, combines beauty perceived through the
senses and chastity in so far as it also resists sensuality. Poem 261
in particular trembles on the edge of allegory, though, characteristically, 262 veers strongly back towards the human figure. In the
final poem in Part 1 the laurel comes strongly through: it is a
poem in praise of the individual *donna*, but also a much more
widely ranging celebration:

> Arbor victorïosa trïumphale,
> honor d'imperadori et di poeti,
> quanti m'ài fatto dí dogliosi et lieti
> in questa breve mia vita mortale!
>
> vera donna, et a cui di nulla cale,
> se non d'onor, che sovr'ogni altra mieti,
> né d'Amor visco temi, o lacci o reti,
> né 'ngano altrui contr'al tuo senno vale.
>
> Gentileza di sangue, et l'altre care
> cose tra noi, perle et robini et oro,
> quasi vil soma egualmente dispregi.
>
> L'alta beltà ch'al mondo non à pare
> noia t'è, se non quanto il bel thesoro
> di castità par ch'ella adorni et fregi.
>
>   (263)

(Victorious triumphal tree, / honour of emperors and poets, /
how many days have you made painful and joyful / in this brief
mortal life of mine ! / true *donna*, and the one who cares for
nothing / except honour, which you, more than any other, reap,
/ nor do you fear the lime of Love, or its snares or nets, / nor
can men's deceit withstand your insight. / Nobility of blood,
and the other / things precious amongst us, pearls, rubies, gold,
/ you equally despise, as if they were some demeaning burden. /

Your high beauty which has no equal in the world / is
wearisome to you, except in so far / as it appears to adorn and
embellish / the lovely treasure of chastity.)

This is the last and strongest celebration in the *RVF* of human
achievement, focused upon poetry but including the achievements
of rulers (line 2). In uniting beauty with moral virtue, clear-
sightedness, and indifference to wealth and high birth, in being
immune to desires of the flesh, the laurel is an emblem of
Petrarch's major humanist ideals, which in the *Africa* and the *Vita
Scipionis* he will bring together in the figure of Scipio Africanus.

Arbor victoriosa is an appropriate conclusion to Part 1, though
that the praise should be built up mostly through negations and
that the poem, like all those since 239, is only a sonnet, are
indicators of adverse pressures. The dangers of loving Laura apply
also to the laurel. Both are objects of desire, and, from that
subjective point of view, which is the most important one, there is
no difference between them. In the *Secretum* Augustine, (broadly
speaking, Petrarch's conscience) charges Franciscus (his ego) with
a perverse obsession with Laura's name (in Latin 'Laurea') and
with all things connected with it, especially the laurel (also 'laurea'
in Latin as well as 'laurus'). Augustine's words suggest that the
coronation was almost as regrettable as a sexual conquest:

Denique quia cesaream sperare fas non erat, lauream poeticam,
quam studiorum tuorum tibi meritum promittebat, nichilo
modestius quam dominam ipsam adamaveras concupisti: ad
quam adipiscendam, quanquam alis ingenii subvectus, quanto
tamen cum labore perveneris, tecum ipse recogitans
perhorresces. (*Prose* 158)

(At last because it was quite wrong to hope for the imperial one,
you conceived a desire for the poetic laurel which had no more
restraint than the love you had felt for your mistress. You will
be horrified if you think over how much effort it cost you to
obtain it, even though your genius had wings that carried you
aloft.)

In this perspective, the sensuality associated with the one is not
uplifted in the desire for the other. And the analogies or identities

can be extended. Both Laura and the laurel may be more illusory than real: both belong to the uncertain world of experience, imagination, literature. In time both are bound to perish, and, therefore, both must be renounced. There may be a difference of scale, but in the end 'immortal' fame and 'immortal' poetry are as transient and delusive as the more obviously fleeting beauty of an individual. Conceptually and imaginatively Laura and the laurel continue to coincide in this negative dimension as they do in the positive.

Poem 142 (*A la dolce ombra de le belle frondi*) had already proposed, in vain, that it was time to turn from the laurel to another tree, that is, the cross. Now at the beginning of Part 2, *I' vo pensando*, the great canzone of aporia in the face of vanity, makes it plain in the simplest of metaphors (taken probably from *Purg.* 11. 100) that not only is love irrational and destructive, but so is the desire for literary immortality:

> Poi che fia l'alma de le membra ignuda,
> non pò questo desio piú venir seco;
> ma se 'l latino e 'l greco
> parlan di me dopo la morte, è un vento:
> ond'io, perché pavento
> adunar sempre quel che un' ora sgombre,
> vorre' 'l ver abbracciar, lassando l'ombre.
> (264. 66–72)

(After the soul is bare of the body, / this desire [for fame] can no longer accompany it. / But if Latin and Greek / continue to speak of me after death, it is [empty] wind: / and so I, since I fear / ever to be amassing what a moment may sweep away, / would wish to embrace the truth, leaving the shadows behind.)

This recognition is not the end, any more than the negative interpretation of love means abandoning Laura in Part 2. Laurels will continue to appear up to three poems from the end of the collection (363.4). As with Laura, the dominant note is regret for the loss of something beautiful, the impermanence of which was previously discounted. Only in one poem will there be a Christian transformation of the laurel, and then an ambiguous one (359: see section 5 below).

The alternation and oscillation between Laura and the laurel throughout the *RVF* signals Petrarch's doubts about whether vernacular poetry can go beyond certain limits except uncertainly and sporadically. But it also signals more troubling fears. Poetry proves unable to dispense with its darker side, its fascination with what cannot fully make sense and desires that are not wholly purified. Laura's loose hair ('sparsi', 'scattered', as in poem 90), the scattered poems (as in the 'rime sparse' of 1. 1 or the 'sparte fronde' (scattered branches) of 333. 7) and the 'unrefinement' of style, which Petrarch also preferred, he said, to be 'uncombed' ('incomptius') (see Chapter 4.2), all converge. So long as poetry refuses to be ordered, it will be surrounded by moral and ontological ambiguities, but conversely the fickle, untrustworthy changefulness, and the disorder, are essential to the beauty of poetry as Petrarch envisages it and writes it.

In the end, as seems more obviously the case with the play on 'l'aura', there may be nothing but the sounds of words and their only half-articulated suggestions. The 'lauro' and Laura may be no more than those words, offering an all too material pleasure that is empty of significance. One of the sonnets in Part 2 has reverberations for the whole collection:

> Quand'io veggio dal ciel scender l'aurora
> co la fronte di rose et co' crin' d'oro,
> Amor m'assale, ond'io mi discoloro,
> et dico sospirando: Ivi è Laura ora.
>
> O felice Titon, tu sai ben l'ora
> da ricovrare il tuo caro tesoro:
> ma io che debbo far del dolce alloro?
> che se 'l vo' riveder, conven ch'io mora.
>
> I vostri dipartir' non son sí duri,
> ch'almen di notte suol tornar colei
> che non â schifo le tue bianche chiome:
>
> le mie notti fa triste, e i giorni oscuri,
> quella che n'à portato i penser' miei,
> né di sé m'à lasciato altro che 'l nome.
>
> (291)

(When I see dawn descend from heaven / with her forehead of roses and her hair of gold, / Love assaults me, at which I turn pale, / and say sighing 'There is Laura now.' / O happy Tithonus, you well know the hour / when you recover your precious treasure: / but what shall I do with the sweet laurel? / If I wish to see it again, I must die. / Your partings are not so hard, / since at least at night she is used to return / who feels no revulsion for your white locks. / She makes my nights sad and my days dark, / who has borne away my thoughts, / and has left me nothing but her name.)

The words with dual meanings which Petrarch has repeatedly exploited are brought together in the rhymes, and the contrast developed between their real emptiness and another world which they may evoke. In a world of literary myth ageing does not affect perpetual return. Tithonus is always revisited by Aurora. For Petrarch there are only the words which point to Laura, fragmented, varied, substituted for each other, but in the end signifying only a name. Time has done its work of destruction, though that is only a revelation of what was always implicit. But the consequence is still not silence or another language: once again Petrarch sets in motion a play of language in which time's power and language's powerlessness are both acknowledged, embracing that defeat, like others, in a poem.

5.5 Transcendence

The *Vita nuova* and the *Divina commedia* had affirmed in the strongest terms that love of the *donna*, or at least of Beatrice, led upwards, its point of arrival being the ultimate reality from which it and Beatrice, its medium and manifestation, sprang. Love was therefore rational, as declared in *Vita nuova* 1; it harmonised with the moral and intellectual choices that a man should naturally make, an advance in goodness or in understanding being also an advance in love. Thus love of Beatrice could never in itself be suspect: however much it seemed to centre on a person, it was simultaneously directed towards the supreme values that manifested themselves in or through her. The educative process might be painful, but the desire of the lover carried him forward; or, from the opposite perspective (and, within this Neo-Platonic scheme, the more truthful one) the love that manifested itself through the beloved in the lover returned stage by stage to its source. If death impeded the ascent, it was only through the weakness of the lover; Beatrice, united with ultimate reality, signalled the ultimate goal through remembered images and words. When the lover's perverseness caused these to fail, it was possible for love to descend to Dante through a chain of mediation that linked the Virgin, St Lucia, Beatrice and Virgil, who then could guide Dante through more numerous grades of mediation eventually back to Beatrice. She, in her turn, would guide Dante through Paradise until she ceded him to St Bernard for the last stages of his pilgrimage.

In its actual unfolding in the *Commedia* it was a subtle, coherent and dynamic system, and one that absorbed into itself its actual medium. Poetry and love were metonymically related, as they had been since the *Vita nuova*. Poetry propelled poet and reader forward towards the truth, whilst never denying its own nature as poetry. It too emerged from an order of things of which the poet was not fully aware, although he would become more expert in its techniques and would gain an increasing intellectual understanding of poetry, in general and in particular, exactly as he would of love. So too would readers. The first poem of the *Vita nuova* would have meanings that would only become apparent after Beatrice's death. Inferno, both as a place and as part of a poem, would only be intelligible (that is, present meanings, as opposed to affecting the emotions and the perceptions) in the light of Paradise. The circular processes of love repeat themselves in poetry.

Nothing of this unified system remained to Petrarch. Everything that surrounded the core of love in Dante – politics, philosophy, history, vatic poetry itself – had been recast in quite different forms in Petrarch's Latin work. But, as I said in Chapter 4.4, there was still the question of the centre. A collection of poems which implicitly defined the limits and the procedures for poetry in Italian for contemporary culture, and did so almost entirely in terms of love-poetry, had to confront the transcendentalism of Dante, if it were not to ignore the most important love-poetry that had been written for centuries. Systematic or not, it had to look at questions of truth that the tradition before Dante had largely ignored and at representations of the beloved of which it had little idea. Most of all it could not discount the posthumous phase, since Dante had closely bound the fulfilment of love and poetry closely to the contact between the dead beloved and his living self. The living Laura is only affected by the Beatrice of the *Commedia* to a limited degree: the dead one is her direct progeny. If a story had emerged at all in the work of a traditional poet writing before Dante, it would have ended rapidly enough with a decent lament (*planh*) for Laura and then perhaps a poem for the Virgin. Outside the *RVF* and the *Triumphs* Petrarch himself drew a predictable curtain down. 'In youth I was troubled by a fierce passion, but a single, honourable one,' he says in his letter to posterity, 'and I would have been troubled longer, if death, cruel but expedient, had not extinguished the already cooling fire.' ('Amore acerrimo sed unico et honesto in adolescentia laboravi, et diutius laborassem, nisi iam tepescentem ignem mors acerba sed utilis extinxisset.' *Prose* 5) And that is all. What need was there to write of the dead Laura in Latin? In Italian it was inevitable.

The result is a major enrichment of his own poetry, not a fundamental change. Petrarch's refusal to rebuild any of the fragments that he took from Dante or any other writer as a coherent whole means that any impulse to transcendentalism cannot be carried through. Instead there is an appropriation of transcendental motifs similar to that which is made of sensualism. The self and poetry absorb into their own sphere what is tendentially transcendent whilst leaving open whether or not questions of ultimate truth can be answered or even seriously asked in poetry.

The first opening in this direction, as in others that the *RVF* explores, comes very early in the collection. The negative implications of loving Laura are suggested in poem 3 by making the experience begin on Good Friday. In the following poem it is the turn of the positives. The incarnation illuminated the obscure prophecies of the Old Testament, elevated obscure men into the Apostles and took place, not amidst the splendours of Rome, but in the obscurity of Judaea. So Laura, an illuminating sun, was born in an insignificant township.

> Que' ch'infinita providentia et arte
> mostrò nel suo mirabil magistero,

che crïò questo et quell'altro hemispero,
et mansüeto piú Giove che Marte,

vegnendo in terra a 'lluminar le carte
ch'avean molt'anni già celato il vero,
tolse Giovanni da la rete et Piero,
et nel regno del ciel fece lor parte.

Di sé nascendo a Roma non fe' gratia,
a Giudea sí, tanto sovr'ogni stato
humiltate exaltar sempre gli piacque;

ed or di picciol borgo un sol n'à dato,
tal che natura e 'l luogo si ringratia
onde sí bella donna al mondo nacque.

(He who infinite providence and art / displayed in his
marvellous mastery [in making the cosmos], / who created this
hemisphere [the Northern] and that other [the Southern], / and
made Jove gentler than Mars, / coming to earth to illuminate
the pages / which for many years past had concealed the truth, /
took John and Peter from their net, / and made them share in
the kingdom of heaven. / He did not grant the grace of his birth
to Rome, / but rather to Judaea, so much over any state / did it
always please him to exalt humility. / And now from a small
township he has given us a sun, / such that nature and the place
give thanks, / since from them so beautiful a *donna* was born
into the world.)

Taken at face value the poem proposes that Laura's birth is a
continuation of God's work comparable with the most important
events in cosmic history. But it is hard to read it in quite that way,
and not only because of the negative suggestions of the poem that
precedes it. Poem 4 has the air of a hyperbolic, almost sacrilegious
compliment in which the analogies are dexterously manipulated in
order to arrive at a final line which is startling in its bare literality:
all that grand preparation has been for 'sí bella donna', a simple
noun with the simplest of adjectives but, in the context,
reverberating with connotations of earthly beauty. Perhaps earthly
beauty is, scandalously, being given the significance that the poem
seems to give it. But at the same time an apparent statement about

the scheme of things is on the edge of dissolving into an elegant projection of feeling and a correspondingly elegant display of the formal and rhetorical possibilities of poetry.

A similarly sacrilegious air will hover over a few other early poems (16, 25, 26). Generally in the none too numerous poems in Part 1 which explicitly celebrate the powers and virtues of love it gives way to the more familiar Neo-Platonic ascent. The basic motif of being guided through love to the highest good ('al sommo ben') and to heaven ('al ciel') appears in 13, but the theme only comes to prominence with the three canzoni on Laura's eyes (71–3), 'the three sisters' (as they are traditionally called from the *congedo* to the second) which form a unique trio in early Italian poetry. No one had written a group of three canzoni with an identical metrical structure (though of different lengths), and no one had devoted the whole of even a single canzone to the eyes of the beloved, though the motif was ubiquitous. Laura's eyes rid Petrarch of vile thoughts, distinguish him from the run of men, guide him like stars. But they are much more than that: they are 'sopra 'l mortal corso sereni' ('serene beyond the course of mortal things': 71. 50), they have 'la divina incredibile bellezza' ('divine, incredible beauty': 71. 62), they are 'vaghe faville, angeliche, beatrici' ('entrancing angelic sparkles, giving blessedness': 72. 37). He sees in their movement 'un dolce lume / che mi mostra la via ch' al ciel conduce ' ('a sweet light / which shows me the way that leads to heaven': 72. 2–3) and, a few lines later, he says, 'Questa è la vista ch'a ben far m'induce / et che mi scorge al glorïoso fine' ('This is the sight that draws me to do good / and which guides me to the glorious end': 72. 7–8). In the next stanza the *via analogica* becomes explicit:

> Io penso: se là suso,
> onde 'l motor de le stelle
> degnò mostrar del suo lavoro in terra,
> son l'altr' opre sí belle,
> aprasi la pregione, ov'io son chiuso,
> et che 'l camino a tal vita mi serra.
>
> (line 16–21)

(I think, 'If there above, / from where the mover of the stars / deigned to show some of his work on earth, / the other works

are so beautiful, / let the prison [the body] be opened, in which I
am closed, / and which bars the road to such life.')

Such lines could obviously be exploited by sixteenth-century
Neo-Platonists, but in the poems in which they appear the Neo-
Platonic motifs lack any coherent development. They emerge from
the flow of other motifs, coming to prominence only in the second
canzone (from which almost all the lines just quoted are taken). In
broad terms the three poems describe a movement of ascent and
descent. The first begins the upward movement, the second holds
it at a pinnacle, and the third, with its stress on the weariness of
the writer and the inexhaustibility of the theme, marks a descent
that will only be finally concluded in the coda of subsequent
sonnets (74–5). Even in the second poem, other themes and motifs
appear which are familiar from other poems – the desire to see
and its frustration, the conflict of pain and pleasure, the joy of
praising what gives delight, a sense of the irrational nature of his
desires and their pleasures (especially at ll 55–60). The centre to the
poems is, of course, the eyes, and essential to their beauty and
power is their movement. Stillness is imagined, not in any steady
gaze, but in the steady contemplation of their changes. It is there
that some approximation to heavenly peace may be found,
although, as in the contemplation of Laura in a rain of flowers in
126 (see Chapter 5.3), there is every awareness that similarity does
not mean identity and that looking is being treated as an end in
itself:

> Pace tranquilla senza alcun affanno,
> simile a quella ch'è nel ciel eterna,
> move da lor inamorato riso.
> Cosí vedess' io fiso
> come Amor dolcemente gli governa,
> sol un giorno da presso
> senza volger già mai rota superna,
> né pensasse d'altrui né di me stesso,
> e 'l batter gli occhi miei non fosse spesso.
>   (73. 67–75)

(Tranquil peace without any tribulation, / similar to that which
is eternal in heaven, / moves from their laughter full of love. / So

might I see with fixed gaze / how Love sweetly directs them, / only for one day from close at hand, / without there ever being movement of wheel of heaven [i.e. without time passing], and might not take thought of others or of myself, / and my eyes blink only rarely.)

Movement is the key to the poems. They are anything but the orderly unfolding of a theme or group of themes. This does not mean that they are unstructured, only that for the relatively rational organisation of the *stil novo* canzone, Petrarch has substituted a flowing structure comparable to the complex tracery of high Gothic decorative art, though classicising readers might feel analogies with the Pindaric ode. It is small wonder that De Sanctis, tired of grace and elegance in Petrarch, praised these poems for their vitality (1971: 137). For around the eyes they interweave their disparate, often contradictory motifs, with rapid transitions from one to another, as from Laura to Petrarch, to the poem being written, and back again. In all this the movement beyond the eyes towards heaven is merely a further repeated gyration that is intensified in the central poem, but there, as elsewhere, comes back inevitably to the moving objects which it had seemed to leave behind. There is no transcendence here, except as one possibility inherent in the beauty of this poetic movement. Benedetto Varchi, writing in the late sixteenth century, spoke for most Italian critics who have commented on the poems when he said that there was in them 'una infinita disusitata dolcezza' ('an infinite, out-of-the-ordinary sweetness': quoted by Carducci and Ferrari, 1899: 102). That peculiar sweetness, like the sweetness that Petrarch saw in Laura and the words about her, may or may not be a way to heaven.

That such ambiguities should surround such celebration had been prepared for specifically by the canzone (70) immediately preceding, which links an emblematic survey of past poetry (see Chapter 4.4) with self-accusation. In the last stanza Petrarch castigates himself for his inability to pass beyond the outer beauty of the world and for his inability to concentrate at those moments when he manages to do so:

Tutte le cose di che 'l mondo è adorno
uscîr buone de man del mastro eterno;

ma me, che cosí adentro non discerno,
abbaglia il bel che mi si mostra intorno;
et s'al vero splendor già mai ritorno,
l'occhio non pò star fermo,
cosí l'à fatto infermo
pur la sua colpa, et non quel giorno
ch' i' volsi inver' l'angelica beltade
nel dolce tempo della prima etade.
                                    (41–50)

(All the things with which the world is adorned / emerged good
from the hand of the divine master. / But I, who cannot look so
deeply into them, / am dazzled by the beauty that displays itself
around me; / and if I make a return to the true splendour, / my
eye cannot remain steady, / so infirm has it been made / only
through its own fault, and not because of that day, / when I
turned towards the angelic beauty / *in the sweet time of my
early years.* [23. 1])

Mobility, which is to be a source of intense pleasure in the canzoni
which follow, is here a source of pain, a mark of congenital guilt
to which there is no solution. The following sisters may contrast
with this poem but they do not forget it.

There is no coherent development of the motifs of ascent in the
remainder of Part 1, though there will be praise sonnets enough
particularly in the second century, which reiterate and vary the
motifs of divine ascent or descent, some moving more obviously in
the direction of the *stil novo* (e.g. 154, 156, 160 (for which see
section 3 above), 191, 192), others merging *stil novo* and
classical phrasing (e.g. 159, 193). None of these, in isolation or
together, are as complex or as strongly affirmative as the three
canzoni. If anything they are more worldly, coming closer in their
subtle hyperboles to poem 4, even if they are not potentially
scandalous. They register the impression of overwhelming beauty,
the significance and status of which is in doubt or suspended.
Poem 220, for example, consists of a succession of questions.
These are superbly ordered and varied amongst themselves, but
there is no answer to any of them, no sense that they are anything
but rhetorical:

Onde tolse Amor l'oro, et di qual vena,
per far due treccie bionde? e 'n quali spine
colse le rose, e 'n qual piaggia le brine
tenere et fresche, et die' lor polso et lena?

onde le perle, in ch'ei frange et affrena
dolci parole, honeste et pellegrine?
onde tante bellezze, et sí divine,
di quella fronte, piú che 'l ciel serena?

Di quali angeli mosse, et di qual spera,
quel celeste cantar che mi disface,
sí che m'avanza omai da disfar poco?

Di qual sol nacque l'alma luce altera
di que' belli occhi ond'io ò guerra et pace,
che mi cuocono il cor in ghiaccio e 'n foco?

(Whence did Love take the gold, and from what vein, / to make
two blonde tresses? And on what thorns / did he gather the
roses [her lips], on what hillside [did he find] the tender fresh
frost [her skin] / and give it pulse and spirit? / Whence did he
take the pearls [her teeth], in which he breaks and reins / sweet,
honourable, special words? / Whence so many so divine
beauties, / in that forehead more serene than heaven ? / From
what angels, from what [heavenly] sphere / came that celestial
singing that is my destruction, / so that I have now little left to
be destroyed? / From what sun was born the lofty nurturing
light / of those beautiful eyes – whence I have war and peace – /
which cook my heart in ice and fire?)

The metaphors do not hint at a symbolic system: they only create
a stream of connotations connected with brightness, beauty and
preciousness, complicated and darkened by intimations of pain.
Words indicating the divine order – 'divine', 'angeli', 'celeste' –
have lost any denotative meaning they may have had in earlier
poetry: though they retain their force of suggestion, they seem to
point to the feelings of the speaker or only to colour the
celebration that the poem is enacting. The poem stays on the
earth, especially in the culminating metaphor of cooking and the
virtuoso alliteration in which it is embedded.

The failure or refusal to transcend runs through Part 1. Again

and again it is outer beauty, transformed into poetry but not
transformed through poetry into something else, that holds the
attention. The alternatives, when there are alternatives, are
envisaged in the form of a renunciation, an escape or a deliverance
that miraculously appears. When a sublimation is projected in
which the same desires assume Christian form, the formulation is
imprecise. In the following lines, which conclude the sestina *A la
dolce ombra de le belle frondi* (142), there is a turning from the
laurel to the cross, but the emphasis falls on the sheer otherness,
with respect to the laurel, of what is projected.

> ora la vita breve e 'l loco e 'l tempo
> mostranmi altro sentier di gire al cielo
> et di far frutto, non pur fior' et frondi.
>
> Altr'amor, altre frondi et altro lume,
> altro salir al ciel per altri poggi
> cerco, ché n'è ben tempo, et altri rami.
>
> > (lines 34–9)

(now the brevity of life and the place and the time / show me
another path to go to heaven, / and how to yield fruit, not just
blossom and foliage. / I seek another love, other foliage, other
light, / another path up to heaven over other hills, / since it is
well nigh time, and other branches.)

On the Dantesque schema Laura's death would have marked
the beginning of a progression, if not the continuation along a
path already entered on during her life. But, as the exact
coincidence between the times and dates of enamourment and
death suggests, the dominant note of Part 2 is regressive or
recursive, not progressive. Petrarch does not surrender old
pleasures lightly. Whether he looks backward or forward, or to
the equally uncertain present, it is Laura as she was, or as he
thought she was, who occupies him. When her image changes, it is
into a further perfection of what he had already imagined. In the
major lamentation in the immediate aftermath of her death (268),
the dead Laura already returns as an enhanced version of the
figure who had appeared in poem 4:

Piú che mai bella et piú leggiadra donna
tornami innanzi, come
là dove piú gradir sua vista sente.
(lines 45–7)

(A *donna* who is more beautiful and more attractive than ever /
returns before me, as to there / where she feels the sight of her
gives most pleasure.)

He was conscious of the risks of vanity or misapprehension
before. The unhealable fracture of her death heightens this
consciousness; but knowing that the tracing of old ground is not a
restoration, does not prevent the action of the imagination or of
the desire that guides it from continuing to repeat itself. Much
that is familiar returns, if always with some thematic or formal
variation – the attempts to defeat the annihilating power of time,
the crises of self-delusion, the possibilities of reaching through the
destruction to some firmer reality, the possibility still that the
poetry has human significance, not divine. There is so little
reorientation that Part 2 seems overall a more concentrated,
darker rewriting of Part 1, its transposition into a minor key.

More specific recurrences are evident too. As Petrarch had
blessed the moment of first seeing Laura (61), so now he blesses
the day that she first returns to him in a vision (284). He projects
understanding onto the landscape now (288) as he had done in the
past (35). He asks rhymes to go to her (333) as he had before
(153). Poetry had previously been written only to release emotion
and so it is now (293, 304, 332); poetry was written to win fame
for her, and so it is now (297, 327). Even the weeping or
lamenting is not new. Petrarch had indicatively declared himself
'un di quei che 'l pianger giova' early in Part 1 (37. 69), and had
made the contrast between 'pianto' and 'canto' the contrast
between two poems (229–30). In Part 2 the motif is merely
accentuated.

In the following poem the contrast of 'pianto' and 'canto' is
only one of a string of features which have appeared in Part 1 and
are now recombined. Petrarch now re-enacts his characteristic
process of poetic composition under the auspices of death,
proclaiming the need for an ending, but also in the last line
allowing for a continuation of lament, if not of song:

Gli occhi di ch'io parlai sí caldamente,
et le braccia et le mani e i piedi e 'l viso,
che m'avean sí da me stesso diviso,
et fatto singular da l'altra gente;

le crespe chiome d'òr puro lucente
e 'l lampeggiar de l'angelico riso,
che solean far in terra un paradiso,
poca polvere son, che nulla sente.

Et io pur vivo, onde mi doglio et sdegno,
rimaso senza 'l lume ch'amai tanto,
in gran fortuna e 'n disarmato legno.

Or sia qui fine al mio amoroso canto:
secca è la vena de l'usato ingegno
et la cetera mia rivolta in pianto.

(292)

(The eyes of which I spoke with such heat, / and the arms, and
the hands, and the face, / which had so divided me from myself,
/ and made me uniquely different from other people, / the
curling hair of pure gleaming gold, / and the flashing of the
angelic smile, / which used to make a paradise on earth, / are a
little dust which feels nothing. / And I live on, which fills me
with grief and rage, / left without the light that I so loved, / in
great storminess and on a boat in disarray. / Now let there be
an end here to my song of love: / the vein of my customary
invention is dry, / and my harp has turned to mourning.)

The catalogue of Laura's beauties, earthly if apparently immortal
or divine, their effects, the loss of a guiding light and the storm-
tossed ship (cf. 80, 132, 189), the very renunciation of poetry (cf.
60, 142), are changed only by the verb-tenses and the finality of
line 8, which should be, but is not, an end. In the very rhetoric of
the poem, as well as in the sense, there is a protraction of a lost
past.

As in life looking back is complemented by looking forward.
Hope of meeting in this world has dissolved, but it re-emerges as a
prospect for the next. Some poems speak of Laura's death having
ironically occurred at a moment when ageing made it likely their

future relations would have been untroubled by sensual desires
(314–17). But such complaints at the apparently arbitrary cruelty
of time are countered by other poems in which the failure to
satisfy sexual desire and Laura's resistance to it are seen as a kind
of agon from which both of them have won moral and spiritual
credit (e.g. 290, 359). She is in heaven; he, through her, may find
his way there too, though the goal of his journey is more a
perfected Laura than God. At most he can conceive of a
conjunction of the two, but not the subsumption of the human in
the divine (so 349, 362). Whilst recognising repeatedly that his
imagination of Laura and ultimate reality is inadequate, he cannot
abandon the fantasy of a fulfilment of desire in morally laudable
terms.

Dante, guided by Beatrice through Paradise, had been sure of
his own eventual salvation and of the validity of his exploration of
the realm of the dead, whether his actual account was to be
considered allegory of the poets or of the theologians. Petrarch,
following Dante, has meetings between himself and Laura. These
occur in dreams or visions, in which Laura is imagined descending
from heaven to visit him on earth, or, alternatively, they occur in
the course of intense thinking, when Petrarch feels that he rises
somehow into heaven. In both kinds of encounter, as has often
been observed, Laura appears a much more alive character than
she did during her lifetime, much as the dead Beatrice also
acquires concreteness and definition in the *Commedia*. Laura and
Petrarch are now intimates: she speaks to him, as she had never
done in previous poems, except in dreams presaging her death,
using the familiar *tu* form rather than the polite *voi* which he had
used in his appeals to her during her life; and she shows concern
and affection for him, letting it be understood that her apparent
coldness was a necessary brake which did not reflect her true
feelings. At the same time, again like Beatrice to Dante, she is an
incentive to him to press on, the castigator of his weakness,
justified in her impatience by her position among the blessed and
her consequent closeness to her Maker.

But question-marks hang over all of this. There is no
progression from poem to poem: there are constant relapses from
visitations or ecstasies into regrets for the lost living Laura. There
is thus no increase in spiritual understanding, no confirmation that
further grades of reality are being probed as the poems go by.

There is no authorisation, no mediation by which Laura's visits or Petrarch's ascents can find a foundation in the order of things. Instead there is merely the force of the encounter itself, which within the individual poem becomes an end in itself, offering and simultaneously denying a happiness similar to that which had been offered and denied by the contemplation of the living Laura's eyes. It is poetry which gives Laura life, not something beyond it.

Levommi il mio penser (302) brings most of these concerns together:

> Levommi il mio penser in parte ov'era
> quella ch'io cerco, et non ritrovo in terra:
> ivi, fra lor che 'l terzo cerchio serra,
> la rividi piú bella et meno altera.
>
> Per man mi prese, et disse: — In questa spera
> sarai anchor meco, se 'l desir non erra:
> i' so' colei che ti die' tanta guerra,
> et compie' mia giornata inanzi sera.
>
> Mio ben non cape in intelletto humano;
> te solo aspetto, et quel che tanto amasti
> et là giuso è rimaso, il mio bel velo. —
>
> Deh perché tacque, et allargò la mano?
> Ch'al suon de' detti sí pietosi et casti
> poco mancò ch'io non rimasi in cielo.

(My thoughts raised me to the place where was / she whom I seek and do not find on earth: / there, amongst those whom the third circle [i.e. the heaven of Venus] encloses, / I saw her again, [now] more beautiful and less haughty. / She took me by the hand, and said, 'You will be in this sphere [of heaven] / with me yet, unless my desire is mistaken. / I am she who fought such warfare with you / and completed my life before its evening came. / My happiness exceeds human understanding. / I wait only for you, and that which you loved so much, / and has remained there below, my beautiful veil [i.e. her body].' / Oh, why did she cease speaking, and release her hand? / For at the sound of such chaste and pitying words / I very nearly remained in heaven.)

It is the sheer force of cogitation which elevates Petrarch into another realm and which then produces a recognition, which, if one poem led narratively to another, would be unnecessary. As in the lines from 268 quoted above and in so many other poems in Part 2, Laura is more beautiful and more sympathetic than in life. Beatrice had unhesitatingly told Dante in the Earthly Paradise that he would join her in heaven (*Purg.* 32. 100–2). Laura adds to her comparable assurance a disturbing qualifier (line 6) that both stresses the strength of her feelings and leaves some room for uncertainty. In the sestet, though she says, as the blessed should, that her happiness exceeds human understanding, she again introduces a qualification. She refuses to forget her body, which he loved and which she now wishes to have again, as she will indeed have it eventually at the Last Judgment. There is much fulfilment of long-standing wishes here: Petrarch is imagining a Laura who is everything he wanted her to be, with a beauty that will only be perfected in eternity, with love for him, and yet morally admirable. It may or may not be that heaven will provide such an impossible reconciliation of opposites: all that is certain is that it can be imagined in a poem, that there the pleasure and power of the imagined or imaginary world in all their uncertainties can be represented.

This poem leaves the issues implicit. *Quando il soave mio fido conforto* (359) is the last major encounter poem, and the most narrative of them all; it is the clearest summary of the constants in Petrarch's long, fragmentary dialogue with Dante over the problem of poetic transcendence. Again Laura takes pity on Petrarch. She descends to him apparently in a dream, though she has come to console rather than to help (line 2), and ominously seats herself on the left side of his bed, not the more auspicious right. Like Beatrice to Dante (*Purg.* 30. 121–45), she argues that Petrarch should have responded to her translation to a better life with rejoicing and with efforts on his part to climb from the mortal to the immortal (lines 39–44). Now at last the laurel is briefly transfigured: she explains that she carries a palm frond signifying victory over the world and herself and a branch of laurel signifying the triumph (that is, a heavenly version of a Roman triumph) which she deserves. But this syncretist solution is quite unsatisfying: Petrarch represents himself as unable to follow her. He is indifferent to the new Christian laurel, and cannot see

beyond the familiar person, with blonde hair, not laurel leaves,
and quite human eyes, whose form Laura tells him she has
temporarily assumed solely for his benefit and which she again
says she will eventually possess in its perfection, that is, after the
Last Judgment:

> 'Son questi i capei biondi, et l'aureo nodo
> – dich'io – ch'ancor mi stringe, et quei belli occhi
> che fur mio sol?' 'Non errar con li sciocchi,
> né parlar – dice – o creder a lor modo.
> Spirito ignudo sono, e'n ciel mi godo:
> quel che tu cerchi è terra già molt' anni,
> ma per trarti d'affanni,
> m'è dato a parer tale; et anchor quella
> sarò, piú che mai bella,
> a te piú cara, sí selvaggia et pia
> salvando inseme tua salute et mia.'
>
> (lines 56–66)

('Is this the blonde hair, and the golden knot' / I say, 'which still
binds me, and those beautiful eyes / which were my sun?' 'Do
not err with fools / or speak,' she says, 'or believe in their
manner. / I am naked spirit, and I take my pleasure in heaven. /
What you seek has been earth for many years now. / But to
draw you from your troubles, / such a semblance has been given
to me: and again I shall be as I was, / more beautiful than ever, /
to you more dear, preserving, through being so untractable and
compassionate, / the well-being of your soul and mine
together.')

But all these potential positives collapse: the *congedo* refuses to
take the steps forward which should be taken.

> I' piango; et ella il volto
> co le sue man' m'asciuga, et poi sospira
> dolcemente, et s'adira
> con parole che i sassi romper ponno:
> et dopo questo si parte ella, e 'l sonno.
>
> (lines 67–71)

(I weep. And she dries my face / with her hands, and then sighs / sweetly, and becomes irate, / saying words capable of breaking stones. / And after this she leaves me, and so does sleep.)

In spite of her attempts at consolation, and her reproaches, nothing happens, except for his weeping. The poem ends with an awakening that may be an awakening to reality from the delusions of sleep or, less likely, an awakening from a truthful vision to the emptiness of the phenomenal world. The poem leaves both options open, though only as curtains around the scene which it has created. As has repeatedly happened throughout the *RVF*, the truth has been mislaid or has vanished into mere possibility. This, the most vivid and the most Dantesque of Petrarch's poems for the dead Laura, is a refusal of any position that Dante himself ever espoused, an accusation that the poetry of Beatrice has really this ambiguous status too.

The doubts surrounding Laura dead might have been expected to lead to greater insistence on the need for renunciation of love and love-poetry than was evident in the poems written for Laura alive. Poem 264, introducing the second part, had presupposed such a need, as poem 1 had presupposed it for the collection as a whole. In fact, the intensity of repetition and variation on previously assumed positions makes it impossible. Only in the concluding poems, as narrative reasserts itself more strongly, does renunciation or transformation appear even with the force that was to be found in poems such as *Padre del ciel* (62).

As the form of its opening line suggests, *Quel'antiquo mio dolce empio signore* (360), Petrarch's longest and most disputatious canzone, is a companion piece to the preceding *Quando il soave mio fido conforto*, but with a strong shift towards the negative. It represents an unresolvable debate between Love and Petrarch, which echoes the debate between Franciscus and St Augustine in *Secretum*, Book 3. The 'I' speaks of Laura as an incubus who has taken the place of any form of truth and caused endless pain. Love dwells on her virtues and beauty, and once again on the possibility of an ascent to the divine through loving her (lines 140–3). But Reason, before whom the two speeches, almost equal in length to each other, are delivered, refuses to come down on either side, much as Truth is silent in the face of the arguments advanced by the two parties in the *Secretum*. There is no resolution even now, as the two following sonnets, which are in the mode characteristic of Part 2, make plain, the first of these (361) being a recognition of the unrepeatable uniqueness of experience, the second (362) a final imagined encounter in heaven.

It is only in the last four poems that there is a gradual turning away from Laura to God and to the Virgin (see Chapter 3.3), though even in the last two poems it is prayers for rescue which are made, not assertions of freedom. It is easy enough to see why the poem to the Virgin is an appropriate conclusion to the collection, thematically, formally and stylistically. Some troubadour lives had ended with the poet turning from the earthly beloved to the mother of God; more specifically, Dante had begun the last canto of the *Commedia* with a prayer to the Virgin (*Par.* 33. 1–39). Petrarch echoes some of Dante's words, but creates a much grander structure, which resembles a liturgical prayer in its repetitions and its scriptural and patristic echoes, which are denser here than in any other poem of the *RVF*. The formal and stylistic shifts accompany a differentiation, unprecedented in the collection, between two aspects of the female. On the negative side and apparently rejected there is Laura: she is now no more than a Medusa (line 111) (as he also calls her in another very late poem (197)) whose awful beauty he allowed to paralyse him. On the positive side, there is the Virgin, with all the virtues, power and beauty previously ascribed by himself to Laura and by Dante to Beatrice; now the 'vera beatrice' ('the one who truly blesses': line 52) might provide the help that is needed.

The final transformation is as much a final poem as a prayer. *Vergine bella* is itself a supreme example of repetition and variation, the vocative returning in the first and ninth lines of each stanza, at first with a series of different attributes, and then in more complex and varied patterns, as Petrarch brings himself to the forefront as he had done before in other canzoni (e.g. 50, 128). In this return which is always different, a simulacrum of the peace that is asked for in the poem is offered, much as other poems had re-created other forms of movement and stillness. Again, if for the last time, it is in the pleasure and power of words that help lies. What lies outside the poem can be perhaps pointed to, but it is in the very request for a peace that is not present that the poem finds its own troubled contentment and expects the reader to do likewise. No vision of the kind that concludes *Paradiso* 33 follows the prayer; nor is there any return to the point from which the work departed, except in so far as repetition and variation have been constant throughout the collection from its beginning. The poem divides the impossible conjunction of the earthly and the unearthly which had been Laura. In that sense it is a new beginning as well as an end. What it concludes is clear. But what it begins is something of which neither it nor any other poem of Petrarch can speak.

6

Art

6.1 Poetic disunity

Everything in the previous chapter could have been put under the heading of Art. The very choice of themes, the shape and emphasis which they are given, the resolution or lack of resolution of the issues they embody, all are matters which presuppose work of selection and combination which could properly be called artistic. Yet though questions of language repeatedly raised themselves, the previous chapter was centred upon the content as opposed to form, upon problems of meaning as opposed to other aspects of poetry. In this chapter I turn to areas where Petrarch's art is more apparent and more apparently art – to sound and rhythm, to the choice of words, to imagery, verbal organisation, the manipulation of poetic forms. It is in these areas that Petrarch most demonstrates that he can do what his predecessors did and much more. It is here that he shows a combinatorial skill which is never artisanal, or simply technical, but always at a level of sophistication and refinement that is only partly attainable by his imitators. It is here, more than in meanings detachable from the poems, that his power as a poet is indisputable. In spite of the truism that poetry is untranslatable, it is usually possible for some shadow of the poet to pass into the foreign language. In Petrarch's case that shadow is very pale: without *those* words in *that* form there is almost nothing; with them there can be delight.

All the parts of a poem are obviously interrelated. The choice of a particular word or words has rhythmical consequences, the arrangement of sentences affects and is affected by poetic form, and all and any of these may affect meaning. Yet the parts are also heterogeneous in the sense that, up to a point which it is impossible to define, they can act independently of each other or against each other. Metre can be a constant, irrespective of what the poem is saying. Particular sound patterns may be established which maintain a certain tone, even though metre and subject change. And so on. An analogy might be drawn with biological cells in an organism, which can be seen as distinct units within a body, but which allow a liquid or colour to pass osmotically from one cell to another through their separating walls, and under certain circumstances, press against other cells to change their shape, in such a way that they work together or, conversely, against each other.

In Petrarch the general relationship of 'form' and 'content' is peculiarly multiform. The latter emerges from the former, but that does not mean that it is subordinate to it. Form is modulated in accordance with the emotions designated in a particular poem, but it rarely has a directly expressive function. Negative states, such as pain, grief, confusion, ignorance, frustration, which figure prominently in the *RVF*, regularly run counter to syntactical and metrical arrangements favouring balance, clarity, order. Looked at experientially, a poem can be a way of dispelling what is unpleasant, 'perché cantando il duol si disacerba' ('because through song pain loses its bitterness': 23. 4), although the specific pleasure of song is one indifferent to whether the poem is 'canto' or 'pianto' (cf. 229 and 230) and the various words indicating pain and pleasure themselves recur as items in a repertory of words which are available for perpetual variation. But not everything moves into the light or is neutralised. The clarity and order are never quite perfect, and not solely because the negatives cannot be wholly suppressed. The music of Petrarch's poetry itself contains a dark element, which is a necessary component of its harmony but which is based in the material, irrational aspects of sound and rhythm. Whilst regular patterns and rules, especially metrical rules, can be identified, there is also the dense, constantly changing complexity of what happens within or against those patterns, which may exert a powerful enough fascination for thoughts of meaning, and notions of order and clarity, to be forgotten. In the end we may just like the way it sounds.

That Petrarch's poetry combined disparate, even opposed qualities was already recognised by Pietro Bembo in the sixteenth century. Bembo identified its particular excellence as a union of 'gravità' (gravity), by which he meant, he said, 'l'onestà, la dignità, la maestà, la magnificenza, la grandezza, e le loro somiglianti' ('honourableness, dignity, majesty, magnificence, grandness and the like'), and 'piacevolezza' (pleasingness), that is, 'la grazia, la vaghezza, la dolcezza, gli scherzi, i giuochi e se altro è di questa maniera' ('grace, charm, sweetness, play, games and whatever else there is of this kind') (Marti ed. 1961: 321–2). He backed up his formula by comparisons with Dante and Cino da Pistoia, for both of whom he had high regard, though less than for Petrarch. Dante, he said, thinking of the *Commedia*, was 'grave' but not always 'piacevole'. The matter was serious enough, but Dante sometimes said vulgar things which should not be said and chose words that were unpleasing. Cino, on the other hand, was 'piacevole' enough, but there was a thinness in what was being said and in the sound quality. Petrarch had the attractions of both: he was 'grave', but not indecorous, 'piacevole' but substantial.

Bembo was writing in the shadow of Renaissance Neo-Platonism, and his formula is easily adaptable to ideas of unity in diversity. But, assuming we do not pin our faith to that idealism or a similar one, it is difficult to formulate with any coherence how far there is a union or unity rather than interrelatedness or superimposition in Petrarch's poetry. I argued in Chapter 3 that in the collection as a whole there is no superior synthesis to be found. Within the individual poems there are strong unitary forces at work in the poetic form itself, in syntactical arrangements and in certain dynamics of contrast and balance. But it is not clear that all the distinctive features of a poem combine in an intelligible whole. The poem remains an event or process in time and space, which, thanks to the written text, is repeatable, with some alterations or fluctuations, so long as the text survives. Within it the various levels, or micro-processes, interact and separate, rather as in polyphony various voices might sing against each other or together. If there is a unity which is total, it is in the completion of an analogical circle. The pleasurability of the poem, in its decorum, variety, divergence, finds a correspondence in the beautiful, fragmented, ever-elusive Laura who emerges from the poems and falls back into the words from which she and they are made. The uncertain pleasure of love and poetry are blurred together, as are the questions of the meaning and status of both which the poems also continually raise and continually reabsorb into themselves.

6.2 Metre and rhythm

Petrarch uses two lines only, one of eleven, the other of seven syllables. These, respectively the *endecasillabo* (hendecasyllable) and the *settenario* (heptasyllable), were the two lines which had dominated thirteenth-century poetry, though other lines were also sometimes used (of nine, five, three syllables, and occasionally lines with an even number of syllables). Sonnets were always written in *endecasillabi*, and most canzoni used mixtures of these and *settenari*. Dante had already proclaimed that the longer line was the 'superbissimum carmen' ('proudest poetic form': *DVE* 2. 5. 5–8) and that next to it was the *settenario*, the rest being lines inappropriate to the highest kinds of poetry. On the whole fourteenth-century practice concurred with Dantesque precept, but was happy to admit other lines, especially in light poems such as *frottole* or *caccie*. Petrarch allows himself no such variations, just as he allows himself no variation on standard poetic forms.

In a similar way he rejects variants on the *endecasillabo* and *settenario*. Median rhymes, which had been particularly favoured by the Guittonians, disappear almost altogether (with exceptions in 29, 105, 135, 366 and the *congedo* of 206). It was possible to have a shortened, oxytonic form of either line by ending in a monosyllable (such as 'giú, 'down') or other words with a final stressed vowel (such as 'virtú', 'virtue'). Petrarch has none of these. It was possible, too, to have a lengthened, proparoxytonic form of either, by ending in a word stressed on the antepenultimate syllable. There are many such *sdrucciolo* words in Italian. Petrarch allows none to end the line, except for occasional borderline cases, such as 'inopia' (24), 'Numidia' (130), 'glorio' (131), in which the final '-ia' or '-io' counts metrically as one syllable. Instead his lines are consistently eleven and seven syllables long, ending with a rhyme-word stressed on its penultimate syllable. Most common and most characteristic nouns, adjectives and verb-forms of Italian might seem to fit with this requirement without effort, though it excludes many verb forms ('pórtano', 'they carry'; 'portávano', 'they used to carry'; 'portò, 'he carried'; 'porterà', 'he will carry', etc), and many Latinisms which later humanist poets will employ for special effects ('plácido', 'placid'; 'celebérrimo', 'most celebrated', and similar).

Such self-restriction is not an impoverishment. The *stil novo* had already tended to make lines regular and to work for poetic richness within regular formations rather than against them. Petrarch develops this tendency to a degree that was unknown to the earlier poets, producing lines which combine regularity and variety, evenness and instability in the ever-changing, ever-constant way which is characteristic of all aspects of his poetry.

Historically it is the regularity, particularly of the dominant *endecasillabo*, which has been most important. Though there have been constant disagreements about exactly what are the regular patterns of the *endecasillabo*, it has been orthodox wisdom since the sixteenth century that in Petrarch are to be found the metrical rules which are to be followed, or, alternatively, which are to be resisted.

The first poem is an exemplar and manifesto of Petrarch's rhythmic brilliance (for text and translation see Chapter 5.1). It is also, in a much simpler sense, an exemplification of almost all the regular patterns of the *endecasillabo*. Like earlier poets, Petrarch inevitably has a metrical stress on the rhyming tenth syllable of any line ('suóno' in line 1, 'córe' in line 2, etc.), and, as was also normal, he has an often more marked stress on either the fourth or sixth syllable, after which there is a presumed metrical break (caesura). According to standard Italian terminology, if this break comes closely after the fourth syllable, then the line is said to be *a minore*, deriving from the fact that it begins with a shorter unit. The first line of poem 1 is an example:

> Voi ch'ascoltáte / in rime sparse il suono

If the break follows the sixth syllable, then the line is *a maiore*, since it begins with a larger unit. So 1. 14:

> che quanto piace al móndo / è breve sogno.

Commonly there was at least one further marked stress in the line, which earlier poetry had allowed to appear in a variety of places. The result had often been lines which were uneven, though energetic, Dante being the prime case. Petrarch establishes as his rule that, if it does not fall on an even syllable (as is the case with 'spárse' in 1. 1 and 'piáce' in 1. 14 just quoted), it should fall on the seventh syllable in an *a minore* line, to give the pattern 4, 7, 10, as in 1. 5:

> del vario stíle / in ch'io piángo et ragióno

or on the third syllable in a line that is *a maiore*, giving the pattern 3, 6, 10, as in 1. 6:

> fra le váne speránze / e 'l van dolóre

Alternatively it could fall on the first syllable, to give an *a maiore* with stresses on 1, 6, 10, as in 1. 10:

> fávola fui gran témpo / onde sovénte

The first syllable of an *a minore* could also be stressed, though more weakly and more evenly in what becomes a four-stress line, with the pattern 1, 4, 8, 10, as perhaps in 1. 1, or more convincingly in 5. 14:

> língua mortál / presumptüósa végna

Such are the regular, imitable patterns, but they are obviously merely the basic elements in Petrarch's metrical art, and at least in part extrapolations from something in practice much more interesting. The regular stresses are not the only stresses in the line nor are they necessarily prominent. Rather than producing lines which are heavily accented (which of course he can do as and when he wishes), Petrarch tends to even out the contrasts, modulating them in a controlled flow, within which diverse rhythmical currents are at work. One important factor in this is that he packs his lines with words much more than earlier poets had done. Lines with only the three canonical stresses are infrequent: it is more normal for there to be four or five possible stresses, with the secondary stresses having almost as much weight as those which traditional analysis would posit as the major ones. The evenness and density which this promotes is complicated and reinforced by exploiting the possibilities of vowel combination offered by Italian. Contiguous vowels within a word normally count metrically as one syllable (synhaeresis); so in poem 1 the diphthongs of 'su*o*no', 'p*i*ango', 'var*i*o', 'f*ui*' have the same value as the simple vowels of 'core', 'sono', etc., though it was permissible in certain cases to give both vowels full weight (as in 'presumptüosa' in 5. 14 quoted above). Consecutive vowels across words are also run together metrically, although both are still heard. Petrarch makes particularly frequent use of synaloephe, as this phenomenon is called. In all the lines from poem 1 quoted above the break at the caesura is mitigated, perhaps even healed: in each instance the fourth or sixth syllable, after which there is, or should be, a metrical break, occurs within a word, and the following syllable ending in a vowel runs into the first syllable of the second part of the line. So in line 1, for example, a better representation of what occurs than the one given above would be:

Voi ch'ascoltá/te⌢in rime spárse⌢il suóno

Although even this, as we shall see, is not the whole rhythmic story, it hints at how both a break and a binding are suggested at the same time, and not solely at the point of caesura. The general effect of frequent synaloephe is both to bind the elements of the line together and to distribute the weight of the line more evenly. Because of their relatively extended and complicated sound texture, unstressed syllables in synaloephe occupy more time than they would otherwise do, pressing against what should be the prominent syllables. Consequently, since these are themselves densely packed, the patterns I confidently identified earlier are often more notional than actual.

Thus, at one extreme, a line such as the one opening 263 is quite unusual:

Arbór victorïósa / trïumphále

(Victorious triumphal tree)

Here there are only three words, no synaloephe, and within the words there is no synhaeresis. Instead the words have their full emphasis, as is appropriate to this final celebration of the laurel at the end of Part 1 (cf. 5. 14 quoted above). But the other extreme is even more rare: 303. 5 is a virtuoso display:

fior', frondi, herbe, ombre, antri, onde, aure soavi

(flowers, leafy branches, grasses, shadows, caves, waves,
soothing breezes)

In this almost outrageous line there are a total of eight stresses, all
of equal weight, and synaloephe between all words but the first
and second and the two final ones; there is no perceptible caesura.
The effect is of overwhelming fullness, which it is hard to believe
is actually contained within eleven syllables (cf. 148. 1–4). Full
lines of this kind are commonly more varied and less flamboyant,
as, for example, in line 4 of poem 1, which has seven stresses
evenly distributed without any trace of strain:

quánd'éra^in párte^áltr'uóm da quél ch'i' sóno

It is more characteristic for there to be more diverse rhythmical
patterns, which vary according to their context and function. I
suggested above that line 1 of poem 1 was *a minore*, with stresses
on the fourth, sixth and tenth syllables, with a further, perhaps
secondary stress on the first, the pattern being complicated by the
bonding between the two parts of the line. A rhythmically
unprejudiced reading will recognise that the line is really much
more interesting. The break-cum-bonding at the notional caesura
is repeated later in the line, so that, if anything, it falls into three
parts bonded together:

Vói ch'ascoltáte / ^in ríme spárse / ^il suóno

The first two parts, though rhythmically different from each other,
correspond: both have four complete syllables and a weakened
syllable at the end, the parallelism being confirmed by the
assonance of '-ate^il' and '-arse^in'. Thus two complementary units
are set against the third, which consists only of 'il suono' and has
only one stress. But what might appear to be imbalance is
functional and, in a sense, balance: the first two parts of the line
establish a counterweight to the rhyme-word, which traditionally
was the climax to the line, and which is strong in itself because of
its rhyme function. Any isolation of the word is countered by
other means: 'suono' is firmly integrated into its own line by

syntax and alliteration, and it is then drawn by the enjambement to the opening phrase of the following line ('di quei sospiri'), to which it is also related by the same means.

As we proceed through the first poem, we are subjected as readers to consistently varied patterns. The stresses move backwards, and forwards in the lines, the pauses shift position, the sound density itself changes. Two moments are particularly important. Line 8 is a much more emphatic line than any which have preceded it:

> spéro trovár pietá / non ché perdóno.

The emphasis is created by various means: there is no synaloephe; there is a strongly accented oxytonic word ('pietà') in the middle of the line at a sense break so that a caesura is definitely imposed; a series of /s/ and /p/ alliterations that had run through the whole octet become pronounced in the initial plosives of three of the five stressed words in the line; and, lastly, a line comes to a definite stop for the first time in the poem. All these features combine to highlight the end of the octet as the culminating point within the poem.

The other point which is normally even more prominent within the economy of the poem is the ending. In poem 1 the slowest line in the poem is line 13. It has only three stresses: the break follows the fourth syllable suggesting that this is an *a minore* line, but unusually there is no stress on this syllable at all, the accent falling on the second syllable ('péntersi'). The effect is of calculated irregularity – an irregularity which was muted in many editions by replacing the unusual 'pentersi' with the more usual 'pentírsi', with its stress on the penultimate syllable, to give an almost acceptable *a maiore* line. In the original there is fading in its middle, which then rises with the two strong stresses to its close, though the alliteration of /c/ will be carried forward into the final line:

> e 'l péntersi, / e 'l conóscer chiaraménte

Apart from the binding alliteration, the final line stands against the irregularity of line 13 because of its regular rhythm. It might be called a hendecasyllable *a maiore* with stresses on the fourth, sixth and tenth syllables, but that would not do justice to the complexity of its rhythm, which is noticeably more insistent than that of any other line in the poem (except, perhaps, line 11, 'di mé medésmo méco mi vergógno', which is its rhythmic preparation). The regularity is created by synthesising two opposed movements, the iambic ($-'$) and the trochaic ($'-$), of which the latter has been barely felt in the rest of the poem. After the introductory 'che' the line consists principally of five trochaic words, which propose the following pattern to the reader:

(che) quánto | piáce | (al) móndo | / (è) bréve | sógno

But of course there are also those apparently insignificant particles, which in fact cannot be eliminated, and which propose the counter rhythm:

che quán | to piá | ce al món | do | è bré | ve só | gno

Both rhythms run through the line, but the trochaic dominates the first part, and the iambic the second. The total result is a rhythmic *tour de force*, achieved in apparently casual fashion with the commonest of words. When we take the dark resonance of its sound into account too, it is small wonder that this line and the poem which it concludes should be sirens that draw us into the labyrinth of the collection, no matter what the line and the poem are saying.

6.3 Sound

How important Petrarch judged the sound of poetry to be can be gauged from a note in which he records his hesitations about the order of some lines in *Non fur ma' Giove et Cesare sí mossi* (155):

Attende quoniam hos .4. versus venit in animum mutare. ut qui primi sunt essent ultimj, et e converso, sed dimisi propter sonum principij et finis et quia sonantiora erant in medio, rauciora in principio et fine quod est contra rethoricam. (Romanò 1955: 83)

(Pay attention here since it came into my mind to change these four verses, so that those which are first should be last and vice

versa. But I abandoned the idea, because of the sound of the
beginning and the end, and because [with the alteration] the
more sonorous [elements] were in the middle and the less
musical ones were at the beginning and end, which goes against
the rules of rhetoric.)

He probably has the order of the quatrains in mind, which could
have been inverted without doing violence to the sense. Whether
he has or not, it is plain that he considered the rearrangement
entirely in terms of the effects on the disposition of different kinds
of sound within the poem, without any thought for the order in
which the presentation of Laura weeping and the hyperbolic
image of its putative effects on Jupiter and Caesar were to appear.
If he did not carry this particular revision through, again and
again his drafts show him working above all on the sound of his
poems, often over a long period, until eventually his particularly
resonant and complex harmonies were achieved. (See Chapter
2.3.)

Pietro Bembo claimed in his *Prose* (ed. Marti 1961: 316) that he
had seen an early version of *RVF* 1, which read as follows:

> Voi, ch'ascoltate in rime sparse il suono
> di quei sospir, de' quai nutriva il core

(You who hear in scattered rhymes the sound / of those sighs
with which it [or I] fed my heart . . .)

The meaning is identical with that of the final version, apart from
the ambiguity in the verb in line 2 or, as Bembo puts it, the
absence of a direct reference to Petrarch himself. But the second
line is quite unsatisfactory because too much of 'di quei' is
emphatically and unmusically repeated in 'di quai'. According to
Bembo, Petrarch first changed the latter phrase to 'di ch'io' ('with
which I'), before arriving at the synonymous 'ond'io' which was to
be the final solution. The attraction of the rarer word 'onde' was
its sound, 'that word being more round, more sonorous on
account of the two consonants which are in it, and more full'
('essendo ella voce piú rotonda e piú sonora per le due consonanti
che vi sono, e piú piena'). All that remained was to lengthen
'sospir' to 'sospiri', because 'it is a fuller word, and sweeter' ('piú

compiuta voce è, e piú dolce'). In fact there was one other difference between Bembo's text and Petrarch's final version: 'nutriva' either became or was already the voiced form 'nudriva'.

We have no way of checking Bembo's account, since the papers to which he refers have been lost. But even if the story is an invention, it illustrates not only Bembo's own interests – which were shared by many other Renaissance commentators – but also criteria we can presume were applied by Petrarch as he surveyed the choices open to him. Generally it is the rounder, fuller, more sonorous words and forms which he prefers. The choice of 'onde' with its closed /o/ merging with the following combination of nasal and voiced dental anticipates a whole register of sound which depends on similar consonant combinations: other words with nasal followed by plosives ('canto', 'spento', 'fronda', 'campi', 'tempo', 'lembo', etc.) or with two nasals ('donna', 'affanno', 'perenne', 'somma', etc.), words with two liquids or a liquid and some other consonant ('perle', 'armi', 'tranquillo', 'carro', 'parte', 'colto', 'salma', 'carco', etc.), words with two sibilants or a sibilant and another consonant ('passo', 'bosco', 'amasti', 'invesca', etc.), words which bring together three consonants ('ambra', 'ombra', 'mostra', 'speranza', 'scalzo', etc. – *z* having the value of a double consonant). There are even, though more rarely, combinations which might seem harsh when the word is heard in isolation: words with two plosives ('gabbo', 'intoppo') or ones which put the plosive or other strong consonant(s) before the liquid ('fabbro', 'adopra', 'aspro', 'nigre', etc.).

The implications will be made clearer by comparison. It is not that such words were unknown to earlier poetry: some of them, such as certain common nouns or verb forms, were almost unavoidable. But there has been a significant shift of emphasis. Dante proposed that the noblest style depended on the combination of two different kinds of words, for which he coined the term 'combed' (pexa) and 'shaggy' (yrsuta). Of the first group he said:

> Et pexa vocamus illa, que trisillaba vel vicinissima trisillabitati, sine aspiratione, sine accentu acuto vel circumflexo, sine *z* vel *x* duplicibus, sine duarum liquidarum geminatione vel positione immediate post mutam, dolata quasi, loquentem cum quadam suavitate relinquunt, ut *amore, donna, disio,* vertute, *donare, letitia, salute, securtate, defesa.* (DVE 2. 7. 5)

(And we call those words combed which have three syllables or
their closest equivalent, without aspiration, without acute or
circumflex accent [i.e. without stress on the final syllable],
without double *z* or *x*, without the coupling of two liquids or
the placing of one immediately after a mute – words which are
as it were smoothed, and which leave the speaker with a certain
sweetness, such as *amore, donna, disio, vertute, donare, letitia,
salute, securtate, defesa*.)

In the second group he put necessary words, such as monosyllables of various sorts, and then ornamental words, that is,
polysyllables and generally words which 'have some asperity of
aspiration, accent, double consonants, liquids or length', amongst
which he cites 'terra, honore, speranza'. What Dante says here
corresponds to a large extent, if not in every detail, with his
practice in his *stil novo* phase and with that of other *stil novo*
poets, which do indeed give emphasis to the words which he
lists and to others with similar sound configurations. Above all,
together with a certain regularisation of metrical patterns, it is the
preference for words dominated by clear vowels and single
consonants which gives the *stil novo* its 'dolcezza'. Dante's
quintessential *stil novo* sonnet, *Tanto gentile e tanto onesta pare*
(*VN* 26) voices a whole aesthetic in its rhymes: pare: saluta: muta:
guardare: laudare: vestuta: venuta: mostrare: mira: core: prova:
amore: sospira.

Such a rhyme-sequence is not characteristic of Petrarch. He
avoids strings of infinitive rhymes (which are triflingly easy in
Italian), and, when he uses rhymes of the type vowel + consonant
+ vowel, he normally mixes them with others that are more
consonantal. Almost all the words listed on page 183 appear in
rhyme as well as outside it. Many of them are words which
Dantesque precept and practice (in his earlier poetry) would
exclude, especially those which contain two liquid consonants or a
liquid and a plosive.

As with consonants, so with vowels. Petrarch has a much
greater propensity than the *stil novo* for vowels in combination.
It is symptomatic that he should choose to focus so much on
'Laura', or 'l'aura', and 'lauro', with their unusual blending of
liquid consonants and a diphthong which was itself only present
in Tuscan in words imported from Latin or Provençal (see

Chapter 5.4). Synaloephe (the running together of contiguous vowels of contiguous words) and synhaeresis (the running together of contiguous vowels within the same word), which were discussed in the previous section in connection with metre and rhythm, are the two most important ways in which vowels are combined in richly resonant patterns. But Petrarch also makes the most of the diphthongised forms of words that were characteristic of Florentine (e.g. 'suono' as in 1. 1), as well as of the non-diphthongised forms (e.g. 'core' as in 1. 2), which had been traditionally identified as poetically superior, no doubt because they were less local and closer to Latin and to Provençal. In, for example, a line such as the following:

> da sí lieti pensieri a pianger volta
> (305. 4)

(from such joyful thoughts turned to weeping)

It would have been possible to write 'leti penseri', with a similar vocalic repetition between the two words. The humbler, less Latinate forms enrich the sound and integrate the phrase more fully into the sound-texture of the line as a whole, since the repetition of /ie/ is closely followed by a similar, though unaccented, repetition of /ia/ (pensieri a pianger). Conversely in a nearby poem it is the undiphthongised form of the same word which appears.

> Levommi il mio penser in parte ov' era
> quella ch'io cerco, et non ritrovo in terra:
> ivi, fra lor che 'l terzo cerchio serra,
> la rividi piú bella et meno altera.
> (302. 1–4)

(My thought raised me to the place where was / she whom I seek and do not find on earth: / there, amongst those whom the third circle [i.e. the heaven of Venus] encloses, / I saw her again, [now] more beautiful and less haughty.)

The reason for the alternation (which is frequent) was perhaps in part the constant impulse to vary almost as something pleasurable in itself. But it is clear that throughout this opening quatrain, and to some degree in the second quatrain, too, there is a remarkable concentration of /er/ repetitions. The first instance is 'penser', which is marked through being quite heavily accented at the break-point in the line. It sets a note which will be repeated and varied until, at the moment when in line 4 we should expect it to recur again, in its place there is 'bella', apparently isolated but unexpectedly in rhyme with 'quella' of two lines previously. The effect is to give prominence to this semantically crucial word.

It is evident that, as we would expect, the sound-quality of Petrarch's poetry depends at least as much on combination as on selection. The absolute values which Dante wished to ascribe to words in the *DVE* and which are reflected in his actual poetry have been displaced. Words are not harsh in themselves, as Petrarch made particularly plain in his rewriting of the *petroso* style (see Chapter 5.3). Nor for that matter are they sweet. And rather than directing his verse towards either extreme, he creates a new *dolcezza* which absorbs both the old sweetness and the old harshness. The texture of the verse has been made darker and denser, its clarity complicated, its music more resonant. Poetic transcendentalism, which Cavalcanti and Dante were in love with in different ways, is questioned in the music of the *RVF*, as it is in its thematics. At the same time, just as there is no reduction to sensuality, so musicality is never abandoned, even when sounds as unacceptable to the *stil novo* Dante as the double *z* appear in rhyme, as in the very word for 'sweetness':

> Cantai, or piango, et non men di dolcezza
> del pianger prendo che del canto presi,
> (229. 1–2)

(I sang, now I weep, and no less sweetness / do I take from weeping than I took from song.)

The emphasis on combination means that Petrarch's poetry has a high density of assonance (repetition of vowel sequences) and alliteration (repetition of single consonants or consonant groups), the two being often brought together or carried across lines, sometimes (as in the first poem or in the lines from 302 quoted above) through an entire octet. Since the patterns are so dense and varied, the verse may register as strongly assonantal or alliterative only relatively infrequently (as in 1. 11: 'di me medesmo meco mi vergogno'). Such moments occur particularly towards the ends of poems. The following concluding tercet is one of the most brilliant musical combinations in the *RVF* and, partly because of its meaning, one of the most disturbing:

> Ben vedi omai sí come a morte corre
> ogni cosa creata, et quanto all'alma
> bisogna ir lieve al periglioso varco.
> (91. 12–14)

(You see well now how every created thing runs towards death / and as for the soul, / we must go unencumbered to the perilous passage.)

The alliteration of /c/ in the first two lines is woven with assonances of 'omai'/'come', 'morte'/'corre'; 'ogni' is echoed in 'bisogna', and 'all'alma' in 'al' of the final line, which, if it picks up these and other sounds, also shifts into a more 'liquid' tone, with the bringing together of /gn/, /r/, /l/, /gli/ with /i/, the vowel with which they are most closely related in their articulation as phonemes. The result is a musical *tour de force*, comparable, in its aestheticisation of a matter of tremendous import, with the concluding line of the first sonnet.

In exceptional lines the sound-patterns may be directly related to meaning, as in the strongly alliterative 1. 11 quoted immediately above. More commonly the repetition and variation of sound work to bind words together in a physical unity, as in almost all the examples I have examined. But it is relatively rare to be able to find balanced, regular structures. When they do occur they can be of remarkable complexity. One well-known case is the conclusion of *I' vo pensando* (264), already discussed in Chapter 4.3 from the point of view of its being an adaptation of an equally famous dictum of Ovid:

> A   B   B   A
> et veggio / 'l meglio, // et al peggior / m'appiglio.

(And I see the better and adhere to the worse)

The chiasmus (AB:BA structure) was already in Ovid:

A   B   B   A
video / meliora proboque, // deteriora / sequor

(I see the better [alternative] and approve, I follow the worse.)

Petrarch has regularised Ovid. He has eliminated the unbalancing (and semantically superfluous) 'proboque', and bound the line together by alliteration and assonance. He has also integrated the sound repetition with the chiasmus. In sound terms 'véggio' is in assonance with 'peggiór' (with which it does not quite rhyme because of the difference in stress), and 'méglio' finds what is half assonance and half alliteration in 'm'appiglio'. So an AB:AB structure is also created:

A   B   A   B
et veggio / 'l meglio, // et al peggior / m'appiglio.

At the same time the two halves of the line are each bonded internally, the first by /e. . . o/ assonance, the second by some degree of assonance and, more pronouncedly, by the alliteration of /p/. Though there are features here which, as is characteristic, fall outside any patterning, the effect is one of remarkable formal unity. Again there is a comparison to be made with the opening poem: here too, at the end of this second introductory poem, there is a line that may be making a negative statement but which, through its sheer virtuosity, also gives pleasure.

The sound-patterns are always intricate, but, as I remarked above, they are rarely so balanced. Even in the line I have just examined, some (perhaps minimal) element of irregularity makes itself felt which prevents a full rationalisation of the pattern and yet which is necessary to Petrarch's particular music. In most lines the irregularities are stronger, introducing differences and implausibilities within a relatively constant register of sound, playing alternatively with and against meaning, with and against the poetic form which they also help to define.

6.4 Words and images

Multiplicity of lexical form is characteristic of Italian. Nouns, verbs, adjectives undergo changes depending on their grammatical function and, to a degree, on their phonetic context. On the whole the commoner the word, the more it varies: so 'bello' (beautiful) appears in eight different guises – 'bello', 'bel', 'begli', 'bei' (reduced often in old Italian to 'be''), 'belli', 'bella', 'belle', 'bell''. In old Italian the rules governing the choice of a particular form were less rigid than they are in the standard modern language. In principle it was possible, at least to a degree, for a poet to select the form which he preferred according to whim or the needs, usually musical needs, of a particular poem. There were also far more multiple forms in the old poetic language than there are now. Poetry of the thirteenth century seems to have delighted in the diversity available to it and to have made it one of its major features. The possibilities offered by 'bello' were much as they are in the modern language. However, the noun 'beauty' was also variable. As well as the now standard 'bellezza', there were 'beltà', 'beltade', 'beltate', plus diphthongised forms of all three ('bieltà', etc.). There were even forms such as 'bellore', 'bellenza', 'bellanza'. The suffixes '-ore', '-enza', '-anza' (and also '-imento') either derived from Provençal poetry or flourished under its influence. They were attached, indiscriminately as it now seems, to adjectives and in certain cases to nouns and verbs to create a plethora of abstract nouns, which commonly figured in rhyme position, such as 'plazimento' (pleasure), 'nutricamento' (nourishment), rhymed by Giacomo da Lentini in *Amor è un[o] desio che ven da core* (*Poeti* 1, 90), or 'usanza' (habit), 'fallanza' (error), 'leanza' (loyalty), rhymed by Guittone d'Arezzo in *Ora parrà s'eo saverò cantare* (*Poeti* 1, 216). Such rhymes were ubiquitous, but they are only the most salient feature of a poetic language which also had a superabundance of alternative verb-forms, and a wealth of terms that seriously overlapped each other in meaning.

The *stil novo* winnowed down the duplicates. It expunged many of the abstract nouns, rejecting on the whole the kind of easy but cumbersome rhyming which they encouraged and finding its own new poetry primarily in combinations of a small number of key terms: apparently simple but semantically rich nouns, such as 'amore', 'donna', 'vertù', 'salute', 'onore', 'spirito', 'umiltà', 'mente', 'occhi', 'cuore'; a small number of rather abstract adjectives, such as 'umile', 'bello', 'gentile' (noble); and some common verbs, such as 'vedere', 'passare', 'parere' (appear), 'gridare' (cry out), 'piovere' (rain). Cavalcanti, in particular, developed the metaphorical effects that could be had from linking such verbs with nouns of the kind I have just listed. But the self-imposed restrictions were severe, the risk, as Cavalcanti himself seems to have recognised, a certain kind of mannerism (see *Poeti* 2, 530). In his later lyric poetry Dante considerably extended the lexical range that he was willing to use. In the *Commedia* his lexicon expanded beyond any bounds which he had previously explored. Popular language, previously excluded from serious poetry, Latin literature, both medieval and classical, dialects other than Tuscan, all furnished Dante with words, and, when there were no precedents, Dante neologised in his determination to say everything, including what was unsayable.

In many ways Petrarch's lexicon seems to look back past the *Commedia* to the *stil novo* and Dante's lyrics. He retains only a very few Provençalising abstractions, most prominently 'speranza' ('hope', appearing alongside the native 'spene' and 'speme'), and also a few others for more occasional use, such as 'dolzore' ('sweetness', which at 191. 13 replaces the much more frequent 'dolcezza'), and 'usanza' ('habit', replacing the normal 'uso' at 258. 10). Generally he limits Provençalisms to those forms or usages which were firmly established in previous poetry, such as 'augello' ('bird', used inevitably in place of Italian 'uccello'), or 'soglio' in the sense of 'I was accustomed' (instead of the expected present significance). Obviously he does not dispense with multiple forms, but he rarely privileges them as rhyme-forms (as he does do exceptionally with 'coraggio' (heart) at 204. 1 and 'ave' (has) at 29. 58 and 105. 54). For the most part those he retain are the common ones, such as 'beltà', 'beltate', 'beltade' alongside 'bellezza', or, among verb forms, 'fia' ('will be', as well as 'sarà'), 'fora' ('would be', as well as 'sarebbe'). In one respect there is a difference with respect to high poetry of the preceding century. The *stilnovisti*, like their predecessors, had, it seems, preferred to use forms of common words which were closer to the more prestigious Sicilian, Provençal and Latin, as opposed to more local Florentine or Tuscan forms. Petrarch admits both or either: he inevitably has 'core' (heart), 'foco' (fire), 'gioco' (play) and usually 'pò' (can), all of which have the simple vowel rather than the Florentine diphthong, but he also has Florentine 'suoi' (his), 'io' (I), and almost always 'mio' (my) and 'suono' (sound). In some of his common words both possible forms appear equally frequently, such as 'pensero' and 'pensiero' (thought), 'inseme' and 'insieme' (together), 'rimanere' and 'remanere' (remain). But his choice is never indiscriminate. Petrarch finely calculates the appropriateness of a form, not in the light of its different associations, which appear to be non-existent, but in view of its place within the musical structure of his verse, as was discussed in connection with 'pensero' and 'pensiero' in the previous section of this chapter. (See also the discussion of the reworkings of 268 in Chapter 2.3.)

Whilst refining on *stil novo* attentiveness to sound-qualities, Petrarch expands the lexicon of their poetry. He increases the number of more concrete items: witness those relating to Laura's person and to the natural world discussed in Chapter 5.3 or the examples cited *à propos* of his favoured sound-combinations in the previous section of this chapter. Many of these words are taken from Dante's lyrics, especially the *rime petrose*, though some come from the *Commedia*. There are also a considerable number of Latinisms, both new and established, the most striking of which are used for fairly precious rhymes, such as the sequence 'palustre' (marshy): 'ilustre' (illustrious): 'trilustre' ('lasting fifteen years') in 145, or 'Ethïopia': 'inopia' (shortage) in 24, or 'bibo' ('I drink', for normal 'bevo'): 'describo' ('I describe', for 'descrivo'): 'delibo' ('I taste, enjoy') in 193; although others which are generally less flamboyant appear relatively frequently within the line, such as 'refrigerio' (refreshment), 'inexorabile' (inexorable), 'importuna' (importunate), 'insania' (madness), 'corporeo' (corporeal), 'divelli' (uproot). Generally his lexicon does not flaunt humanist culture, of which the major sign in this respect is a negative one: the abandonment of the scholastic terminology which had figured so prominently in all intellectually ambitious poetry in Italian from Guinizzelli to Dante. Many of his none too numerous neologisms have the air of Italian formations rather than of conversions from Latin, as, for instance, in a significant series of metaphors for release from love or life: 'smorsa' ('release the bit': 152.5 and 195. 2), 'mi spetro' ('I free myself from stone': 89. 13, 105. 19), 'si scapestra' ('frees from the halter': 86.8) and others. And once at least, in spite of his hostility to French poetry (see Chapter 4.4), he is willing to assimilate, again for reasons of sound, a French verb, 'retentir' ('to make resound'), which he applies to bird-song (291. 2).

In fact his lexicon is not closed. If we count multiple forms such as 'beltà', 'beltade', 'beltate' as one word (though 'bellezza' as another), then, according to the concordance to the *RVF* published by the Accademia della Crusca in 1971, there are 3,275 words ('lemmi') in the vocabulary of the collection. Of these, 1,199 appear only once. The great majority of the Latinisms and neologisms cited in the preceding paragraph, for example, appear no more than once or twice. In one sense, therefore, the collection is in continuous progression, as it constantly assimilates and discards new lexical material. But its drive is towards a taking in, not a reaching out. The words which appear only once or twice rarely stand out, even in rhyme position, since they are always deeply embedded in sound-structures and rhythms which tend to treat the unusual word as one element amongst many others. They are also countered by other words which recur. The Crusca concordance gives 1,593 words as occurring three times or more. Some of these are remarkably frequent. 'Occhio/i' (eye(s)) appears 263 times, 'bello', in one form or another, 342 times, 'dolce/i' (sweet) 251 times, 'sole' (sun) 133 times. Whatever the incidence of novelty, there is an outstanding degree of repetition. New combinations, rather than new items, are the outstanding feature of Petrarch's lexicon, as of so much else in his work.

It is a lexicon which is disposed to avoid precise reference. The *RVF* belongs much more in the human world than the *stil novo* had done, but sound possibilities and the associations of words, often the literary associations, count much more than poetic or conceptual definition of anything that could be imagined as existing outside the poetry, whether in the world of historical experience or in some other, apparently objective realm. Other worlds are neither denied nor forgotten, as the previous chapter tried to make plain, but it is in the world of words that Petrarch's centre lies. Evocations of Vaucluse and Laura are fragmentary listings of the appropriate nouns, qualified by imprecise adjectives: psychological unease shades into uncertain combinations of 'affanni' (wearying distress), 'fatiche' (labours), 'doglia' and 'dolore' (pain), 'desio' (desire), 'stanchezza' (weariness), in which generic and generalisable possibilities always remain. So too with imagery: though Petrarch has much to say about the experience of seeing, and images in plenty which could be said to be visual, exact images which, perhaps through simile or metaphor, cast things in a new, revelatory light are largely absent. Birds are birds, with at best a nightingale or a sparrow, though, when specified, the birds are more often the phoenix and eagle of the bestiaries, the dove of the Bible; animals are just beasts, with an occasional emblematic lion, bear or tiger; trees, when they are not just trees, woods or forests, are beeches, elms, myrtles, palms, oaks, any of which, like the laurel to which they are commonly compared, also readily turn into literary emblems; flowers are roses, violets, lilies, narcissi; mountains, paths, roads, fields, hills, cities are little more than that. The fire, ice, snow, winds, mists, rain, seas, the rivers (even when named), the streams, flowers, precious stones, jewels, springs and winters, which together furnish the elements for figurative language as well as for the apparently literal evocation of a person and a landscape, all recur in constantly indeterminate realisations.

And so too the epithets. The favoured ones are melodious, but notoriously difficult to pin down. The most constant epithet for Laura and any part of her is 'bello' (beautiful), a quite unemphatic word in Italian which none the less returns in almost every poem as a marker less of her objective beauty than of her power to please and to excite. Then there are also other adjectives whose connotations overlap with those of 'bello': 'soave', used of words, sounds, breezes, suggesting something flowing and soothing; 'leggiadro', used of women, clothing, parts of the body, language, suggesting delicate refinement, perhaps insubstantiality, 'vago', still retaining some of its etymological associations with wandering or erring, but suggesting also a beauty which is unstable, hence almost vague; and lastly 'dolce', suggesting softness and sweetness of sound, gentleness of colour and shape. When other adjectives appear with meanings which would have been objective, if not well-defined, for Dante and most of the poets of the previous generation, such as 'celeste' (heavenly), 'divino' (divine), 'angelico' (angelic), they indicate at most a perhaps momentary apprehension of a possibility and hover on the edge of turning into the conventional compliments which they will in time become (see, for example, 220 discussed in Chapter 5.5). Generally, adjectives indicating subjectively apprehended qualities, such as 'vivo' (alive), 'tranquillo' (peaceful), 'triste' (sad), 'accorto' (shrewd), 'casto' (chaste), 'onesto' (honourable), outweigh visual adjectives such as those indicating colour – 'verde' (green), 'aureo' (golden), 'biondo' (blonde), 'bianco' and, more rarely, 'candido' (white), 'nero' (black), all of which, when they do appear, appear in unqualified form. Shades of colour, like shapes of objects, are unknown to Petrarch.

Indeterminacy is part of a general tendency to accentuate the distance between poetry and any reality to which the poems might point. In place of direct naming, Petrarch prefers to use language in slightly unusual, literary ways (catachresis) or to indicate a part for the whole (synecdoche), as occurs especially in evocations of Laura. Above all, unlike any previous Italian writer of lyric poetry, he is a poet whose language is constantly more figurative than literal. Once again it is the repetitions, not the innovations, which are striking. Along with other, similar metaphors, 'foco' (fire), 'fiamma' (flame), 'gelo' (freezing) and 'ghiaccio' (ice) are used more densely and more elliptically by him than by any of his predecessors to indicate the passion and the paralysis of love, just as Laura (or her eyes) can be variously evoked as 'sole' (sun), 'stella' (star), 'dea' (goddess), 'dolce nemica' (sweet enemy), 'fera' (wild animal), 'fonte' (spring), 'tesoro' (treasure), 'angioletta' (young angel), 'fenice' (phoenix) and so on, whilst various parts of her face and body can turn into 'perle' (pearls), 'rose' (roses), 'neve' (snow), and, above all, her hair can be turned to gold. These are only the most notable instances of a metaphorical disposition which constantly returns to familiar, not novel transferences and which chooses even to absorb its own inventions (such as the metaphors of release mentioned above) into the texture of the verse, in such a way as to diminish any innovative force they may have.

It is a mistake to see such metaphors simply as a kind of coding or shorthand. They may have that function, but they are not restricted to it. They have a particularly rich part to play in the serious game of repetition and variation both within and across poems. Just as words generally change their reference from one context to another (see Chapter 3.4), so metaphorical terms become literal and vice versa, and take on varying degrees of metaphorical realisation, ranging from almost colourless ciphering to emblematic brilliance. Petrarch's concern is primarily with the processes of meaning as they occur within language or within poetry, though these internal changes are always conducted in the light of a reality which language may mask or which eludes language. At any given moment there is an awareness that metaphor, like poetry generally, may distance reality, but it cannot annul it.

The most conspicuous metaphoric (and metonymic) cluster is Laura – 'l'aura' – 'lauro' (see Chapter 5.4). But other terms are caught in similar nets. One such is 'sole' (sun), which is one of Petrarch's most frequently repeated words, and one which has particular importance in relation to Laura. Obviously it can be used literally – as a marker of time, a giver of warmth and light or as an element in a landscape, in any of which roles it will be more or less elaborated as an image depending on the context (for an extensive development of the theme of sunset see 50). But then, in more than forty instances, it is also an image of Laura, or her eyes, as well as becoming more occasionally an image of Apollo (60; 115) or God (214. 30; 306; 366. 2 and 44) or both (188). The very first introduction of the metaphor in poem 4 is as flat as possible:

> ed or di picciol borgo un sol n'à dato,
> tal che natura e 'l luogo si ringratia
> onde sí bella donna al mondo nacque.
> (4. 12–14)

(And now from a small township he has given us a sun, / such that nature and the place give thanks, / since from them so beautiful a *donna* was born into the world.)

The poem moves from metaphor to literal statement. Its expectation is that the simple literal 'bella donna' of the last line will emerge as both sound and image to override the metaphor. It is as if a verbal cloak has been removed to reveal what it concealed, although as always the revelation may be illusory. Poetically, the metaphor functions because of its inertness, not in spite of it. (See also Chapter 5.5 on this poem.)

There is a much more complex metaphorical action in 219, and in the opposite direction. Here the literal is eliminated in an effacement of reality by language:

Il cantar novo e 'l pianger delli augelli
in sul dí fanno retentir le valli,
e 'l mormorar de' liquidi cristalli
giú per lucidi, freschi rivi et snelli.

Quella ch'à neve il volto, oro i capelli,
nel cui amor non fur mai inganni né falli,
destami al suon delli amorosi balli,
pettinando al suo vecchio i bianchi velli.

Cosí mi sveglio a salutar l'aurora,
e 'l sol ch'è seco, et piú l'altro ond' io fui
ne' primi anni abagliato, et son anchora.

I' gli ò veduti alcun giorno ambedui
levarsi inseme, e 'n un punto e 'n un'hora
quel far le stelle, et questo sparir lui.

(The new singing and the weeping of the birds / towards
daybreak make the valleys resound, / and the murmuring of
liquid crystals / down clear, fresh, swift-flowing streams. / She
whose face is snow, whose hair gold, / in whose love were never
deceits or failings, / wakes me to the sounds of amorous dances,
/ combing the white locks of her old [husband]. / Thus I awaken
to greet the dawn, / and the sun that is with her, and, more, the
other [sun] by which I was / dazzled in my youthful years, and
am still. / Some days I have seen both / arise together, and in
one single moment / that [sun] cause the stars to disappear, and
this one [Laura] do the same to him.)

The sonnet gives its metaphors prominence from the very
beginning, in its presentation of birdsong as weeping and of
running water as liquid crystals, and it goes on to heighten them.
In the second quatrain a personification, Aurora, the dawn, is
herself described in metaphorical terms, her face (the sky towards
sunrise?) becoming snow, her hair (lines of cloud?) becoming gold,
only for reference to the real world to fade through the amorous
dances (birds in the trees?) into the almost entirely literary image
of Tithonus, whose white locks (bars of clouds?) are mingled –
absurdly from the point of view of representation – amongst the
gold of Aurora's hair. Reference to the real world is slipping away
in an evocation of colour, music and myth. The opening of the

sestet turns to the literal in a way that explains the sense of the preceding quatrain, but this lowering of the tone is only the prelude to raising it again. The sun in the sky and the sun which is Laura come together in a poetically powerful synthesis. The real and the metaphorical sunrise are as rapid in the poem as they are said to be in Petrarch's eyes, the pronouns compelling the reader to perform the substitutions and to set them in relation to each other. It is this swift reordering of meanings which triumphs. Laura (or the poem) effaces everything outside. And then the poem ends. The illusion is over.

But suns can be quite differently related. Here is the opening of a sonnet for the dead Laura:

> Quel sol che mi mostrava il camin destro
> di gire al ciel con glorïosi passi,
> tornando al sommo Sole, in pochi sassi
> chiuse 'l mio lume e 'l suo carcer terrestro.
> (306.1–4)

(That sun which showed me the right road / to go to heaven with glorious steps, / returning to the highest Sun, closed within a few stones, / my light and her own earthly prison.)

Laura is a sun who illuminated the path to heaven, and has now been assumed into the divine light that was her source. The light which she cast has been enclosed in the grave as has the body in which she was confined during her life. In part the metaphors appear here because there are no other terms readily available: what other language is there for talking about such things within the context of a Christian civilisation than one that evokes divine light or the path to heaven? As always Petrarch accepts and adapts traditional motifs. But they also retain something of their power as images, even if it has been severely qualified. One image of a sun is set against another, which absorbs it; but this opening into something larger, reflected in the relatively grandiose outward movement and expansive syntax of the first two lines, is countered by a succession of ideas of closure: the body, which gave Petrarch light, was itself an earthly prison, and is now enclosed in the grave – the grave being designated not by its expected term but by what might be described either as a periphrasis or as an unexpectedly exact almost brutal designation of reality. With clarity and compression these four lines evoke a complex progression of thought and feeling, in which the largely pre-established associations of the images are made to enclose each other. An illusion of depth is created, though again within the language of poetry, not as an image of external reality.

In both the poems I have just examined, the emblematic quality of the image of the sun is evident. In my final example of a 'sun' poem, the image-content of 'sole' is itself almost, though not quite, effaced. Poem 135, a canzone which largely reworks traditional bestiary imagery, opens with a general prelude followed by a comparison to the phoenix;

> Qual piú diversa et nova
> cosa fu mai in qual che stranio clima,
> quella, se ben s'estima.
> piú mi rasembra: a tal son giunto, Amore.
> Là onde il dí vèn fore,
> vola un augel che sol senza consorte
> di volontaria morte
> rinasce, et tutto a viver si rinova.
> Cosí sol si ritrova
> lo mio voler, et cosí in su la cima
> de' suoi alti pensieri al sol si volve,
> et cosí si risolve,
> et cosí torna al suo stato di prima:
> arde, et more, et riprende i nervi suoi,
> et vive poi   con la fenice a prova.
>
> (1–15)

(The most diverse and strange / thing that ever was in some exotic clime / – that, if one assesses it well, / most resembles me: to such a point have I come, Love. / There from where the day comes forth, / flies a bird, which, alone without mate, / from its willed-for death / is reborn, and completely renewed for life. / So my will finds itself alone, / and so at the highest point / of its lofty thoughts it turns to the sun, / and so it is annihilated, / and so it returns to its previous state. / It burns and dies, and recovers its strength, / and lives then in competition with the phoenix.)

The fabulous bird which dies and is born again from its own ashes becomes a symbol of uncontrollable recurrence. This is, in effect, the subject of the stanza, iterated in the verbs of repetition and in the succession of 'così', but diffused in other ways at various levels. One of the elements which recur is 'sol', which first appears as 'sol' (alone) (lines 6 and 9), and then as 'sol' (sun) in line 11, before becoming no more than part of a verb, 'risolve' (line 12). The syllable 'sol' rhymes and is interwoven with 'vol', which is similarly repeated in a series of senses, or half-senses, in lines 6, 7, 10, 11. But both 'sol' and 'vol' are only two threads in a web of repetition which winds into itself almost everything in the stanza: its two main structural features are the unusual reappearance of rhymes from the first part of the stanza in the second (see Section 5 below) and the merging of the tenor and vehicle of the simile in the subsequent string of metaphors. Only the identification of the bird in the last line brings a pause, though it is one that will be broken in the continuation of recurrence in the following stanzas with other traditional images, and, particularly in the fourth stanza, with a return to the image of the sun that has appeared here.

Such linguistic play hovers between meaninglessness and the representation of poetic and psychological processes of the most serious kind. On the whole it is more evident in Part 1. Part 2, as a poetry of death and the dead, reduces vitality and variety in style as in much else. Some readers have felt that the poems consequently become less mannered and hence more genuine. But there is reduction, not elimination – see, for example, the shifting senses of 'nido' (nest) between 318, 320 and 321, or the triple 'sol' in 306, or the continuation of the 'l'aura' and 'lauro' variations in many poems. The words continue to repeat themselves, and, for as long as they do, fresh combinations continue to appear, if now cast in a more sombre light.

6.5 Syntax

With rare exceptions Petrarch's syntax is characteristically lucid. Though it may be hard to define meanings precisely, internal relations between the parts of a sentence are clearly marked. Assuming we know the rules, subject, verb, object, main and subordinate clauses all emerge with perfect clarity. This lucidity, and the fact that it can be described in the kind of terms which I have just used, is a distinguishing feature of Petrarch's poetry, and one that bears the imprint of a humanist approach to sentence organisation. For at this basic level, irrespective of any specific arrangements which derive from Latin, Petrarch has given syntactical relations the clarity and subtle regularity which all humanists admired in the Latin writers whom they took as their models. This is not true to the same degree of earlier Italian poetry, which, for all its sophisticated attention to rhetoric, often by Latin canons had a syntactic roughness and uncertainty to it. For example, the particle 'che' had often been used, as it still is in many dialects, as a fairly loose connective indicating subordination of the following clause in an imprecise way. Continuing a process already well developed in Dante, Petrarch makes clear the relations that later prescriptive grammar will consider normal and normative: 'che' is a relative pronoun, a conjunction introducing indirect speech, or (later to be usually printed with an accent) a subordinating conjunction meaning 'since'. Functions that were previously indistinct have been distinguished in the same way as similar functions are distinguished in Latin. The writing has become 'grammatical' in the sense that it accords with the relations prescribed for and by Latin grammar.

That such a clarification should have taken place does not mean that sentence structures are habitually those which seem 'natural' in Italian, as in Romance languages generally. Partly under the influence of Latin, initially medieval rather than classical, Italian poetry had always made some use of inversions of the normal subject–verb–object order. Again under the influence of Latin, it had also favoured a certain degree of subordination, especially in poetry aiming at a high style, though co-ordination was also widely used. Part of the pleasure of poetry, part of the skill of the writer, was in the appropriate manipulation of language 'artificially', that is, with an art of which the rudiments were learnt at school and which was quite 'natural' in contemporary culture. In a broad sense Petrarch's syntax simply grows out of the tradition, heightening already established tendencies towards varied word-order and subordination of clauses in fairly complex sentences. The novelty is partly in his characteristic clarity, partly in a new ductility, whereby the modulations of the syntax seem to adhere to the often complex progression of thought and to the formal

demands of a particular poem more closely than the relatively
rigid impositions of stylistic rules had allowed in the past, and
partly in a constant tendency towards a highly flexible middle
style, which appropriates to itself many of the elements of the
traditional high style whilst avoiding its formality.

Two opposed examples from the not too distant extremes of
Petrarch's rhetoric will make this clearer. In the political canzoni
(for which see Chapter 5.4) Petrarch tries to speak with an
Apollonian, vatic voice, although even there his characteristic
mode of writing continually asserts itself. The opening of 28 is one
of the few places in which a high style is evident:

> O aspectata in ciel beata et bella
> anima che di nostra humanitade
> vestita vai, non come l'altre carca:
> perché ti sian men dure omai le strade,
> a Dio dilecta, obedïente ancella,
> onde al suo regno di qua giú si varca,
> ecco novellamente a la tua barca,
> ch'al cieco mondo à già volte le spalle
> per gir al miglior porto,
> d'un vento occidental dolce conforto;
> lo qual per mezzo questa oscura valle,
> ove piangiamo il nostro et l'altrui torto,
> la condurrà de' lacci antichi sciolta,
> per dritissimo calle,
> al verace oriente ov'ella è volta.
>
> (28. 1–15)

(O soul awaited in heaven to be blest and beautiful / who go
clothed in our human form, / not burdened by it like others, /
that the roads may now be less hard for you, / (obedient
maidservant beloved of God) / whereby one passes from earth
below into his kingdom, / see now before your boat, / which has
already turned its back on the blind world / to sail to the best
harbour, / the sweet comfort of a wind from the west, / which,
through the midst of this dark valley, / where we bewail our
own wrongdoing and that of man [i.e. Adam], / will guide it,
free from the snares of old, / along the straightest path / to the
true east where it is bound.)

In part the tone is raised by the elaborate flow of traditional
metaphors, which are drawn together in one long sentence, with
its main clause pushed well forward into the stanza (line 13), and
prefaced and succeeded by complex subordinations. From the very
beginning words are set in unusual relations: the participle
('aspectata') appears well before its noun ('anima') and the
interposed adjectives 'beata et bella' have a compressed (proleptic)
sense ('to be blessed and beautiful'). The rest of the stanza
continues in the same way, inverting the normal position of
adjectives and phrases, adding a further vocative address, inserting
one relative clause after another.

At the opposite extreme is a sonnet to Petrarch's friend
Sennuccio del Bene:

> Qui dove mezzo son, Sennuccio mio
> (cosí ci foss'io intero, et voi contento),
> venni fuggendo la tempesta e 'l vento
> ch'ànno súbito fatto il tempo rio.
>
> Qui son securo: et vo'vi dir perch'io
> non come soglio il folgorar pavento,
> et perché mitigato, nonché spento,
> né-micha trovo il mio ardente desio.
>
> Tosto che giunto a l'amorosa reggia
> vidi onde nacque l'aura dolce et pura
> ch'acqueta l'aere, et mette i tuoni in bando,
>
> Amor ne l'alma, ov'ella signoreggia,
> raccese 'l foco, et spense la paura:
> che farei dunque gli occhi suoi guardando?
>
> (113)

(Here where is half of me [i.e. half remains with his friend or
Laura], my Sennuccio, / (so were all of me here and you
contented!) / I came fleeing the storm and the wind / which
suddenly brought about ill weather. / Here I am safe: and I
want to tell you why I / do not fear the lightning as I used to do,
/ and why I do not find my burning desire at all diminished, / let
alone extinguished. / As soon as, on reaching the palace of love
[i.e. Laura's house], / I saw from where was born the sweet,

pure breeze, / which calms the air and banishes thunder, / in my soul where she [i.e. Laura] rules, Love / rekindled the fire and extinguished fear. / What would I do then if I were to look into her eyes?)

The tone is much lower than in 28, partly because the language is more literal or hovers uncertainly between the metaphorical and the literal. But there are also three sentences here, parts of which are almost independent syntactic units. There is subordination and inversion, but some of the phrasing has an unelaborate air. From a purely syntactic point of view, the first five lines need little adjustment for them to become standard modern Italian prose. By fourteenth-century and Renaissance standards they border on the colourless, though, of course, there is a justification: this is a poem to a friend, and in writing to friends a deliberately conversational style is in order.

Petrarch does use elsewhere than in the political canzoni fairly elaborate structures, but rarely with the concentration which they have in the opening to 28, Generally the canzoni, as the major form (see section 6 below), are syntactically more elaborate than the sonnets. Overall the sonnets, whilst making constant inversions, are more flowing, particularly in the quatrains. They make more of strings of clauses, and phrases, linked by 'and' or another repeated conjunction (as, for example, in 224, which consists of a succession of 'if' clauses, followed by a main clause in the final line), or by the repetition of a construction or key word (see, for example, 92, 192, 312, 351), although a much more complex rhetorical progression is always possible, as with the very first sonnet (for which see Chapter 5.1).

Whatever the specific syntactical arrangement, the unfolding of any poem demands the same kind of attention as that demanded by prose which is unfolding an argument, or by Latin poetry. There is an expectation that the reader will follow and enjoy the steps in the discourse, although the poem may well treat its argument playfully or draw the reader into making disconcerting imaginative leaps.

One of the most powerful canzoni is 129, the culmination of the group of canzoni in the middle of Part 1. It opens with a highly lyrical passage:

Di pensier in pensier, di monte in monte
mi guida Amor, ch'ogni segnato calle
provo contrario a la tranquilla vita.
Se 'n solitaria piaggia, rivo o fonte,
se 'nfra duo poggi siede ombrosa valle,
ivi s'acqueta l'alma sbigottita;
et come Amor l'envita,
or ride, or piange, or teme, or s'assecura;
e 'l volto che lei segue ov'ella il mena
si turba et rasserena,
et in un esser picciol tempo dura;
onde a la vista huom di tal vita experto
diria: Questo arde, et di suo stato è incerto.
                                    (129. 1–13)

(From thought to thought, from mount to mount / Love guides
me, for every marked path / I find contrary to tranquil life. / If
there is a stream or spring on a solitary hillside, / if there is a
shady valley between two hills, / there my bewildered soul finds
rest. / And, as Love invites it, / now it laughs, now cries, now is
afraid, now reassured. / And my features, which follow it [i.e.
my soul] where it leads them, / become disturbed and then
serene, / and remain in one condition for only a little time. /
Wherefore, at the sight, someone with experience of such a life /
would say, 'This man burns [with passion], and is uncertain of
his state.')

The first three lines demand that the reader understand the
guiding to be from thought to thought as well as from mountain
to mountain, and then apply to both elements in the first clause
the reasoning of the second; the progress from thought to thought
is also pathless. The next three lines forget the psychological
movement, and elucidate the tranquillity to be found in the
mountains. But rather than being allowed to contemplate the
scene, however briefly, the reader has still to continue actively
making connections: 'siede' (line 5) has been read back into line 4
as the verb of which 'rivo o fonte' is the subject. Now the poem
shifts to the psychological instability suggested in the opening
words, only to lead rapidly from the inner state to the outward
appearance. The soul follows the invitations of desire (line 7),

passing constantly from one emotion to another, and the outer expression follows the movement of the soul, at which point (line 9) the reader is caught in a similar pursuit of what it is that the pronouns are referring to, only to emerge into what is a reasonable, but actually quite unexpected conclusion: *hence* ('onde', line 12) an experienced observer (if there were one) would conclude that passion makes the speaker uncertain of his state of mind or state of being. We cannot but agree with this non-existent observer who voices our own thoughts. But how did we reach this conclusion?

Apparently there is a progression of thought in this stanza. Processes of reasoning, which are dependent on the syntax, are invoked ('if . . . , then . . .'; 'hence . . .'); substitutions and insertions are demanded in accordance with quite complex syntactic rules (cf. the conclusion of 219 discussed in section 4 above): but there are also analogical movements which require less secure leaps backwards and forwards, especially in the parallelisms between the physical and the mental. The remaining stanzas of this poem will reiterate this particular progression, with variations. If not always to this degree, many other poems, the first one of all being perhaps the most notable example, also build up a discourse in this way, bringing together imagination, argument, association in an unstable unity. Rhetorically they might be classed as enthymemes, were it not that they do not try to persuade the reader of a particular truth or case. Whether they are cast as monologues or formally addressed to some other person, they draw the reader into themselves because, in part thanks to their rhetorical skill, they seem pleasurable, beautiful or revealing.

Driving to a conclusion which is then succinctly and strikingly formulated is in itself a particular form of literary pleasure, and Petrarch writes many poems (again *RVF* 1 being canonical) which culminate in such *sententiae*. But the journey to the conclusion is never solely for that purpose. It has also to provide pleasures of its own. Sentence patterning is one source of pleasure that is open to infinite variation within the general lines I have so far discussed. It is possible, for instance, to make a canzone entirely of gnomic *sententiae* (105), in which there is no flow at all, or to create an abrupt, and unusually expressive, contrast by setting an accumulative listing of a kind which Petrarch is particularly fond of in descriptions of Laura and the landscape (see Chapter 5.3) against a similar listing in which the connectives have been omitted:

> Or che 'l ciel et la terra e 'l vento tace
> et le fere e gli augelli il sonno affrena,
> Notte il carro stellato in giro mena
> et nel suo letto il mar senz'onda giace,
>
> vegghio, penso, ardo, piango;
>   (164. 1–5)

(Now that heaven and earth and wind are still / and sleep restrains beasts and birds / and Night guides the starry chariot in its round / and the sea lies waveless in its bed, / I watch, brood, burn, weep; . . .)

These are exceptions: it is normal for Petrarch to prefer an apparently regular or even structure for his sentences as for his rhythms, and to complicate and diversify within evenness.

So far as sentence structure is concerned, the evenness is largely created by balancing one unit against another. Petrarch frequently repeats, in fairly close proximity, a word or a phrase, or, still more often, he repeats the grammatical or rhythmic structure of a word, phrase or clause, creating between the two units an air of equivalence. He sometimes follows the habit common in Romance poetry of juxtaposing words which are as close to synonymous as can be imagined. The 'passi tardi et lenti' ('slow and tardy steps': 35. 2) and the 'vecchierel canuto et biancho' (literally, 'the old man white-haired and white': 16. 1) are two frequently cited (though exceptional) cases where the second adjective reiterates the meaning of the first, the one adjective in each case being Latinate, the other more vernacular. Commonly there are differences of meaning, even strong ones. For Petrarch regularly sets against each other units which are semantically divergent or opposed. In part antitheses express conflict, but, as ancient rhetoric recognised, there is also a pleasure in semantic opposition, if a formal parity is established through and against it. Antithesis is an adornment, not just an expression of discord. 'If we embellish our speech with this figure,' says the *Ad Herennium* (4. 15. 21), speaking for most ancient and Renaissance rhetorical thinking, 'we shall be able to be both impressive and distinguished (et graves et ornati)'. One reason why antithesis should convey dignity is that, like any other form of balance, the very fact of counterposing one unit to another shows the movement of the verse down rhythmically, and, because it always refers backwards, it focuses attention on the immediate environment rather than on an eventual point of arrival. It is also patently artificial: because we have to read one unit against another, we are constantly aware that the words have been *set* against each other. To the horror of every romantic, antitheses are made, not born.

In Petrarch balance, whether it takes the form of antithesis or not, is evident and insistent. The patterns are themselves characteristically complex, and, almost inevitably, include some element of divergence or imbalance, either in the form of words themselves or in their meanings. As in other ways, there is a disturbance of regularity which seems to be part of the questionable pleasure of poetry itself.

In a poem such as 113, which I quoted earlier in this section, balance is one of the means by which the prosaic tendencies of the syntax are corrected and the language made to call attention to itself. Five lines out of fourteen contain noteworthy balanced units (lines 2, 3, 10, 11, 13). All work to establish a harmonious order in the poem. At the same time variation, even conflict, is at work, primarily, though not exclusively, in the semantic relations between the balanced units. Line 2 ('cosí ci foss'io intero, et voi contento') creates an antithesis between 'io' and 'voi', as if they are contrasted, which in turn creates the expectation of a contrast between 'intero' and 'contento'. But there is no opposition: the second part of the line is a logical and temporal consequence of the first, not in parallel or in opposition with it. In line 11 ('ch'acqueta l'aere, et mette i tuoni in bando') there is a different relationship: the two parts seem to be contrasted, the one emphasising peace, the other thunder, but they mean almost the same thing; if they are distinct, they should logically be reversed. Then in line 13 rather more elements in the two parts are set in balance; each part consists of verb, article, noun, the two verbs being plainly antithetical. But again precise parity is avoided: 'foco' and 'paura' are not opposites in the way the two verbs are, even if Aristotelian physiology associated fear with coldness (cf. *RVF* 264. 127–8). Only the minor equivalences of lines 3 and 10 are almost free of this kind of disturbance.

In the opening lines of 164, also quoted a little earlier, an atmosphere of night calm is evoked. The first two lines accumulate a number of similar units connected by 'and', the repetition seeming (somehow) to contribute to the suggestions of tranquillity emerging in other ways from the verse. But an attentive reading will reveal that all is not as calm as it might be: each of the phrases is slightly varied and the cumulative effect is of a not quite regular undulation. There is then a shift in the following pair of lines, which are rhythmically complementary to each other as they are in their overall syntactic structure, even though they have very few syntactic or lexical features in common. Conversely the four emphatic verbs of line 5 ('vegghio, penso, ardo, piango'), which together give an impression of psychological conflict or obsession, are rhythmically and syntactically identical, just as their associations in meaning are made to overlap and to merge. In this line, for once, repetition is turned towards expressive violence.

The subtlety of the patterns created and the elements of disturbance incorporated into them distinguish Petrarch's poetry from that of most of his imitators. Even at his most Petrarchist, Petrarch avoids falling into mannerism, if only by a hair's breadth. There is always an element of darkness which suggests a lack of literary complacency at the very moment when his contrasts, repetitions and balances seem on the edge of a harmony in which all would – spuriously – be resolved.

Chaucer translated the following sonnet in his *Troilus and Criseyde* (1. 400–20), which, like some others from the same area of the *RVF*, is striking for its antithetical play:

> S'amor non è, che dunque è quel ch'io sento?
> Ma s'egli è amor, perdio, che cosa et quale?
> Se bona, onde l'effecto aspro mortale?
> Se ria, onde sí dolce ogni tormento?
>
> S'a mia voglia ardo, onde 'l pianto e lamento?
> S'a mal mio grado, il lamentar che vale?
> O viva morte, o dilectoso male,
> come puoi tanto in me, s'io nol consento?
>
> Et s'io 'l consento, a gran torto mi doglio.
> Fra sí contrari vènti in frale barca
> mi trovo in alto mar senza governo,

sí lieve di saver, d'error sí carca
ch'l' medesmo non so quel ch'io mi voglio,
e tremo a mezza state, ardendo il verno.

(132)

(If it is not love, what then is what I feel? / But if it is love, by
heaven what thing is it and of what kind? / If it is good, whence
comes its harsh, deadly effect? / If ill, wherefore is every torment
so sweet? / If I burn voluntarily, whence the tears and lament? /
If in spite of myself, what profit is there in lamenting? / O living
death, O delightful malady / how do you have so great power in
me, if I do not give my consent? / And if I consent, I am greatly
amiss to complain. / Amongst so contrary winds in a fragile
boat / I find myself on the high sea without tiller, / [my boat] so
light in wisdom, so laden with error / that I myself do not know
what I want, / and I tremble in midsummer, burning in winter.)

The sonnet is an elaborate but concise example of *complexio* or
dilemma in which one alternative is set against another with
which it is irreconcilable. An example given in the *Ad Herennium*
(2. 24. 38) is: 'You treat me, father, with undeserved wrong. For if
you think Cresphontes wicked, why did you give me to him for
wife? But if he is honourable, why do you force me to leave such a
one against his will and mine?' As usual when he incorporates
established rhetorical practices, Petrarch has directed against
himself what was traditionally directed to others, producing, in
the first part of the poem, a string of questions to which there are
different kinds of reply or in some cases no reply, as if these
questions were either equivalents or antithetically related. In fact
there is a free progression from what love is, to its effects, and
from there to the question of responsibility. There is also constant
formal variation, with inversions, displacements, imbalances,
notably in the last line, where the exact balance which could have
been created by writing 'et ardo il verno' ('and I burn in winter') is
avoided in preference for the more resonant and expressive
'ardendo'.

In a sense the poem is a game; but the game element is more in
evidence in the octet. There is a shift into a different register with
the repetition-cum-variation which connects lines 8 and 9. The
poem now says what it has said before, but more seriously, before

reaching a conclusion. This in turn marks another change through its different imagery (though 'ardo' has already appeared as a more muted metaphor in line 5): otherwise the conclusion (like some other conclusions) is a repetition and clarification of what the poem has reiterated throughout: that the state of desire is uncategorisable and unintelligible. The rhetoric of this lucid, beautifully organised poem works to an analogous end: what the poem is, is continually changing, moving from one category to another, from one set of images to another, denying that it can be included in any or that any can be denied. It is a game: it is a tragedy. Petrarch holds both in suspense.

6.6 Poetic forms

The small number of poetic forms that Petrarch uses – sonnet, canzone, ballata, madrigale and sestina – are distributed in a complex combination of order and disorder through the *RVF* (see Chapter 3). All are less fixed than might appear. Within regular forms there is always some degree of anomaly, and, on a much larger scale, there are reworkings of the relations of the parts within what may be established as a prevalent dynamic. With forms which are constitutionally varied, particularly the canzone, the differences are much larger.

The 317 sonnets, coming mostly in substantial sequences, provide a base of continuity and regularity that none of the other forms possess, except perhaps the sestina. But within their constant fourteen-line length much can happen, particularly with rhymes. The octet is the most stable part, though fourteen sonnets do not have the ABBA ABBA scheme (i) that had become normal with the *stil novo*. Of these, ten have the more old-fashioned ABAB ABAB scheme (ii) (56, 79, 134, 187, 280, 281, 307, 310, 311, 318), two a variant on this, which inverts the scheme of the second quatrain to give ABAB BABA (iii) (260, 279), and two the stranger variant ABAB BAAB (iv) (210, 295). In the sestet there is a more constant variation between three major alternatives, with four other possibilities admitted which also, coincidentally, I presume, add up to a total of fourteen, The table on the next page gives the figures first for three-rhyme and then for two-rhyme schemes.

The prevalent schemes, using the lower-case Roman figures given in brackets, are thus (i) in the octet with either (v), (vi) or (ix) in

Scheme	Part 1	Part 2	Total
CDE CDE (v)	82	37	119
CDE DCE (vi)	55	14	69
CDE EDC (vii)	1	0	1
CDE DEC (viii)	1	0	1
CDC DCD (ix)	79	36	115
CDC CDC (x)	4	4	8
CDD DCC (xi)	3	1	4
Total	225	92	317

the sestet. These are mixed together in more or less random arrangements, alternating at some points, at others appearing in groups that may or may not be thematically linked. Irregularities are mostly concentrated. All seven sestet types appear as a sequence between poems 91 and 97: 91 (vi), 92 (v), 93 (vii), 94 (xi), 95 (viii), 96 (ix), 97 (x). There is another strong disturbance early in Part 2, involving octet and sestet, once in the same poem: 278 (x), 279 (iii), 280 (ii + x), 281 (ii), 282 (x). Other poems which, like 280, have unusual schemes in both octave and sestet, are 56 and 311 (ii + x), both of which are set close by other abnormal poems: 58 (x), and 310 (ii). Poems 310 and 311 are thematically linked. Poems 56 and 58 figure in a string of poems with different forms (54 madrigal, 55 ballata, 56–8 sonnets, 59 ballata). As with the other irregular sequences, diversity seems the sole convincing reason for their introduction.

I have already spoken at various points about the organisation of individual sonnets. If there is a structure which is canonical, it is the one blazoned in poem 1, which recurs, with variations in much of the *RVF*, and then becomes the model for subsequent sonnet writers, which they follow or which (like Petrarch himself) they react against, whilst never being able to forget it (cf. the sonnets by Boiardo and Gaspara Stampa quoted in Chapter 5.1). It is what we think of as the inevitable, the natural structure for a sonnet, though there is little sign that anyone before Petrarch felt that this was the case.

This structure is articulated around a marked sense-break coinciding with the end of the octet, the sestet then rising against the octet, whether or not there is an actual counterstatement being made of the kind that appears in the first poem. The imbalance between the two parts is redressed by weighting the sestet in various ways. The octet commonly flows with a more even rhythm. Its internal sense-breaks, usually much less pronounced than the one at the end of line 8, occur at the end of the first quatrain, and, still less marked and often ignored altogether, at the end of the couplets (i.e. lines 2 and 6). There are normally no strong sense-breaks within the lines, and there may be strong enjambement within the quatrains, particularly between odd and even lines. Thus there is a tendency, though it is not usually quite carried through in Petrarch (as the model *RVF* 1 shows), for the rhyme-scheme and the sense-breaks to make interlocking anti-thetical movements – ABBA against ABAB – unobtrusively reconciling the flow of enjambement and the regularity which is created by end-stopping. The sestet is also broken into two equal parts, normally with a lesser sense-break between them, corresponding to the break between the quatrains. But the evenness is disrupted; the rhythms are more uneven within lines and more varied between them; there are commonly pauses within the line; and there is a strong final line, a *sententia* which seems to be the culmination and conclusion of the poem both for its sense and for the force and beauty of its expression. (For these features see the discussion of poem 1 in section 2 above.)

It is a dynamic structure which emphasises closure. The sonnet on this model is an in-turned form, the octet looking forward, the sestet looking back, neither complete without the other but the whole needing nothing but itself. In it all that is floating, indeterminate, disordered, fragmented or meaningless in Petrarch's poetry finds a place, whilst not being denied for what it is and only within the individual sonnet. In the next sonnet, or next poem, there has to be another opening and another closure.

These take many forms, although, thanks to the first sonnet, all seem like variations on the canonical schema. In many poems the element of contrast between octet and sestet is reduced to a minimum, and in some annulled altogether. Some poems have a particularly even development, perhaps with some formula which is repeated at intervals through the poem (e.g. 145, 224). Others have barely any break between octet and sestet (51, 57, 69, 282 – which is also one of the poems with an unusual rhyme arrangement – 320, 333, 348). At least one, 164 (quoted in the previous section) makes its major contrast between the first quatrain and the second. Others delay it to the final tercet or the last line (e.g. 268), or even half-line (307). Many end with a quite unemphatic line in which no trace of the epigrammatic is to be found (e.g. 163, 319, 329). But the implicit principle is always followed: structurally order is assured even if in other respects it is not.

Petrarch makes his limited variations on sonnet schemes within the fixed fourteen-line frame, and gives more weight to exploring the form's dynamics than to modifications of its frame. The framework of the canzone, the major form of the Italian tradition, made it a more varied and more demanding entity, which could not be so readily schematised as the sonnet. Later poets will find the Petrarchan sonnet a highly imitable form. His canzoni are much more difficult. Apart from the inherent complications of the form itself, it is in his canzoni that Petrarch is most diverse, most refined and most individual. Metrically he has done little more than take up some of the possibilities which the tradition offered, whilst, characteristically, discarding virtuoso extremes. But within those possibilities he creates and explores strikingly divergent dynamics, ranging from apparently free development to complex cycles of repetition. Though the sonnets are more amenable to critical analysis, it is in the canzoni that Petrarch's art is at its most dazzling.

All canzoni were constructed on the same basic principles, but there was no reason, theoretically, why any two canzoni should have an identical form or length. All of Petrarch's twenty-nine canzoni are formally different to some degree, though for special reasons some are made almost identical. The three canzoni on the eyes (71–3), which are thematically bonded together (see Chapter 5.5), are closest to each other: they have exactly the same metrical structure, though they are of different lengths. Two other thematically bonded poems (125 and 126), though again of different lengths, are almost identical metrically, the one difference being in the final line of each stanza. But then the opposite occurs: 270 and 325, two poems which are related thematically only in so far as they both treat of the dead Laura and which are set at a distance from each other, have exactly the same structure and length. Only their *congedi* are different.

At the basis of the canzone is the stanza, a metrical unit which changes from poem to poem but which is repeated in identical form within the poem. Though his predecessors sometimes wrote canzoni that were longer, all of Petrarch's canzoni consist of between five and eight stanzas, except for the two last (360 and 366), which have each ten stanzas, the additional length contributing to their concluding and culminating roles within the *RVF* as a whole. Unlike many of the poets before him, Petrarch also adds to his canzoni a *congedo*, a leave-taking, usually addressed to the poem, which is a short appendage in the metrical form of the last few lines of the stanza, though two canzoni (70 and 105) are without *congedi*.

The stanza itself is divided into two parts which may be of equal length, though it is commoner in all Italian poetry for the second part to be longer. The first part (*fronte*) is itself divided, and its two parts (*piedi*) have the same number of lines, in Petrarch between two and four, in the same combination of hendecasyllables and *settenari*, though the rhyme-pattern may vary. So, following the Italian convention of representing hendecasyllables by capitals and *settenari* by small letters, examples of perfectly regular *fronti* are: ABC ABC (129), AbC BaC (128), ABbC BAaC (264). The second part of the stanza (*sirma*) is not divided. Though earlier poets had not always done so, Petrarch opens it with a connecting line (*chiave*) which takes up the final rhyme of the first part. Then follows a sequence of lines normally using different rhymes from those of the first part and bound together in a different combination, an exception being made in 135, in which there is a repetition of some of the same rhymes as part of the particular rhetoric of this poem (see section 4 above). The examples just given continue as follows: cDEeDFF (129), cDEeDdfGfG (128), CDEEDdFfGG (264), the second being unusual amongst Petrarch's stanzas in not ending in a rhyming couplet. Some earlier poets had extended the *sirma* to give stanzas as long as twenty-five lines or more. Petrarch's longest stanza, of twenty lines, all but one hendecasyllables, appears in the first canzone in the collection (23), which is also the longest overall (160 lines). Again position is a factor: a long canzone, almost entirely in the superior hendecasyllable (see section 2 above), is a demonstration of poetic dignity and prowess, as traditionally conceived. Subsequently Petrarch prefers a more moderate stanza length: nineteen of his canzoni have stanzas of between thirteen and sixteen lines, whilst only two have stanzas with less than ten. He also prefers the more varied patterns of sound and rhythm that come from combining hendecasyllables with a number of *settenari*. Only two poems apart from 23 have only one *settenario* (53 and 331); the rest, which include some of the most serious poems, have two or more in various positions. They outnumber the hendecasyllables only in 125 and 126, where they are an essential component of the special musicality and lightness of the two poems (see Chapter 5.3).

There are three canzoni which deviate more strongly from the stanza pattern just outlined. The Provençal *canso*, from which the Italian canzone derived, often repeated the same rhymes throughout as well as the same rhyme-schemes. The *unissonans* arrangement had never been widespread in Italy, though there are examples from the Sicilians onwards. After showing his mastery of what had been thought the supreme Italian version of the canzone in 23, in his second canzone (29) Petrarch turns to virtuoso construction of the Provençal kind with a *unissonans* pattern that owes something to Arnaut Daniel. In this poem the rhymes are not repeated within the stanza, but only across the stanzas, each one having the following scheme: ABC(d3)EF(g5)Hi, where the bracketed symbols represent internal rhymes after the third and fifth syllables respectively. Petrarch managed eight stanzas, plus a *congedo*, in this remarkably constraining form, to produce a poem which is uncharacteristically unmusical (as Bembo noted (ed. Mari 1961: 327)), but which is both less harsh and less flamboyant in advertising its technical virtuosity than Arnaut Daniel's poems had been. Once again past extremes are assimilated, before being abandoned.

Later in the *RVF* there is a further variant on the *unissonans* principle, though one that looks more to the *trobar leu* of Bernart de Ventadorn than to the difficult style of Arnaut: 206 is a 'light' poem, based on repetitions of particular phrases. Here the same three rhymes (–ella, –ei, –ia) are used throughout in different combinations in the unusual but in fact not irregular scheme ABBA AcccA.

On the whole, Petrarch avoids the internal rhymes which had been cultivated particularly by the Guittonians as a mark of virtuosity, just as he eliminates similar tricks from the sonnet. But again there is an exception which is a *tour de force*. This is the deliberately obscure 105, in which almost every line is a dictum, and the sequence of thought is bewilderingly difficult. Petrarch is plainly concealing thought here, not expressing it, and it is part of the conception of the poem that the metrical scheme should be correspondingly hard to follow, though in fact the poem is not metrically irregular. It has a canzone stanza with the following quite anomalous but just about permissible scheme: (a)B(b)C(c)D (a)B(b)C(c)D (d)E(e)F(f)EeF(f)GHhG, in which all the rhymes except the last two are repeated internally and the first rhyme of the following stanza (a) is identical to the last rhyme of the preceding (G). As elsewhere at one time or another with almost every other rule that his practice implies, here Petrarch breaks his rules for formal grace and moderation, as well as for lucid writing. Freedom, or ineluctable disorder, has in some degree always to be affirmed.

The same tendency shows itself in other ways. As is to be expected, given his mistrust of intellectual systems, none of Petrarch's canzoni are constructed as arguments, in which a thesis is proposed and developed after the manner of the doctrinal canzoni of Guittone, Cavalcanti and Dante. Instead the overwhelming impression is of dynamic diversity, with changes occurring even within patterns that appear to become firmly established in a particular poem. Within that freedom there are two extreme points, represented by the first and last canzoni, though it is plainly not the case that there is a journey through the other canzoni from the one to the other.

Nel dolce tempo (23) narrates a succession of Ovidian metamorphoses. Whilst the sense-breaks overall follow the main metrical divisions, as is normal in Petrarch's canzoni, the story proceeds almost independently, coinciding with and departing from the metrical divisions at different times. Some metamorphoses occupy far more lines than others, and the sequence of changes comes to an end simply with a list of others which have occurred, implying that there is only an arbitrary limit to the metamorphoses or to the poem. At the opposite extreme to this apparently uncontrolled freedom, there is the canzone to the Virgin, with its complex pattern of repetitions. Each stanza begins with the word 'Vergine' which, for the first six and the last two stanzas, is then followed by phrases which are traditionally addressed to the Virgin and which occupy the whole of the first *piede*. The word 'Vergine' then reappears five lines from the end of each stanza, with more appositional phrases in stanzas 3, 4, 5, 7, 8 and in the *congedo*. As against the dynamism of 23, there is here a structure based on repetition, though a repetition with carefully wrought variations (see Chapter 5.5 for further discussion of the poem).

Other canzoni occupy different positions on a notional scale running from one of these to the other. Some are built up on the basis of repetition, though not with the evident liturgical air of the last poem. Poem 50 opens each stanza with a description of a calm evening scene, which is then contrasted with Petrarch's own torment. Similarly but more subtly 129 (for which see section 5 above) opens with a declaration of isolation and obsession amongst the mountains which is then reformulated to occupy the first *piede* of every stanza except the fourth. Most rigid of all is 135, which builds each of its stanzas on a comparison between an image from the bestiary or from commonplace mythology, occupying the first part of the stanza, and a representation of Petrarch's psychological state occupying the second (see section 4 above). In none of these poems, however, is the pattern unbroken: as it progresses, the external element, whether it is the evening, the fabulous springs, or the Virgin, comes to occupy less space and the self to occupy more, before some order is re-established towards the end of the poem. The development is dynamic as well as cyclic.

Other poems move away from repetition in the direction of 23. The political canzoni are more like formal exhortations, opening with an appeal to the addressee and continuing through to a peroration in the *congedo*. The two debate poems of Part 2, 264 and 360, set one argument against another, making each main point occupy a stanza. In the latter each of the speakers speaks for the same number of stanzas; in the former there is an internal debate between one thought or wish and another, which eventually resolves itself in the final stanzas as Petrarch comes forward to speak in his own person. This tendency to follow change, even at the risk of confusion, is especially cultivated in the canzoni on the eyes, in which (see Chapter 5.5) the flow of change around moving points which is the subject of the poems is represented in the ever-changing flow of the rhetoric, which keeps going away from its centres and returning to them, using the pivotal metrical points as points of redirection. Rather than running against the divisions of the poems, as occurs in 23, the formal articulations are springboards from which the poem continually launches itself.

Of the remaining three poetic forms which appear in the *RVF*, two, the ballata and the madrigale, are marginal, the first notably so. The ballata, in the form which it had taken in Tuscan poetry, consisted of a *ripresa* (refrain) normally of three or four lines, though longer ones are to be found, which was set at the beginning of the poem, followed by a number of stanzas resembling those of a canzone, each of which ended with a line rhyming with the last line of the *ripresa*. Originally, as its name indicates, the ballata was a form which accompanied dancing ('ballo' being the word for 'dance'), and the *ripresa* was repeated after each stanza, although it may well be that already in the thirteenth century the *ripresa* was sensed as making only one appearance, at least in literary ballate. The *stil novo* had particularly favoured the form, and, on occasion, had developed it on something like the scale of the canzone, though in the *DVE* (2. 3. 5) Dante had rated it intermediate in worth between the sonnet and the canzone. Petrarch carries out a reduction in scale that implies a serious devaluation. Although he wrote others (*RD* 7–9), he includes only seven ballate in the *RVF*, six in Part 1 (11, 14, 55, 59, 63 and 149) and one in Part 2 (324). Only two (55 and 59) have two stanzas, and even then the length in each case is only seventeen lines, whilst the last (324) is actually shorter than a sonnet. None of the ballate are particularly significant. They seem to have been included primarily as part of the pattern of formal variation which is at its most intense in the earlier poems of Part 1, but also as a qualified acknowledgment of the form's right to exist within the gamut of poetic possibilities which the collection represented.

In contrast the other minor form represents a qualified innovation, at least with respect to poetry of the previous century. The madrigale seems to have come into favour in the fourteenth century principally as a sung form, the possibilities of which were developed particularly by the composers of the *Ars nova*. It consisted of tercets and couplets, arranged in no fixed pattern but linked by rhyme to each other. Its outstanding feature was its brevity. Petrarch's four madrigali (52, 54, 106, 121) consist of eight, ten, eight and nine lines, respectively, making them the slightest poems in the collection, if also some of the most graceful both for their musicality and for their particularly light use of familiar imagery. Noticeably Petrarch creates a strikingly contrastive pattern, by setting one of the weighty political canzoni, *Spirto gentil* (53), between two of his madrigals.

The form which I have left to last is a special form of canzone and a much weightier matter. So far as we know, there had been only two isolated sestine written before Petrarch's example established it as an unusual but regular form, which was as available as any other, at least for moderate use. Arnaut Daniel's *Lo ferm voler* was the first. Dante, in the full flood of experimentation in his *rime petrose* along lines suggested by Arnaut, produced the second in *Al poco giorno*, although he then went on to write 'something new and untried' ('aliquid novum et intentatum': *DVE* 2. 13. 12) with *Amor tu vedi ben* in which he took to extremes the repetitions upon which the sestina is based. The normal sestina consists of six stanzas, each six lines long, plus a *congedo* of three lines. The same six words, which do not rhyme together, though they may show some degree of assonance, appear in rhyme-position in each stanza, their order changing from stanza to stanza according to a fixed pattern. After the first stanza (ABCDEF), subsequent stanzas construct their sequences by working inwards from the two extremities of the one preceding, to give FAEBDC in the second stanza, CFDABE in the third, and so on, until, with the last stanza, all the combinations which this system allows have been covered. In the three lines of the *congedo* all six rhyme-words are repeated, two appearing in each line. After the first four of Petrarch's nine sestine, the order in the *congedo* in the remainder is that of the first stanza. Eight of the sestine appear in Part 1 (22, 30, 66, 80, 142, 214, 237, 239). The ninth (332) is a double sestina (as the poem itself announces at precisely the point where it should have ended (lines 36–40)) in which the sequence is followed through for a second time.

Both Arnaut's and Dante's sestine connected the repetition of difficult, harsh rhymes with sexual obsession, and, in Dante's case, with resistance on the part of the *donna di petra*. Traces of this overt sexuality, transmuted into mythic guise, remain in the two Petrarchan sestine which enclose much of the poetry of Part 1 (22 and 237: see Chapter 5.3), but Petrarch refuses to hold either to this thematic restriction or to the emphasis on harshness and difficulty. Three of his sestine (80, 142, 214) are amongst the most religious poems of Part 1. None, even the last double sestina, make a display of overcoming technical problems. The attraction of the form for him is different. The recurrence of the same words, primarily nouns, in different combinations and with different meanings or resonances (see the discussion of *Là ver' l'aurora* in Chapter 5.4) is an extreme formalisation of fundamental qualities in his poetry generally. In the sestine his emblematic imagery attains a glittering intensity, and the deep, even resonance of his music becomes most consistent. Here, more than anywhere else, the power of repetition and variation in poetry is affirmed as an alternative to the sad wastes of time, even if it cannot ultimately triumph and is debarred from suprahuman refuges. Far from being artificial or restrictive, the sestina is the form in which Petrarch's poetic self is most explicit.

Bibliographical notes

1 Introduction

1.1 For P's reputation see Bonora (1954), Sozzi (1963), Dionisotti (1974). For general studies on P see Bosco (1961), Noferi (1962), Quaglio (1967), Foster (1984), Mann (1984), and specifically on P's humanism, De Nolhac (1907), Billanovich (1947 and 1965), Trinkaus (1979). For the development of P's thought see also Baron (1968). For P as scholar see also Reynolds and Wilson (1974: 113–17). On P's life see Wilkins (1961). For a survey of recent criticism see Turchi (1978).

1.2 For the Sicilians see Folena (1973). For Guittone see Marguéron (1966). For *poesia giocosa* see Marti (1953). For the *dolce stil novo* see Marti (1973), Favati (1975). For the diffusion of the *Divina commedia* see the introduction to Petrocchi ed. (1966). For the general situation in fourteenth-century Italy see Larner (1980). For fourteenth-century poetry see Dionisotti (1967), Tartaro (1971), Balduino (1973), Lanza (1978), Russell (1982). For Niccolò de' Rossi see Brugnolo ed. (1974–7). For music and poetry see Roncaglia (1978).

1.3 See Bibliographical Notes to subsequent chapters.

1.4 For Sennuccio see Altamura ed. (1950) and Billanovich (1965). For P and Sennuccio see also Barber (1982). For Antonio da Ferrara and texts of *tenzoni* with P see Bellucci ed. (1972). For P and vernacular Boccaccio see Branca (1981: 300–32). For a discussion of Boccaccio's lyrics see Branca (1981: 250–76).

2 Composition

2.1 For possible differences between earlier and later poems see Alonso (1961). For *RVF* as a book see Santagata (1979) and Gorni (1984).

2.2 For composition see principally Wilkins (1951) and Rico (1976). See

221

also Viscardi (1970) and Martinelli (1973 and 1976). For V1 see also
Romanò ed. (1955). For Chigi form see also the introduction to De
Robertis ed. (1974). For Correggio form see also Gorni (1978). For
Quiriniano see also Gaffuri (1976).

2.3 For the work of revision see Contini (1943) and Romanò ed. (1955).
On the composition of individual poems, for 23 see Dutschke (1977),
for 194 see Chiappelli (1967), for 323 see Chiappelli (1971).

3 Structure

3.1 For the *RVF* as *poema* see the introduction to Zingarelli ed. (1963:
17–28).

3.2 and 3 For the calendrical structure see Roche (1974), Jones (1983
and 1984a). For views of moral structure see Martinelli (1976), Rico
(1976) and Foster (1984: 48–92). For a view of the lack of structure
see Wilkins (1951: 154ff).

3.4 For connections between poems see Santagata (1979: 1–56) and
Freccero (1975).

4 The tradition

4.1 For the presentation of the self as poet in *RVF* see Sturm (1975). On
P and Cino see Lo Parco (1930) and Boggs (1979). On P and recent
Latin poetry see Velli (1976).

4.2 For P's view of imitation see Greene (1982). On his poetics generally
see Barberi Squarotti (1959) and Ronconi (1976). On his Latin see
Martellotti (1951 and 1961).

4.3 and 4 For P and classical Latin poetry see Petrie (1983). For P and
the troubadours see Scarano (1900), Zingarelli (1935), Ferrero
(1958), Peirone (1967), Fontana (1975). For P and Guittone see
Pierantozzi (1948). For P and the *dolce stil novo* see Suitner (1977).
For P and Dante see Bernardo (1955), Feo (1970), Trovato (1979)
and Waller (1980).

4.5 For P's attitude to scholasticism and Aristotelianism see Foster
(1984: 150–6).

5 Themes

5.1 On *RVF* 1 see Noferi (1974), Almansi (1974) and Jacomuzzi (1977).

5.2 For the historical Laura see Carrara (1959) and Jones (1984b). For
P's note in his Virgil and other time-notations see De Nolhac (1907:
2, 286–8). For the name Laura and its significance see Contini (1957)
and Zingarelli (1935). For fabrication in Boccaccio see Branca (1981:
191–249). For the significance of 6 April see Calcaterra (1942b) and
Martinelli (1973). For the confusion of life and literature in P see
Mann (1984: 1–9). For P's view of historical time see Mommsen

(1942) and Greene (1982). For the absence of history in the *RVF* see Bosco (1961).

5.3 For ideas of woman in medieval literature see Renier (1885). On P's descriptions see Raimondi (1970), Poole (1980), Vickers (1981). On P and the *rime petrose* see Neri (1951) and Possiedi (1974) and references to P and Dante at note to Chapter 4.3 and 4, above.

5.4 On 'l'aura' see Contini (1957). On the myth of Daphne in the Middle Ages see Giraud (1968). On the myth in the *RVF* see Calcaterra (1942a), Dotti (1969), Durling (1971), Hainsworth (1979). For resemblances of Laura to Scipio see Bernardo (1962). For non-love-poems in the *RVF* see Momigliano (1937), Bernardo (1950). For the political canzoni see Petronio (1961).

5.5 On the dead Laura see Bosco (1961) and Foster (1962; and 1984: 48–92).

6 Art

6.1 For P's style generally see Fubini (1947), Bigi (1954), Fulco (1969) and Forster (1969).

6.2 For *endecasillabo* see Di Girolamo (1976). For metre in P see Bigi (1961) and Fubini (1962).

6.3 For sound-patterns see Simonelli (1978).

6.4 For P's language generally see above all Contini (1951). For metaphors see Velli (1980) and Hainsworth (1988). For word-frequency see the Accademia della Crusca concordance (1971).

6.5 For P's syntax see Bigi (1954) and Herczeg (1976). For antithesis see Herczeg (1961) and Sansone (1971).

6.6 For technique see Di Pino (1957). For earlier sonnets see Biadene (1889) and Kleinhenz (1986). For P's sonnets see Figurelli (1961) and Kleinhenz (1975). For canzoni see Galdi (1965). For sestine see Shapiro (1980). For ballate see Bigi (1974).

Bibliography

1 Editions

(a) Petrarch

Italian poems
All quotations from the *RVF* are from Francesco Petrarca, *Canzoniere*, ed. G. Contini, Turin, 1964 (originally, Paris, 1949). I have also made use of the following editions and their commentaries and introductions:
G. Carducci and S. Ferrari, F.P., *Le rime*, Florence, 1899: reissued, with presentation by G. Contini, Florence, 1965.
F. Neri, G. Martellotti, E. Bianchi and N. Sapegno, P., *Rime, Trionfi, e Poesie Latine*, Milan and Naples, 1951.
N. Zingarelli, *Le rime di F.P.*, Bologna, 1963.
M. Vattasso, *L'originale de'l Canzoniere di F.P., Codice Vaticano Latino 3195, riprodotto in fototipia*. Milan 1905.
 Unless otherwise indicated, quotations from the *Rime disperse*, the *Frammenti* and the *Triumphi* are from the texts given in: P., *Rime, Trionfi*, etc.
 Unless otherwise indicated, quotations from earlier versions of poems are taken from: A. Romanò, *Il codice degli abbozzi (Vat. Lat. 3196) di F.P.*, Rome, 1955. I have also used: *Il codice Chigiano L.V. 176. Autografo di Giovanni Boccaccio,* phototypic edition, with introduction by D. De Robertis, Rome and Florence, 1974.

Latin works
For the *Posteritati, Secretum, De vita solitaria, Invective*, references are to F.P., *Prose*, ed. G. Martellotti, with P.G. Ricci, E. Carrara, E. Bianchi, Milan and Naples, 1955 (cited as *Prose* in text with page number).
 For the *Familiares*, I have used *Epistolae familiares*, 4 vols, ed. V. Rossi and U. Bosco, Florence, 1933–42; for the *Africa*, the edition by N. Festa, Florence, 1926; for the *Collatio laureationis* and *De otio religioso*, the edition given in *Opere latine di F.P.*, ed. A. Bufano, with B. Acacri and

C.K. Reggiani, Turin, 1975; for the *Bucolicum carmen*, the edition by
T. Mattucci, Pisa, 1970, with for *Buc. carm.* 10, *Laurea occidens*, the
edition by G. Martellotti, Rome, 1968: for the *Sine nomine* the edition by
U. Dotti, Bari, 1974.

For the *Seniles* and the *De remediis* I have used the selections in *Prose*,
ed. Martellotti and *Opere latine*, ed. Bufano. For the *Epistole metrice* I
have used the selections in *Rime, Trionfi*, etc. In default of a complete
modern edition of the three works, I have also used F.P., *Opera omnia*,
Basle, 1554 (republished, New Jersey, 1965).

(b) Other authors

Italian poetry of the thirteenth and fourteenth centuries
For the Sicilians, Guittone d'Arezzo and other Tuscan poetry up to and
including the *dolce stil novo*, all references are to *Poeti del Duecento*, 2
vols, ed. G. Contini, Milan and Naples, 1960 (cited as *Poeti* with volume
and page number). For fourteenth-century poets, other than those cited
below, references are to *Rimatori del Trecento*, ed. G. Corsi, Turin, 1969
(cited as *Rimatori* with page number).

Otherwise I have used the following editions:

Antonio da Ferrara	*Le rime di Antonio da Ferrara (Antonio Beccari)*, ed. L. Bellucci, Bologna, 1972 (cited as *Rime* with poem number).
Boccaccio	*Rime* and *Trattatello in laude di Dante* in *Opere minori in volgare*, ed. M. Marti, Milan, 1972 (cited as *Rime* with poem number in the first case, and *Opere* with page number in the second).
Dante	*Rime*, ed. G. Contini, Turin, 1946. *Vita nuova*, ed. M. Barbi, Florence, 1932. *La divina commedia*, ed. G. Petrocchi, Turin, 1975 (originally Milan, 1966). *De vulgari eloquentia*, ed. A. Marigo (3rd ed.), Florence, 1957.
Francesco di Vannozzo	*Le rime*, ed. A. Medin, Bologna, 1928.
Niccolò de' Rossi	*Il canzoniere*, ed. F. Brugnolo, Padua, 1974–7.
Sennuccio del Bene	*Il canzoniere*, ed. A. Altamura, Naples, 1950 (cited by poem number).

*Fifteenth-
and sixteenth-century authors*

P. Bembo	*Prose della volgar lingua* in *Opere in volgare*, ed. M. Marti, Florence, 1961.
M.M. Boiardo	*Orlando innamorato. Amorum libri*, ed. A. Scaglione, 2 vols, Turin, 1966.
G. Stampa	*Rime*, ed. G.R. Ceriello, Milan, 1954.

Other authors

John of Garland   *Parisiana poetria*, ed. T. Lawler, New Haven
                           and London, 1974.
Antonio da Tempo   *Summa artis rithimici vulgaris dictaminis*, ed.
                           R.A. Andrews, Bologna, 1977.

2 Critical works cited

Abbreviations

GSLI   *Giornale storico della letteratura italiana*
IMU   *Italia medievale e umanistica*
IS   *Italian Studies*
LI   *Lettere italiane*
MLN   *Modern Language Notes*
MLR   *Modern Lanugage Review*
PMLA   *Proceedings of the Modern Language*
               Association
SP   *Studi petrarcheschi*

Accademia della Crusca (1971), *Concordanza del Canzoniere di Francesco
   Petrarca*, 2 vols, Florence.
Almansi, G. (1974), 'Petrarca o dell'insignificanza', *Paragone* 296,   ·
   pp. 68–73.
Alonso, D. (1961), 'La poesia del Petrarca e il petrarchismo (mondo
   estetico della pluralità)', *SP* 7, pp. 73–120.
Amaturo, R. (1971), *Petrarca*, Bari.
Balduino, A. (1973), 'Premesse ad una storia della poesia trecentesca', *LI*,
   pp. 3–36.
Barber, J.A. (1982), 'Il sonetto CXIII e gli altri sonetti a Sennuccio',
   Lectura Petrarce, Padua, pp. 21–39.
Barberi Squarotti, G. (1959), 'Le poetiche del Trecento in Italia',
   *Problemi ed orientamenti critici di lingua e di letteratura italiana.
   Momenti e problemi di storia dell'estetica. Parte prima. Dall'antichità
   classica al barocco*, Milan, vol. 5, pp. 255–324.
Baron, H. (1968), *From Petrarch to Leonardo Bruni*, Chicago.
Bernardo, A.S. (1950), 'The importance of the non-love poems in
   Petrarch's *Canzoniere*', *Italica* 27, pp. 302–12.
Bernardo, A.S. (1955), 'Petrarch's attitude towards Dante', *PMLA* 70,
   pp. 488–517.
Bernardo, A.S. (1962), *Petrarch, Scipio and the Africa*, Baltimore.
Biadene, L. (1889), 'Morfologia del sonetto nei sec. XIII e XIV', *Studi di
   filologia romanza*, 4, pp. 1–234.
Bigi, E. (1954), 'Alcuni aspetti dello stile del *Canzoniere* petrarchesco',
   Dal Petrarca al Leopardi, Milan and Naples, pp. 1–22.
Bigi, E. (1961), 'La rima del Petrarca', *SP* 7, pp. 135–45.
Bigi, E. (1974), 'Le ballate del Petrarca', *GSLI* 151, pp. 481–93.

Billanovich, G. (1947), *Petrarca letterato,* l, *Lo scrittoio del Petrarca,* Rome.

Billanovich, G. (1965), 'Tra Dante e Petrarca', *IMU* 8, pp. 1–45.

Boggs, E.L., IIIrd (1979), 'Cino and Petrarch', *MLN* 94, pp. 146–52.

Bonora, E. (1954), 'Lineamenti di storia della critica petrarchesca', in *I classici italiani nella storia della critica,* ed. W. Binni, Florence.

Bosco, U. (1961), *Francesco Petrarca,* (2nd ed.), Bari.

Branca, V. (1981), *Boccaccio medievale* (5th ed.), Florence.

Calcaterra, C. (1942a), 'Giovene donna sotto un verde lauro', *Nella selva del Petrarca,* Bologna, pp. 35–87.

Calcaterra, C. (1942b), 'Feria sexta aprilis', *ibid.,* pp. 209–45.

Carrara, E. (1959), 'La leggenda di Laura', (1934), *Studi petrarcheschi e altri scritti,* Turin, pp. 77–111.

Chiappelli, F. (1967), 'Dall'intenzione all'invenzione: una lettura petrarchesca (*Rime* CXCIV)', *GSLI* 144, pp. 161–9.

Chiappelli, F. (1971), *Studi sul linguaggio del Petrarca: la canzone delle visioni,* Florence.

Contini, G. (1943), *Correzioni del Petrarca volgare,* Florence. Now in *Varianti e altra linguistica,* Turin, 1970, pp. 5–31.

Contini, G. (1951), 'Preliminari sulla lingua del Petrarca', *Paragone* 2, pp. 3–26. Now as introduction to Petrarca, *Canzoniere,* Turin, 1964.

Contini, G. (1957), 'Préhistoire de *l'aura* de Pétrarque', *Actes et Mémoires du 1er Congrès international de Langue et Littérature du Midi de la France,* Avignon. Now in *Varianti e altra linguistica,* Turin, 1970, pp. 193–9.

De Nolhac, P. (1907), *Pétrarque et l'humanisme,* 2 vols, Paris.

De Sanctis, F. (1971), *Saggio sul Petrarca,* ed. E. Bonora, Milan (originally 1869).

Di Girolamo, C. (1976), *Teoria e prassi della versificazione,* Bologna.

Dionisotti, C. (1967), 'Geografia e storia della letteratura italiana', *Geografia e storia della letteratura italiana,* Turin, pp. 25–54.

Dionisotti, C. (1974), 'Fortuna del Petrarca nel Quattrocento', *IMU* 17, pp. 61–113.

Di Pino, G. (1957), 'Poesia e tecnica formale nel canzoniere petrarchesco', *Stile e umanità,* Messina and Florence, pp. 33–63.

Dotti, U. (1969), 'Petrarca: il mito dafneo', *Convivium* 37, pp. 9–23.

Durling, R.M. (1971), 'Petrarch's *Giovene donna sotto un verde lauro',* *MLN* 86, pp. 1–20.

Dutschke, D. (1977), *Francesco Petrarca: Canzone XXIII from First to Final Version,* Ravenna.

Dutschke, D. (1981), 'The Anniversary poems in Petrarch's *Canzoniere',* *Italica* 58, pp. 83–101.

Favati, G. (1975), *Inchiesta sul 'dolce stil novo,* Florence.

Feo, M. (1970), 'Petrarca', *Enciclopedia dantesca,* ed. U. Bosco, vol. 4, 450–8.

Ferrero, G.G. (1958), *Petrarca e i trovatori,* Turin.

Figurelli F. (1961), 'L'architettura del sonetto in Francesco Petrarca', *SP* 7, pp. 179–86.

Folena, G. (1973), 'I Siciliani', *Dizionario critico della letteratura italiana*, ed. V. Branca, Turin, vol. 3, p. 386.

Fontana, A. (1975), 'La filologia romanza e il problema del rapporto Petrarca–Trovatori', *Petrarca. Beiträge zu Werk und Wirkung*, ed. F. Schalk, Frankfurt, pp. 55–70.

Forster, L. (1969), *The Icy Fire*, Cambridge.

Foster, K. (1962), 'Beatrice or Medusa', *Italian Studies presented to E.R. Vincent*, ed. C.P. Brand and U. Limentani, Cambridge, pp. 41–56.

Foster, K. (1984), *Petrarch: Poet and Humanist*, Edinburgh.

Freccero, J. (1975), 'The fig-tree and the laurel: Petrarch's poetics', *Diacritics*, 5, pp. 34–40.

Fubini, M. (1947), 'Il Petrarca artefice', *Studi sulla letteratura del Rinascimento*, Florence, pp. 1–12.

Fubini, M. (1962), *Metrica e poesia: lezioni sulle forme poetiche italiane*, vol. 1, *Dal Duecento al Petrarca*, Milan.

Fulco, G. (1969), *Lezioni sul Canzoniere*, Naples.

Gaffuri, R. (1976), 'Nuove indagini sul codice petrarchesco D. II. 21', *SP* 8, pp. 76–91.

Galdi, L. (1965), 'Les origines provençales de la métrique des "canzoni" de Pétrarque', *Actes du Xe Congrès Internationale de Linguistique et Philologie Romane (Strasbourg 1962)*, ed. G. Straka, Paris, vol. 2, pp. 783–9.

Giraud, Y. (1968), *La fable de Daphné*, Geneva.

Gorni, G. (1978), 'Metamorfosi e redenzione in Petrarca. Il senso della forma Correggio del Canzoniere', *LI* 30, pp. 3–13.

Gorni, G. (1984), 'Le forme primarie del testo poetico', *Letteratura italiana*, ed. A. Asor Rosa, Turin, vol. 3, *Le forme del testo. 1. Teoria e prassi*, pp. 439–518.

Greene, T.M. (1982), *The Light in Troy. Imitation and Discovery in Renaissance Poetry*, New Haven and London.

Hainsworth, P. (1979), 'The myth of Daphne in the *Rerum vulgarium fragmenta*', *IS* 34, pp. 28–44.

Hainsworth, P. (1988) 'Metaphor in Petrarch's *RVF*', in *The Languages of Literature in Renaissance Italy*, edited by P. Hainsworth, V. Lucchesi, C. Roaf, D. Robey and J.R. Woodhouse, Oxford, pp. 1–18.

Herczeg, G. (1961), 'Struttura delle antitesi nel *Canzoniere* petrarchesco', *SP* 7, pp. 195–208.

Herczeg, G. (1976), 'La struttura della frase nei versi del Petrarca', *SP* 8, pp. 169–96.

Jacomuzzi, A. (1977), 'Il primo sonetto del *Canzoniere* come modello di lettura', *Letteratura e critica. Studi in onore di Natalino Sapegno*, ed. W. Binni et al., Rome, vol. 4, pp. 41–58.

Jones, F.J. (1983), 'Laura's date of birth and the calendrical system implicit in the *Canzoniere*', *Italianistica* 1, pp. 13–33.

Jones, F.J. (1984a), 'Arguments in favour of a calendrical structure for Petrarch's *Canzoniere*', *MLR* 79, pp. 579–88.

Jones, F.J. (1984b) 'Further evidence of the identity of Petrarch's Laura', *IS* 39, pp. 27–46.

Kleinhenz, C. (1975), 'Petrarch and the art of the sonnet', in Scaglione (ed.) (1975), pp. 177–91.

Kleinhenz, C. (1986), *The Early Italian Sonnet. The First Century (1220–1321)*, Lecce.

Kristeller, P.O. (1955), 'Il Petrarca, l'umanesimo e la scolastica', *LI* pp. 367–88.

Lanza, A. (1978), *Studi sulla lirica del '300*, Rome.

Larner, J. (1980), *Italy in the Age of Dante and Petrarch*, London.

Lo Parco, F. (1930), 'La leggenda dell'insegnamento bolognese e dell'amicizia personale di Cino da Pistoia con Francesco Petrarca', *GSLI* 96, pp.193–240.

Mann, N. (1984), *Petrarch*, Oxford.

Marguéron, C. (1966), *Recherches sur Guittone d'Arezzo: sa vie, son époque, sa culture*, Paris.

Martellotti, G. (1951), 'Clausole e ritmi nella prosa narrativa del Petrarca', *SP* pp. 35–46. Now in *Scritti petrarcheschi*, Padua, 1983, pp. 207–19.

Martellotti, G. (1961), 'Latinità del Petrarca', *SP* 7, pp. 219–30. Now in *Scritti petrarcheschi*, Padua, 1983, pp. 289–301.

Marti, M. (1953), *Cultura e stile nei poeti giocosi del tempo di Dante*, Pisa.

Marti, M. (1973), *Storia dello stil nuovo*, Lecce.

Martinelli, B. (1973), 'Feria sexta aprilis. La data sacra nel *Canzoniere* del Petrarca', *Rivista di storia e di letteratura religiosa* 8, pp. 449–84. Now in *Petrarca e il Ventoso*, Bergamo, 1977, pp. 103–48.

Martinelli, B. (1976), 'L'ordinamento morale del *Canzoniere* del Petrarca', *SP* 8, pp. 93–167. Now in *Petrarca e il Ventoso*, Bergamo, 1977, pp. 217–300.

Momigliano, A. (1937), 'L'elegia politica del Petrarca', *Annali della cattedra petrarchesca* 7, pp. 77–91. Now in *Introduzione ai poeti*, Rome, 1946, pp. 7–19.

Mommsen, T. (1942), 'Petrarch's conception of the Dark Ages', *Speculum* 17, pp. 226–42.

Neri, F. (1951), 'Il Petrarca e le rime dantesche della pietra', *Letteratura e leggende*, Turin, pp. 32–72.

Noferi, A. (1962), *L'esperienza poetica del Petrarca*, Florence.

Noferi, A. (1974), 'Il *Canzoniere* del Petrarca: scrittura del desiderio e desiderio della scrittura', *Paragone* 296, pp. 3–24.

Peirone, L. (1967), 'La prospettiva occitanica di Petrarca', *Giornale italiano di filologia* 20, pp. 235–41.

Petrie, J. (1983), *Petrarch: The Italian Tradition and the Canzoniere*, Dublin.

Petronio, G. (1961), 'Storicità della lirica politica del Petrarca', *SP* 7, pp. 247–64.

Pierantozzi, D. (1948), 'Il Petrarca e Guittone', *SP* 1, pp. 145–65.

Poole, G. (1980), 'Il topos dell "effictio" in un sonetto del Petrarca', *LI*, 22, pp. 3–20.

Possiedi, P. (1974), 'Petrarca petroso', *Forum italicum* 8, pp. 523–45.

Quaglio, A.E. (1967), *Francesco Petrarca*, Milan.
Raimondi, E. (1970), 'Ritrattistica petrarchesca', *Metafora e storia*, Turin, pp. 163–88.
Renier, A. (1885), *Il tipo estetico della donna nel medioevo*, Ancona.
Reynolds, L.D. and Wilson, N.G. (1974), *Scribes and Scholars. A Guide to the Transmission of Greek and Latin Literature* (2nd ed.), Oxford.
Rico, F. (1976), ' "Rime sparse", "Rerum vulgarium fragmenta". Para el título y el primer soneto del *Canzoniere*', *Medioevo romanzo* 3, no. 1, pp. 101–36.
Roche, T.P. (1974), 'The calendrical structure of Petrarch's *Canzoniere*', *Studies in Philology* 71, pp. 152–71.
Roncaglia, A. (1978), 'Sul "divorzio" tra musica e poesia nel Duecento italiano', in *L'Ars nova del Trecento*, Certaldo, vol. 4, pp. 365–397.
Ronconi, G. (1976), *Le origini delle dispute umanistiche sulla poesia*, Rome.
Russell, R. (1982), *Generi poetici medievali. Modelli e funzioni letterarie*, Naples, 1982.
Sansone, G.E. (1971), 'Assaggio di simmetrie petrarchesche', *Lingua e stile* 6, pp. 223–40.
Santagata, M. (1979), *Dal sonetto al canzoniere*, Padua.
Scaglione, A. (ed.) (1975), *Francis Petrarch, Six Centuries Later*, Chicago.
Scarano, N. (1900), 'Fonti provenzali della lirica petrarchésca', *Studi di filologia italiana* 8, pp. 250–360.
Shapiro, M. (1980), *Hieroglyph of Time. The Petrarchan Sestina*, Minneapolis.
Simonelli, M.P. (1978), *Figure foniche dal Petrarca ai petrarchisti*, Florence.
Sozzi, B.T. (1963), *Petrarca*, Palermo.
Sturm, S. (1975), 'The poet-persona in the *Canzoniere*', in Scaglione (ed.) (1975), pp. 192–212.
Suitner, F. (1977), *Petrarca e la tradizione stilnovistica*, Florence.
Tartaro, A. (1971), *Forme poetiche del Trecento*. (Letteratura Italiana Laterza 7), Bari.
Trinkaus, C. (1979), *Petrarch and the Formation of Renaissance Consciousness*, New Haven and London.
Trovato, P. (1979), *Dante in Petrarca. Per un inventario dei dantismi nei RVF*, Florence.
Turchi, M. (1978), 'Il centenario del Petrarca e la critica', *Italianistica* 7, pp. 378–99.
Velli, G. (1976), 'La memoria poetica del Petrarca', *IMU* 19, pp. 171–207.
Velli, G. (1980), 'La metafora del Petrarca', *Simbolo, metafora, allegoria. Atti del IV Convegno Italo-Tedesco, Bressanone, 1976*, ed. D. Goldín, Padua, pp. 123–31.
Vickers, N.J. (1981), 'Diana described: scattered woman and scattered rhymes', *Critical Enquiry* 8, pp. 265–79.
Viscardi, A. (1970), 'Il *Canzoniere* e i suoi canzonieri', *Ricerche e interpretazioni mediolatine e romanze*, Milan and Varese, pp. 623–31.

Waller, M. (1980), *Petrarch's Poetics and Literary History*, Amherst, Mass.

Wilkins, E.H. (1951), *The Making of the 'Canzoniere' and other Petrarchan Studies*, Rome.

Wilkins, E.H. (1961), *Life of Petrarch*, Chicago.

Zingarelli, N. (1935), 'Petrarca e i trovadori', *Scritti di varia letteratura*, Milan pp. 384–428.

Principal references to individual poems in the RVF

The numbers of the poems are given in brackets

A la dolce ombra (142), 151, 162, 220
Amor che meco (303), 178–9
Amor et io (160), 125–6
Amor m'à posto (133), 88–90
Amor, se vuo' (270), 213
Anima bella (305), 185
Apollo, s'anchor vive (34), 141
A qualunque animal (22), 119, 220
Arbor victorïosa (263), 51, 61, 62, 136, 149–50, 178
Aspro core (265), 87–8

Beato in sogno (212), 47
Benedetto sia 'l giorno (61), 58, 63, 70–4

Cantai, or piango (229), 163, 173, 186
Cesare, poi che 'l traditor (102), 24–8
Che debb'io far? (268), 34, 42–5, 111, 113, 162–3
Chiare, fresche et dolci acque (126), 91, 126, 128–34, 213, 215

Di pensier in pensier (129), 203–5, 214, 217

Dodici donne (225), 112, 113, 136–7

Erano i capei d'oro (90), 111, 140–1

Gentil mia donna (72), 69, 120, 157–9, 213, 217–18
Geri, quando talor (179), 21, 76
Giovene donna (30), 141–2

Il cantar novo (219), 195–7
Il figliuol di Latona (43), 65–70
Il mal mi preme (244), 22
In qual parte del ciel (159), 86
In quella parte (127), 80
Italia mia (128), 59, 61, 110, 145–8, 214
I'vo pensando (264), 35, 38, 39, 61–2, 64, 85–6, 95, 151, 169, 187–8, 214, 217

La bella donna (91), 187
Lasso me (70), 79, 92, 159–60
Là ver l'aurora (239), 62, 136–8, 220
Le stelle, il cielo (154), 91
Levommi il mio penser (302), 166–7, 185–6

232

Mai non vo' piú cantar (105), 205, 216

Ma poi che 'l dolce riso (42), 65–70

Mia benigna fortuna (332), 57, 59, 136, 163, 219

Ne la stagion (50), 195

Nel dolce tempo (23), 21, 35, 41–2, 79, 93, 173, 214, 216–17, 222

Ne l'età sua piú bella (278), 137

Non al suo amante (52), 137

Non à tanti animali (237), 57, 119

Non fur ma' Giove (155), 181–2

O aspectata in ciel (28), 144–5, 201–2

Oimè il bel viso (267), 52

Onde tolse Amor (220), 160–1

Or che 'l ciel (164), 205–8

Or vedi Amor (121), 37, 38, 39

Pace non trovo (134), 91

Padre del ciel (63), 58, 63, 70–4

Perché la vita è breve (71), 69, 120, 157–9, 213, 217–18

Piangete, donne (92), 78–9, 92

Poi che per mio destino (73), 69, 120, 157–9, 213, 217–18

Ponmi ove 'l sole (145), 86, 191

Qual piú diversa (135), 198–9, 214, 217

Quand'io veggio dal ciel (291), 136, 152–3, 192

Quando dal proprio sito (41), 65–70

Quando il soave (359), 63, 72, 151, 165, 167–9

Que' ch'infinita (4), 155–7, 195

Quel' antiquo mio (360), 63, 72, 169–70, 214, 217

Quelle pietose rime (120), 24, 26

Quel sempre acerbo (157), 123–4

Quel sol che mi mostrava (306), 197–8

Qui dove mezzo son (13), 202–3, 207

S'Amore o Morte (40), 67–8

S'amor non è (132), 102, 208–10

Se l'onorata fronde (24), 22

Se 'l pensier (125), 91, 100–1, 126–8, 213, 215

Se Virgilio et Homero (186), 142–3, 148

Sí è debile (37), 121–2

S'i' fussi stato (166), 148

S'i' 'l dissi mai (206), 215

Solo et pensoso (35), 33, 42, 134–5, 206

Spirto gentil (53), 57, 59, 74, 145, 219

Standomi un giorno (323), 42, 222

Tacer non posso (325), 213

Tornami a mente (336), 46, 109, 117

Una donna piú bella (119), 26

Verdi panni (29), 215

Vergine bella (366), 40, 57, 72, 111, 148, 170–1, 175, 195, 214, 216–17

Vincitore Alexandro (232), 59, 69

Vinse Hanibàl (103), 21

Voglia mi sprona (211), 45–7, 53, 109, 117

Voi ch'ascoltate (1), 35, 103–8, 176–83, 211–12

Name index

Absalom, 16
Accademia della Crusca, 191, 223, 226
Acciaiuoli, Niccolò, 147
Almansi, G., 222, 226
Alonso, D., 221, 226
Altamura, A., 221, 225
Amaturo, R., 226
Andrews, R.A., 15, 226
Angiolieri, Cecco, 73
Antonio da Ferrara, 14, 22–7, 221, 225
Antonio da Tempo, 15, 226
Apollo, 21, 118–19, 123, 139, 143, 195, 201
Apuleius, 16
Aquinas, St Thomas, 4
Arezzo, 2
Aristotle, 4, 16, 100, 207
Arnaut Daniel, 45, 79, 87, 89, 90, 93–5, 113, 126, 138, 215, 219
Arquà, 3
Augustine, St, 4, 7, 16, 81, 88, 150, 169
Aulus Gellius, 43
Averroes, 4
Avignon, 2, 13, 23, 57, 59, 91, 95, 96, 109, 133
Azzo da Correggio, 22, 36, 38, 145

Balduino, A., 221, 226
Bambaglioli, Graziolo, 13
Barber, J.A., 221, 226
Barberi Squarotti, G., 222, 226
Baron, H., 221, 226
Beatrice (Bice Portinari), 19, 64, 98, 99, 113–15, 131, 135, 154, 165, 167–70
Bellucci, L., 25, 221
Bembo, Pietro, 173–4, 182–3, 215, 225
Benevento, 10
Bernard, St, 154
Bernardo, A.S., 222, 223
Bernart de Ventadorn, 88, 98, 113, 215
Bertran de Born, 93
Biadene, L., 223, 226
Bigi, E., 223, 226
Billanovich, G., 96, 221, 227
Boccaccio, Giovanni, 13, 16–17, 25, 26, 29, 30, 37, 38, 56, 79, 92, 96, 97, 114–15, 135, 221, 222, 224, 225; *Amorosa visione*, 26; *Decameron*, 14, 56; *Rime*, 17, 25, 26, 27–9, 112, 221, 225; *Trattatello in laude di Dante*, 13, 14, 225
Boggs, E.L., (IIIrd), 222, 227
Boiardo, Matteo Maria, 106–7, 211, 225

Bologna, 10, 11, 96
Bonagiunta da Lucca, 11, 90
Bonora, E., 221, 227
Bosco, U., 221, 222, 223, 227
Branca, V., 221, 222, 227
Brescia, 39
Brugnolo, F., 14, 221, 225
Bufano, A., 224

Caesar, Julius, 24, 27–9, 182
Calcaterra, C., 116, 222, 223, 227
Carducci, G., 52, 88, 159, 224
Carrara, E., 112, 222, 227
Catullus, 103
Catulus, Q., 43, 44
Cavalcanti, Guido, 11–12, 14, 21, 79, 89, 91, 93–5, 98, 101, 114, 115, 186, 190, 216
Ceriello, G.R., 105, 225
Chaucer, Geoffrey, 208
Chiappelli, F., 222, 227
Chigi, Agostino, 37
Cicero, 3, 4, 54, 80, 81, 147
Cino da Pistoia, 13, 16, 78, 79, 89, 90, 92–4, 113, 114, 135, 174, 222
Cola di Rienzo, 3, 4, 145, 147
Colonna (family), 3, 22, 23; Agapito, 22; Giacomo, 3, 109, 113, 115, 139; Giovanni, 22, 23, 59, 67, 111, 144; Stefano, 22
Compiuta Donzella, 10
Contini, G., 53, 91, 101, 113, 222, 223, 224, 225, 227
Corsi, G., 225

Dante, 1, 6, 12–15, 17, 18, 26, 33, 37, 38, 52, 64, 78–80, 84, 89, 90, 91, 93, 94, 95–100, 114–17, 120, 126–7, 131, 148, 153–5, 165, 167–70, 174, 175, 176, 183–4, 186, 190–3, 200, 216, 218, 219–20, 222, 225; *Convivio*, 33, 96; *De vulgari eloquentia*, 1, 12, 84, 93, 175, 183–4,

186, 225; *Divina commedia*, 1, 12–13, 19, 33, 37, 50, 80, 90, 91, 92, 95–100, 115, 153–4, 165, 190–1, 221, 225; *Inferno*, 96, 97, 100, 154; *Purgatorio*, 11, 80, 99, 100, 116, 131, 151, 167; *Paradiso*, 14, 96, 120, 170–1; *Rime*, 37, 89, 90, 91, 95, 126–7, 186, 190–1, 219–20, 223, 225; *Vita nuova*, 12, 18, 33, 37, 52, 64, 91, 98, 101, 107, 115, 153–4, 184, 190–1, 225
Daretes Phrygius, 16
Davanzati, Chiaro, 88, 90
David, 68
De Nolhac, P., 116, 221, 222, 227
De Robertis, D., 37, 222, 223, 224
De Sade (family), 112
De Sanctis, F., 159, 227
Dietisalvi, Ser Pietro, 21
Di Girolamo, C., 223, 227
Dionisotti, C., 221, 227
Di Pino, G., 223, 227
dolce stil novo, 11, 13, 16, 79, 91, 93, 94, 95, 101, 120, 124, 133, 160, 176, 184, 186, 190, 210, 218, 221, 222
Donati, Forese, 91
Dondi, Giovanni, 22
Durling, R.M., 223, 227
Dutschke, D., 222, 227

Ennius, 22, 139

Fabricius, C., 145
Favati, G., 221, 227
Feo, M., 222, 227
Ferrari, S., 52, 88, 159, 224
Ferrero, G.G., 222, 227
Figurelli, F., 223, 227
Florence, 11, 13, 14, 23
Folena, G., 221, 228
Fontana, A., 222, 228
Forster, L., 223, 228
Foster, K., 221, 222, 223, 228

Franceschino degli Albizzi, 23, 94
Francesco di Vannozzo, 14, 15, 225
Francesco da Carrara, 3
Freccero, J., 222, 228
Frederick II, 9
Fubini, M., 223, 228
Fulco, G., 223, 228

Gaffuri, R., 222, 228
Galdi, L., 223, 228
Geri dei Gianfigliazzi, 21, 39, 76
Giacomo da Lentini, 10, 90, 101, 189
Giraud, Y., 223, 228
Giraut Riquier, 93
Gorni, G., 221, 222, 228
Greene, T.M., 222, 228
Griselda, 56
Guido delle Colonne, 89
Guilhem IX, 91
Guilhem de Montanhagol, 93
Guilhem de Saint-Gregori, 93
Guinizzelli, Guido, 11, 78, 91, 94, 191
Guittone d'Arezzo, 6, 10, 78, 93–5, 98, 114, 189, 216, 221, 222, 225

Hainsworth, P., 223, 228
Hannibal, 24, 27–9
Henry VII, 23
Hercules, 21
Herczeg, G., 223, 228
Homer, 78, 80, 142
Horace, 45, 54, 81, 86–7, 102, 103

Incisa, 2
Isidore of Seville, 136, 143
Isolde, 16

Jacomuzzi, A., 222, 228
Jacopo di Dante, 13
Jaufré Rudel, 93
Jeremiah, 89, 107
John of Garland, 54, 226

Jones, F.J., 113, 222, 228
Junius Brutus, 145

Kleinhenz, C., 223, 229
Kristeller, P.O., 229

Lana, Il, 13
Lanza, A., 221, 229
Lapo Gianni, 89
Larner, J., 221, 229
Laura, 6, 8, 19, 21, 32, 33, 40, 42, 44–6, 49, 51–3, 57–9, 61, 64–75, 99, 108–71, 174, 182, 192–9, 205, 213, 222, 223
Lawler, T., 54, 226
Lelio de' Lelii, 25
Livy, 4, 116
Lombez, 3
Lo Parco, F., 222, 229
Lucia, St, 154

Machiavelli, Niccolò, 148
Malatesta, Pandolfo, 22, 32, 38, 39, 40
Mallarmé, S., 45
Malpaghini, Giovanni, 30, 38, 39, 42
Mann, N., 221, 222, 229
Maria d'Aquino, 114
Marigo, A., 225
Martellotti, G., 222, 224, 229
Marti, M., 174, 182, 215, 221, 225, 229
Martinelli, B., 116, 222, 229
Martini, Simone, 110
Mattucci, T., 225
Medea, 85, 86
Medin A., 15, 225
Medusa, 76, 170
Milan, 3, 38
Momigliano, A., 223, 229
Mommsen, T., 222, 229
Monte Andrea, 89

Neri, F., 53, 223, 224, 229
Niccolò de' Rossi, 14, 15, 17, 221, 225
Noferi, A., 221, 222, 229

Onesto Bolognese, 94
Orso dell'Anguillara, 22, 67
Ottimo (commentary), 13
Ovid, 85–6, 134, 138–40, 187–8, 216

Parma, 22, 36, 145
Paul, St, 16
Peire Vidal, 93
Peirone, L., 222, 229
Peruzzi, Luigi, 112
Petracco, Ser 2
Petrarch, *passim; Af.*, 5, 8, 22, 55, 82, 83, 112, 116, 139, 143, 148, 150, 224; *Buc. carm. (Eclogues)*, 7, 8, 83, 113, 139, 225; *Collatio laureationis*, 5, 139, 224; *De rem.*, 5, 55, 82, 83, 225; *De viris illustribus*, 55, 116; *Ep. met.*, 7, 21, 35, 82, 92, 225; *Fam.*, 5, 18, 22, 35, 36, 55, 56, 81, 82, 83, 96, 100, 101, 109, 110, 224; *Invective*, 83, 224; *Ot. rel.*, 55, 82, 224; *Posteritati*, 5, 116, 155, 224; *Psalmi penitentiales*, 83; *RD*, 6, 20–4, 91, 136, 218; *Rerum memorandarum*, 55, 67, 96; *RVF, passim; Sec.*, 5, 7, 150, 169, 224; *Sen.*, 5, 17, 18, 32, 37, 39, 56, 82, 97, 100, 225; *Sine nomine*, 148, 224; *Triumphi*, 6, 23, 26, 93–5, 109, 155, 224–5; *Var.*, 32, 39, 40, 41; *Vit. sol.,*, 54, 55, 133, 140, 224
Petrie, J., 222, 229
Petrocchi, G., 221, 225
Petronio G., 223, 229
Philip VI, 144
Pierantozzi, D., 222, 229
Polycletus, 16
Polyxena, 16
Pompey, 24, 68
Poole, G., 223, 229
Possiedi, P., 223, 229

Quaglio, A.E., 221, 230
Quintilian, 54

Raimondi, E., 223, 230
Ravenna, 12, 14
Renier, A., 223, 230
Reynolds, L.D., 221, 230
Rhetorica ad Herennium, 107, 206, 209
Rico, F., 33, 35, 38, 221, 222, 230
Rigaut de Barbezieux, 90
Robert d'Anjou, 147
Roche, T.P., Jnr., 222, 230
Roman de la Rose, 92
Romanò, A., 21, 34, 35, 36, 41, 42, 45, 46, 181, 222, 224
Rome, 3, 4, 144–7
Roncaglia, A., 221, 230
Ronconi, G., 222, 230
Ruggieri Apugliese, 91
Russell, R., 221, 230
Rustico Filippi, 10, 90–1

Sansone, G.E., 223, 230
Santagata, M., 73, 74, 221, 222, 230
Scaglione, A., 106, 225, 230
Scarano, N., 94, 222, 230
Scipio Africanus, 22, 139, 145, 147, 150, 223
Seneca, 4
Sennuccio del Bene, 2, 16, 22–3, 45, 79, 92, 94, 202–3, 221, 225
Shapiro, M., 223, 230
Sicilian school, 9–10, 19, 79, 93, 215, 221, 225
Simonelli, M.P., 223, 230
Solomon, 16
Sordello, 93, 98
Sozzi, B.T., 221, 230
Stampa, Gaspara, 105–7, 211, 225
Stefano Protonotaro, 90
Stramazzo da Perugia, 22
Sturm, S., 222, 230

Suitner, F., 94, 222, 230
Sulla, 70

Tagliacozzo, 10
Tartaro, A., 221, 230
Trinkaus, C., 221, 230
Trovato, P., 100, 222, 230
Turchi, M., 221, 230

Ulysses, 96, 97

Varchi, Benedetto, 159
Vattasso, M., 224
Vaucluse, 3, 133, 192
Velli, G., 222, 223, 230
Vellutello, Alessandro, 52, 112
Venice, 3, 37

Verona, 4
Vickers, N.J., 223, 230
Virgil, 3, 16, 78, 81, 83, 109,
    134, 142, 15 4, 222: *Aeneid* 8,
    13, 50
Viscardi, A., 222, 230
Visconti (family), 3; Brizio, 16,
    121

Waller, M., 222, 231
Wilkins, E.H. 21, 33, 34, 35, 36,
    37, 38, 39, 41, 45, 47, 49, 52,
    54, 62, 221, 222, 231
Wilson, N.G., 221, 230

Zingarelli, N., 87, 88, 222, 224,
    231